L. Jean Watson
Endowed
Fund

PRIMITIVE

PRIMITIVE

Tapping the Primal Drive That Powers the World's Most Successful People

MARCO GREENBERG

hachette
BOOKS

New York

Hachette Go, an imprint of Hachette Books
Hachette Book Group
1290 Avenue of the Americas, New York, NY 10104
HachetteGo.com
Facebook.com/HachetteGo
Instagram.com/HachetteGo

First Edition: April 2020

Published by Hachette Books, an imprint of Perseus Books, LLC, a subsidiary of Hachette Book Group, Inc. The Hachette Go and Hachette Books name and logos are trademarks of the Hachette Book Group.

The Hachette Speakers Bureau provides a wide range of authors for speaking events. To find out more, go to www.hachettespeakersbureau.com or call (866) 376-6591.

The publisher is not responsible for websites (or their content) that are not owned by the publisher.

Print book interior design by Abby Reilly.

Library of Congress Cataloging-in-Publication Data

Names: Greenberg, Marco, author.
Title: Primitive: tapping the primal drive that powers the world's most successful people / Marco Greenberg.
Description: First edition. | New York: Hachette Books, 2020. | Includes bibliographical references and index.
Identifiers: LCCN 2019047944 | ISBN 9780316530378 (hardcover) | ISBN 9780316530361 (ebook)
Subjects: LCSH: Successful people—Psychology. | Success. | Personality.
Classification: LCC BF637.S8 G6947 2020 | DDC 158.1—dc23
LC record available at https://lccn.loc.gov/2019047944

ISBNs: 978-0-316-53037-8 (hardcover), 978-0-316-53036-1 (ebook)

Printed in the United States of America

LSC-C

10 9 8 7 6 5 4 3 2 1

*This book is dedicated to the memory of the ultimate
primitive, Danny M. Lewin.
(May 14, 1970–September 11, 2001)*

CONTENTS

PRIMITIVE

INTRODUCTION

About a decade ago I received an offer I couldn't refuse.

I was running my own public relations firm, and even though I was fortunate enough to make a good living, I could already sense the economy taking a turn for the worse. I had been bracing for months by cutting costs, hustling for clients, and networking. Then, a former colleague called me up and asked if I'd like to rejoin the PR agency I'd worked for years before, Burson-Marsteller, one of the world's largest. They were looking for a managing director, he said, somebody who knew the company and its culture well, but who could also serve as a change agent and inject a healthy dose of creative thinking. And they thought I'd be a great fit.

I discussed the offer with my wife over dinner. "I know how much you love being your own boss," she said gently, "but is it really worth all the hassle?" Wisely, she argued that with three small children to care for, a high-level position with a large agency would be a blessing. I'd no longer be worrying about making payroll, paying the rent on my office, or any of the other challenges that small business owners face. Together, we imagined all the new job's perks, from traveling the world to working with executives of Fortune 500 companies. Plus, it felt good to know that, having started at the bottom of the company's ladder, I was now being asked to come back and occupy a spot near the top. Feeling hopeful, I accepted the offer.

However, as soon as I walked back into the firm's Park Avenue South office, I knew I had made a mistake.

The wall-to-wall carpeting smelled just as musty as I'd remembered. The halls were dark and eerily quiet, and they led to a maze of cubicles where stressed-out employees glared at their computer screens and clicked away at their keyboards. My inbox was already jammed with emails from human resources summoning me to mandatory orientations and automated reminders about filling out my time-tracking spreadsheet. I told myself that occasional busywork was simply the price I had to pay for working in corporate America; I'd soon be wheeling and dealing with high-powered clients. I set out to do the best job I could. But that proved difficult. Like any large organization, Burson-Marsteller was not above petty office politics; I learned that if I wanted to be assigned to the firm's high-profile accounts, I had to campaign for them. This meant everything from sucking up to the bosses to figuring out which of my colleagues I could trust and which ones were after my job.

I became depressed. I'm a competitive guy, and I loved the work itself, but life in the office felt less about applying my creativity to get and serve clients and more about billing as many hours as humanly possible to prevail in some c-suite version of the Hunger Games. Each week my department posted a running tally of our billable hours that read like a baseball scorecard. If your "bill-ability"—and thus your value to the company—began to shrink, everyone knew it. We were so obsessed with accumulating hours that we barely spoke to each other.

I was caught between the push of the controlling company culture and the pull of my more free-spirited temperament. I let my frustrations seep in and take over. To fight the blues, I took some Zoloft my doctor prescribed, which made me feel dry-mouthed and numb. To give myself a jolt of adrenaline, I woke up before dawn every morning, left the house while my family was still sleeping, and started my day with an intense CrossFit workout. But in the end, no amount of air squats and burpees could fix my sense of despair at work. I was hardly alone in feeling such deep frustration: In a 2018 poll of about thirty thousand American workers, Gallup found that despite an increase in the number of people who report themselves satisfied at work, most of the respondents were still not emotionally connected to their work and classified themselves as "not engaged." They generally showed up and did the minimum required of them, but they'd leave the job if they found a slightly better option. Of those, 13 percent described themselves as "actively disengaged" with "miserable work experiences." Meanwhile, 67 percent said they were sometimes, very often, or always burned out at work.

This certainly would have described a lot of people at Burson-Marsteller, but not everyone. There was one guy who seemed immune to the petty infighting and the ambient malaise that seemed to infect everyone else. His name was Michael Claes, but we called him "007" because he was the consummate mystery man. After the office adopted business casual attire, Michael stubbornly stuck to his pressed white shirts, suits, and solid red and blue ties. No one knew exactly what he was working on, but he counted big blue-chip companies, including Clorox, among his clients. Once, somehow, he brought in the government of Indonesia for an assignment that went on for years. He came and went as he pleased. His office looked like the aftermath of a tornado. He had no clear supervisor because most of the company was afraid of him. "I wasn't interested in people's time sheets," he reflected to me recently. "I didn't worry about concepts like bill-ability or how many hours people worked. Hence, I was considered to be a lousy manager, which didn't bother me at all."

We used to joke that if Michael stopped showing up for work, it would take someone six months to muster the courage to ask where he went. Once, when his office phone stopped working,

Michael called IT to get a new one sent up. Like at any big corporation, an IT ticket had to be created, approved, and then wind its way through the queue, which could take days. But Michael had no patience for bureaucracy, so he smashed the phone and sent the head of the New York office shards of plastic and wire in interoffice envelopes with a note: *Replace my phone.*

Michael got away with all kinds of off-the-wall behavior because, at the end of the day, he was valuable to the agency and brought in millions of dollars per year. He was like a hunter who ventured into the jungle, shot a meaty animal, and dragged it back to feed the village. He was moved by the thrill of the chase, and he relied on gut instinct rather than on some elaborate playbook. The farmers—like many of my colleagues at Burson-Marsteller—were "civilized" folks. They respected precise divisions of labor, valued collaborative work, and kept exacting schedules. They made it possible for Michael to disappear for weeks at a time to haul in a whale of a client. Just like early human civilizations did, the modern workplace needs both hunters and farmers to thrive. The more I've experienced workplaces like Burson-Marsteller, the more I've discovered renegades like Michael Claes who seem to be operating by their own set of rules. In HR corporate speak, they are considered "nontraditional hires." They constantly butt heads with their more civilized colleagues, but are allowed to remain somewhat autonomous because of the immense value they bring to the organization.

When I eventually quit my job and restarted my own communications boutique, I intentionally sought to work with people like Michael. One day I was speaking with my business partner, Liel, trying to understand what it was about these square pegs in round holes that was so refreshingly *different.* I thought about the most successful people I had worked with, from members of the *Forbes* billionaires list to government ministers to surgeons to startup founders. As I told the story of Michael Claes interofficing the mangled remains of his phone to the head of Burson-Marsteller's New York office, we brainstormed about what separated accomplished people like him from the rest of the pack.

Without thinking, I blurted out: "They're totally fucking crazy."

Liel pressed me for a real answer. "Why? Because they are original? Pure? Primal? Uncorrupted by civilization?" We kept naming adjectives until one made me pause: "...Are they kind of primitive?"

I looked at Liel and smiled. "That's it. They're *primitive*."

We throw around plenty of terms to define personality types. Left-brained people are analytical and methodical, while right-brained people are creative and artistic—or so the theory goes. The Myers–Briggs Type Indicator assigns individuals an alphabet soup of letters that align with one of sixteen personality types. There are famed psychiatrist Carl Jung's introverts and extroverts. Type As and Type Bs. Entrepreneurs and employees. Gryffindors and Slytherins. People who see the white-and-gold dress and people who see the blue-and-black dress. I won't pretend to have the expertise to establish yet another scientific framework for categorizing the human mind. Rather, I want to recapture a word and identify a mindset—being primitive—to describe some of the people around us who are quietly and not-so-quietly living life on their own terms. They are talented, creative people whose instincts and unconventional ideas can contribute to innovation if only they are not stymied.

While most of us have been trained in schools and offices to act civilized, we have done little to cultivate our primitive side. And we all have a primitive side: It's the drive that leads us to obsess over our mission. It's the thrust that propels us to fight until we win. It's the tick that lets us ignore conventions and think up new solutions to old problems. It's the urge to jaywalk instead of waiting for the light. Most important, it's taking a social or financial risk when convention says not to.

As Dr. Richard A. Friedman, a professor of psychiatry at Cornell University, explained, "Culture is essentially giving the message that people should be safe and that risk is always a bad thing. So people are supposed to minimize their exposure. We're supposed to be safer, even when taking some risk might be beneficial." The good news, he said, is that "people can be taught to be take more intelligent risk often by just giving them more information about it."

And that information can be found in our primitive brains.

I realize that *primitive* is a loaded term. It's not politically correct. It even sounds a little bit offensive. I don't mean that we should be rude or coarse or unthinking, and I'm not suggesting that we should just let frat boys be frat boys. I'm also not here to tout trends like paleo diets, "primitive technology," "digital nomads," or calling coworkers "beasts" when they nail assignments. While these trends all point to many people's genuine desire to live more simply and more instinctively, this idea is actually much deeper than that.

In fact, *primitive* is the perfect word to describe a certain sort of energy that, as old institutions are uprooted and new economic players rise, is becoming more and more essential. And not only in our era: for approximately 90 percent of our history as a species, we thrived in large part because we roamed the world in tight-knit groups searching for sustenance and opportunity rather than sitting still and waiting for good fortune to come to us.

By the 1920s, the majority of Americans had left their farming communities and relocated to urban environments. But modern city living brought with it not only a new set of conveniences, like indoor plumbing, electricity, and heating, but also a new way of life. In the country, people resided in small communities, where everyone lived together and worked together. In the city, life was far more fragmented: you had your modest apartment, your factory job, your small circle of friends, and you were often sealed off from the millions of people from all backgrounds living below and above and beside you. Instead of roaming to new places to hunt and gather for survival, our society evolved into compliant adults with very different values than their primitive ancestors.

This is not some evolutionary abstraction. It's a process we've each experienced ourselves. We were enrolled in elementary schools that taught us that the most important things were to be polite, to play well with others, to obey our teachers, and to follow the rules. Then we went to college, and there we were told that if we did well—if we studied hard, earned enough As, and chased down the right internships—we'd have good jobs waiting when we graduated. As we entered the workforce, we were reminded that if we wanted to get anywhere in our careers, the only way to do it was by understanding the intricate set of guidelines that governed our professional lives, things like not challenging our boss and knowing our place in the corporate pyramid. Or as "The Logical Song" by the English rock band Supertramp goes, *They send me away to teach me how to be sensible, logical, oh responsible, practical.*

Don't get me wrong: Being civilized has done a lot of us a lot of good. But it's time to consider the alternative.

Why? Because our economy and our society are both changing, rapidly and radically. Some of the changes are technological: according to a 2019 study conducted by the Brookings Institution, 25 percent of American jobs are at "high risk" of being lost due to automation, and another 36 percent are at "medium risk." As a coauthor of the study explained, "If your job is boring and repetitive, you're probably at great risk of automation." Other changes are economic: when my father joined the workforce in the early 1960s, 88 percent of Americans working in the private sector could count on having a pension; today, that percentage is closer to 30, which means that more of us are being left to fend for ourselves in retirement. And some changes are institutional: instead of the large corporations that moved slowly and took few risks, the advent of the internet and the availability of venture capital funding enabled the rise of companies committed to moving fast and breaking things, as Facebook's old motto used to go. As new industries, from ridesharing to coworking spaces, emerge almost overnight, and the job market offers less long-term security than ever before, there is an opportunity to do something about that feeling of frustration so many of us experience each morning as we head out to work. It's time to be more primitive. Luckily, we have a primitive brain that's already making far more decisions than we realize.

For decades, neuroscience was comfortable telling us that we had two brains: a primitive one and a more evolved one. The primitive one contains a group of structures collectively called the basal ganglia. It's that big thing right in the center of the brain that looks like a swirly cinnamon bun, and it's in charge of, among other things, our voluntary motor actions. Then there's the cerebral cortex, the outer layer of neural tissue in your cerebrum that is in charge of complex cognitive functions like long-term memory, language, and abstract thought—all the smart and complex stuff. It's why we often call thoughtful or intelligent people "cerebral."

With this breakdown in mind, scientists assumed that there was a simple relationship between the basal ganglia and the cerebral cortex. The former was the part of the brain where our cave-dwelling ancestors made "gut decisions" that helped them survive. Aggression, dominance, territoriality—all these come to us courtesy of the basal ganglia and other primitive regions of the brain. But as humans evolved, our survival no longer relied on grunting and growling and grabbing, but rather on inventing and theorizing and thinking in the abstract. That's why we developed a big cerebral cortex, a civilized brain for a more civilized existence. Meanwhile, the primitive part of our brain was considered less critical to our modern way of life. Or so we thought, anyway. About a decade ago, scientists at MIT began conducting experiments that revealed the striatum—the part of the basal ganglia that receives input—adapted far more quickly to stimuli than the cerebral cortex. It was the primitive brain, they observed, that was first to identify change and learn to adapt.

You don't have to be a neuroscientist—and I'm certainly not one—to know that for all our material comforts, emotionally and psychologically we aren't that far removed from our cave-dwelling forebearers. We may have iPhones and Netflix and Instagram, but the moment danger arises we do what our species has always done and let our fight-or-flight instinct kick in. This means our brains are still geared to immediately identify threats and opportunities, without too much thought or complication, before handing all that data over for more sophisticated analysis. For all our adaptations, it means that we still have a primitive brain, one that is often faster and more accurate than its civilized counterpart. The key, as we'll see in this book, is to learn how to listen to it.

Take a look around your workplace. How many of your peers seem drained, or simply not connected with their work? My friend Linda went into journalism years ago because she loved the adventure and her ability to constantly explore new subjects. But as she climbed the ladder of managerial success, she feels less creative and fulfilled, and more boxed in by her bosses. Another friend, Kevin, has a great career as a transactional lawyer. But he can't stop dreaming about quitting his job to open a health food store. It's a fantasy he's had since he left college, but one that seems to loom larger in his imagination as his professional status rises. Then there's Matt, who has done very well in corporate real estate, but hates it to the point that he wonders if his work life would not have been happier and more successful if he had followed his early dream of becoming an athletic trainer. You probably know people like Linda, Kevin, and Matt. Maybe their struggles even remind you of your own.

Business, among other professions, trains us to depend on our civilized brains rather than our instincts and our emotions. Our professors and mentors and colleagues teach us to keep the personal and the professional separate, to depend on metrics and data and other tangible, objective yardsticks. The way we're socialized in business is often antisocial; we're taught to be "professional," to not take business problems "to heart." This can be sage advice that is necessary to the effective functioning of a big organization.

But in the information economy, where innovative ideas can often go from inception to implementation—and even world-changing fortune—in a matter of months, I would argue that we need to think differently about the ways we, and our organizations, work. In many realms, business as usual is increasingly an imprudent plan. Yes, "disruption" is already becoming a tired buzzword, but many of us are still searching for ways to engage more genuinely with our work, and to find more satisfaction in it. Part of the solution, I think, is to let that faster brain, the primitive one, loose. To do that, we need a guide that helps us understand just how it works, and how we can tap into the instincts each of us already possesses.

Which is the purpose of this book.

Organizations require a balance between the civilized and the primitive to thrive—you can't have one without the other. And to thrive within an organization, we can't seek some bogus one-size-fits-all prescription for instant happiness. We need a blueprint for a new model that can help us understand our ingrained strengths—including some we didn't even know we had—and chart our professional course accordingly.

To simplify decades of experience and reams of research into clear, easy-to-follow principles, I've come up with two stream-lined sets of acronyms that neatly capture the primitive and the civilized mindsets.

Civilized people are HOMING, which stands for Hierarchical, Occupational, Measured, Insulated, Nonconfrontational, and Grounded. These are all fine qualities that may also, unfortunately, stand in the way of much needed change and growth. I like to think of primitives, on the other hand, as ROAMING. Each letter describes a different trait that each of these personalities embodies. Those traits inevitably overlap, so that people may have several of them and find themselves within a range.

R stands for Relentless, which doesn't just mean trying hard or never giving up or having grit or any of that stuff you'll find on inspirational blogs. Relentless primitives have a radical way of charging forward with their careers, and it colors everything from how they approach rewards to how they bounce back from failure. It's the instinct that guided my client Austin McChord from his father's basement, where he was building his first prototype out of Legos, to founding a billion-dollar company. But as much as relentless primitives know how to barrel full steam ahead, they know when to pump the brakes and abruptly change direction.

O is for Oppositional. Often wild and pugnacious, oppositional primitives know that a healthy dose of discord is the best source of energy. They despise groupthink and are never afraid to say, "You're wrong and here's why." My best friend Danny Lewin, who tragically lost his life during 9/11 trying to thwart the hijackers aboard American Airlines Flight 11, was the consummate oppositional primitive. I watched Danny, once a teenager sweeping the floors of a Jerusalem gym, argue and trash-talk until he became an internet 1.0 billionaire at age twenty-nine. Like other oppositional primitives, Danny sought out impossible challenges and found innovative ways to solve them.

A stands for Agnostic, the ability to jump from one field to the next without getting too attached to any one industry, method, or goal. A former coworker of mine, Love Whelchel III, is familiar with this skill, having been a roadie for hip-hop group N.W.A, an IT recruiter, a chief talent officer, the CEO of his own company, and the right-hand man for rapper and entrepreneur Sean Combs among many other zigs and zags. Agnostic is when my friend Tanya Valle gave up her lucrative job at an entertainment PR firm to become a zookeeper.

M is for Messianic, or having a zealous attachment to a mission that is not necessarily grounded in solid projections and reliable facts. It's the capacity to see oneself as destined for a unique mission that drove the neuroscientist Ali Rezai to devote himself to finding a cure for Alzheimer's, Parkinson's, addiction, and countless other diseases using cutting-edge technology. Messianic primitives like Ali are guided by a singular calling to achieve a seemingly unreachable goal, fix a daunting problem, and to change the world.

I stands for Insecure, which you sometimes have to be to push yourself hard enough to get the best results. Insecure primitives are near and dear to my heart because I am one. As an agency guy serving an array of clients, I've been fired and let go more times than I can count. I've had my professional life upended time and again, and I've lived to tell my story. Insecure primitives are survivors who never rest on their laurels; they scratch and claw their way to success by embracing their shortcomings and turning them into powerful advantages. Take it from Riki Drori, a marketing executive at YouTube, who has become one of the highest-rated managers at the company by being honest and open with her team about her weaknesses and insecurities.

N is for Nuts, or being just plain crazy and, on occasion, taking chances that no careful or rational person would advise. Being nuts is what led a successful physician named Dorian Paskowitz to abandon his lucrative practice, load his young family into a rickety camper, and spend the rest of his life surfing. These are rare souls who follow their dreams, no matter how crazy, insane, or downright dangerous they might be. Nuts primitives may allow civilization to rein in their worst impulses, but they are the ultimate risk-takers, eccentrics, and misfits.

And, finally, the *G* is for Gallant, a trait that combines both courage and nobility, and one that compels primitives to protect those to whom they're loyal and who are loyal to them. It's what drove India Howell, a successful American businesswoman, to give up her privileged life, move to Tanzania, and adopt dozens of homeless children off the streets. Gallant primitives measure their impact by how much good they do for others. It may sound surprising, but being gallant is perhaps our most primal instinct of all.

Each chapter of this book will present these principles at work, backed by everything from neuroscience and organizational psychology to anecdotes I've observed throughout my own life exploring both the civilized and primitive ends of the spectrum. Having been raised by primitives—my father, in a nuts primitive move, pulled me out of school at the age of eight to go live on a sailboat in Mexico—I eventually embarked on my own, different path and pursued a career in a host of civilized institutions, from Capitol Hill to the United Nations to some of the world's most influential marketing agencies. I then returned to my primitive roots, starting my own businesses—some failed, some very lucrative—while making highly unorthodox decisions along the way. Learning how to balance these two dueling parts of my brain has been a defining feature of my life.

Humans are complex animals, and just as we don't all fit neatly into a Myers–Briggs personality type, primitives don't fall perfectly into one of seven archetypes. Some are mutts who identify with two, three, or four traits. Some primitives successfully tap their civilized side; others are über-primitives who are inspiring, but exhausting to be around. By learning from the characters in this book, even the most civilized among us can make a primitive move now and then to advance our careers—or pivot to new ones.

Maybe you've been at the same job for years and it's time to shake things up. Maybe you're just starting out, and you know the same civilized rules that got your parents lifetime employment with the same company no longer apply for your generation. Maybe you'd like to do things differently at work, but all you keep hearing from your colleagues is, "It's always been this way" or "That can't possibly be done." Maybe you're finally launching that business you've always dreamed of starting. Or maybe you're a primitive manager who'd like to light a fire under your civilized employees. Whatever the case, this book is here to offer inspiring stories and applicable to-dos designed to help you discover and rekindle the primitive spark, that urgent and irreverent temperament lying dormant in your belly.

Don't worry, this is not an invitation to have a *Jerry Maguire* moment and declare war on everything and everyone civilized. It's not a call to arms for brutish behavior. There are certainly some primitives among us who have been accused of highly inappropriate conduct—think of Uber's disgraced former CEO, Travis Kalanick, who reportedly had knowledge of sexual harassment at Uber and did nothing; or Carlos Ghosn, the former CEO of Nissan accused of misappropriating company funds; or former WeWork CEO Adam Neumann, whose freewheeling style likely contributed to the infamous failure of his company's IPO in 2019. Like everything in life, the key is to find balance, to unleash the right primitive elements and give them just enough energy to move us along.

I will encourage you to advance your career by tapping into your primitive instincts, but it's equally important to be civilized when the situation calls for it. For example, I sat down with Alex

Konrad, an editor at *Forbes* who has written extensively about tech entrepreneurs and founders, including the highly primitive CEO of Salesforce, Marc Benioff. You may know Benioff as the creative genius behind a long list of marketing and PR stunts that have propelled Salesforce to a $160 billion valuation at the beginning of 2020, but you may not have heard of his cofounder Parker Harris. Alex explained that Harris is "a total civilizing factor" who is able to temper the mercurial CEO's more extreme instincts. Benioff has even learned to emulate his civilized cofounder: "While Benioff is still that primal instinct guy, he listens to more folks," Alex said. "He may not do what they say, but he listens to them."

Primitives often thrive when clashing with a more civilized counterpart. In his excellent book *Powers of Two*, author Joshua Wolf Shenk writes that "for centuries, the myth of the lone genius has towered over us like a colossus." But he goes on to argue that, in fact, the greatest creative breakthroughs came not from single minds, but from sometimes-contentious partnerships. Think John Lennon and Paul McCartney, Susan B. Anthony and Elizabeth Cady Stanton, or Steve Jobs and Steve Wozniak.

While many of these great minds were consummate primitives, others, like Parker Harris, were highly civilized. Of course, we know that not all partnerships are harmonious. When we understand where we fit along the civilized-primitive spectrum, we become more aware of our strengths and weaknesses and can minimize unnecessary conflict and misunderstandings.

Many of the characters in this book are founders, executives, titans of industry, and philanthropists, while some are mid-level managers, artists, and young people at the dawn of their careers. Primitives come in all races, ethnicities, genders, sexual orientations, religions, and socioeconomic classes. One of the most primitive people I've ever met is an artist named Huckleberry Elling, who spent six years hitchhiking across the country using her handmade hats and dolls as currency. Heavily tattooed, Huck has quite literally turned her weirdness into an art form, crocheting wearable masks and five-foot-tall prehistoric creatures. A mom who works out of an Airstream trailer in Great Barrington, Massachusetts, Huck has never designed an app, built a company, or made a million dollars, but she is the very definition of successful. While civilized people measure success with more traditional barometers—such as net worth, 401k contributions, and promotions—primitives think in terms of their lasting impact on the earth and other people. Many primitives insist on being well compensated, sure, but they crave the freedom to roam, to explore their interests, and to leave their mark—all while having fun.

I've had the privilege of knowing and advising some of the world's most successful primitives, and I've seen many go from struggling with hurdles and frustrations to finding unimaginable fulfillment and success. I believe we all have the ability to follow in their footsteps if we tap into our ancient, indestructible, and absolutely essential primitive spirit.

CHAPTER ONE

RELENTLESS

It was the spring of 2007, and Austin McChord was running out of options. A student at Rochester Institute of Technology, he sported a 2.2 GPA and had failed to graduate on time. Austin's peers were, in the go-go days before the Great Recession, accepting jobs at Apple, Google, Wall Street banks, and hot new startups flush with Silicon Valley cash. Austin, on the other hand, had no job, no degree, and a pile of Legos in his father's basement office.

But he had a vision. As a geek who'd spent his high school and college years messing around with computers, Austin understood the importance of protecting data in the digitized economy. While big companies could afford to hire professionals to deal with storing and protecting sensitive data, smaller businesses needed cheaper and faster ways to make sure their files were always accessible. With zero startup capital, Austin used the Legos, hot glue, parts from a Linksys router, and a soldering iron to create a series of barely functional prototypes of a product that could replicate data to servers in the cloud. Before long, he had racked up $80,000 in credit card debt and his closest friends and advisers were urging him to cut his losses before he went bankrupt.

But Austin pushed on. Later that year he founded his company,

Datto, and eventually managed to secure patents. But he still wasn't making any money, and he was constantly making mistakes. When his friends talked about their civilized jobs, Austin talked about his mission, sounding, they often told him with an awkward smile, like some crazy, obsessed person. It was hard not to wonder whether he had done the right thing by staying at home in small town Connecticut while his friends left and made real money.

Yet after hustling for several years and crisscrossing the country to build his customer base, Austin had a devoted following of IT professionals who trusted and relied on Datto's products. His hardware had allowed businesses in New York City to retrieve their data and get back on their feet after Hurricane Sandy destroyed billions of dollars' worth of infrastructure. Impressed, a large company offered Austin $100 million for Datto. Not bad for a C student who took six years to graduate from college. Austin called his lawyer and asked if he should take the deal.

"Absolutely accept this offer," the lawyer urged him. "You can then spend the rest of your life regretting it from your own private island in the South Pacific."

But Austin wasn't so sure. He had a hunch that his company could do even more, that cashing out now would be wrong, that his employees deserved a cut of the action, that the best was yet to come. He turned down the money. Austin continued to grow his company, and five years later another offer for north of $1.5 billion came along from Vista Equity Partners, one of the largest private equity firms in the country. This time Austin accepted, and the erstwhile Rochester Institute of Technology slacker became one of the nation's wealthiest people.

If you ask me what made Austin succeed—and many have—I can give you a simple answer: Austin succeeded because he is a primitive. More specifically, Austin is a *relentless primitive* who is able to distinguish the signal from the noise and maintain his focus. He knew when to charge full steam ahead and when to slow down. He knew when to cut corners and when to be a perfectionist. He knew when to say "Yes" and he knew when to say "No."

In the traditional sense, relentless means being oppressively constant. Context matters, naturally: an advancing band of bloodthirsty orcs is relentless, just as Amazon.com's march toward retail hegemony is relentless. While Jeff Bezos may not have conquered middle-earth (yet), the meaning of the word *relentless* is essentially the same.

When it comes to building a career, a civilized person may cruise relentlessly onward like a marathon runner, but not necessarily smartly or successfully. Take me, for example. The fall of 1991 was one of the most hopeful periods in my life. I had earned my master's degree in international affairs from Columbia University a few years earlier, and I was fortunate enough to have secured a string of promising entry-level jobs, including as an aide to then–California congressional representative Mel Levine and as an intern on the foreign desk of CBS News. With a little bit of experience and a few impressive lines on my résumé, I eagerly jumped into what I imagined would be the rest of my life. I dreamed of a challenging and meaningful career in diplomacy, public policy, or media. I thought I had everything it took to get me where I wanted to go. I applied to every job I could find and prepared a portfolio of enthusiastic recommendation letters. I was sure it wouldn't be long before I was invited to join the educated and the skilled in some dynamic office. Like every American success story, all I had to do was hustle and play by the rules to get that dream job—or so I believed.

And yet, time after time, I was turned down.

Rationally, I knew I shouldn't take the rejections personally. The notes I received were form rejection letters, probably sent to dozens if not hundreds of other job seekers. But in reality, I thought that I wasn't just any other job seeker. I was *special.* Yet, with each "We regret to inform you…," I began to wonder if there was, in fact, something wrong with me. I had relentlessly sent out résumé after résumé, but that strategy clearly hadn't worked. To make matters worse, I was running out of cash; I had already quit my PhD program after falling behind on tuition payments. As my father, who was also nearly broke at the time, told me: "Don't be overeducated and underemployed."

One day, a friend casually mentioned a name that piqued my interest: Elias "Buck" Buchwald, who helped start Burson-Marsteller, which was then the world's largest PR firm. A World War II veteran, Buchwald had counseled the leaders of industry giants including IBM, General Motors, DuPont, and General Electric—iconic brands that owed their success in no small part to Buck's ability to help tell their stories in a clear and truthful way. He even trained the senior diplomats of the Israeli foreign ministry. Having worked for the Israeli diplomatic mission to the United Nations, I thought maybe I had a personal connection. I had to meet this guy. But how?

At first I considered trying the same thing I'd done earlier: submitting an application to Burson-Marsteller's human resources department. But that approach had already failed me. What's more, Buck was surrounded by an impenetrable wall of assistants; my résumé would be buried among hundreds of others. It was time to try something radically different. Instead of hoping to outlast my competition, I had to make a primitive move and sprint to the front of the pack.

The next day I was at Columbia University's business school library, twisting the knobs of the old microfilm and microfiche machines and scouring archived publications for intel about Buck and his firm. What today takes a few seconds with a smartphone took, back in the prehistoric days of the early 1990s, an entire afternoon. But climbing up the stairs to my fourth-floor walk-up that evening, I knew everything I needed to know about the man I was trying to impress. This time I'd write a letter that would get noticed.

"Dear Mr. Buchwald," I began. "I've been practicing public relations without a license...."

I went on to talk about my experience, but not as dull bullet points on a curriculum vitae. I had some fun, giving obvious but playful hints to get Buck interested in me. I sent the letter. A few days later, I picked up the phone and called Burson-Marsteller's offices. Buck's secretary picked up. My voice quivering, I explained to her that I'd written Mr. Buchwald and wanted to speak with him briefly. Shockingly, she put me through.

"I got your letter, Mr. Greenberg, but we're not hiring anyone right now," Buck told me gruffly.

"I understand, sir," I replied. "All I want is just a few minutes of your time."

Finally, he relented. "Be here Friday, 9:00 a.m.," he said, then hung up the phone.

I showed up in his office at the appointed hour. Like a drill sergeant, he asked me a series of rapid-fire questions: Could I write well and fast? Could I work with the media? Was I able to handle myself well in crisis situations? I gave my best answers, and Buck summoned the company's head of HR. The following Monday, I took a writing test. On Tuesday, I received a job offer.

Why did I succeed? I hadn't followed the rules. I didn't wait in line like everyone else. I wasn't particularly qualified. Instead, I acted like a primitive. I was still relentless with respect to my goal—getting a job—but I bent the rules. I took a shortcut.

Contrast my experience with the prescriptions contained in *Battle Hymn of the Tiger Mother*. In that international bestseller, the author, Amy Chua, a professor at Yale Law School and the daughter of Chinese immigrants, advocates for strict, no-nonsense parenting that stresses self-motivation, sweat, and a perpetually positive attitude that never wavers even when hard work yields little or no results. Former British prime minister David Cameron, a big fan of the book, explained that Chua's message was especially important for children: "Work, try hard, believe you can succeed, get up and try again," he said. Or, as another famous British prime minister once said at the dawn of World War II: "I have nothing to offer but blood, toil, tears, and sweat!"

When I was applying to job after job and being rejected from all of them, Chua might have told me to keep at it. I needed to stay positive and keep relentlessly sending out résumés—eventually, one of them would find its way to the right person. Chua's and Cameron's idea of being relentless might have its merits when it comes to conquering algebra, practicing piano, and maybe fending off a Nazi invasion, but it's not necessarily helpful in the modern economy.

By the time I was joining a much more rapidly growing workforce, amid economic changes accelerated by the advent of the internet, the traditional "apply and wait" approach was already feeling antiquated. Today, it's positively ancient. While LinkedIn and Indeed have replaced snail mail, the same idea applies for the civilized: you drop your line in the water, sit back, and wait for a bite. As I learned all those years ago, the relentless primitive doesn't have the patience for any of this; she grabs her spear and goes hunting. She understands that being relentless doesn't just mean trying hard—it means leapfrogging ahead. As we'll see in this chapter, a primitive isn't afraid to reach her goals by telling white lies, being selfish, and flashing that chip on her shoulder. Most important, when she's headed in the wrong direction, she isn't afraid to stop moving, turn around, and find a new road.

THINK LIKE A FIVE-YEAR-OLD

A decade ago I was hired by a nonprofit, Iran180, to help publicize human rights abuses by the Iranian regime. Human rights, I thought, was a topic everyone understood instinctively; you didn't need a master's degree in international relations to grasp that executing people because they were gay was a horrendous crime, or that a state that supported terrorism shouldn't be allowed to develop nuclear weapons. Our task was to find simple ways to explain the horrors of the Iranian regime to the general public. Sitting on the roof deck of our office, we threw around ideas about how to get the attention of people with only a passive interest in foreign affairs. My buddy David Galper, just riffing, began talking about the furry mascots that dance in between innings at baseball games. These mascots are crowd favorites, David said, because they are garish and over the top. You can't help but watch.

So instead of taking our campaign to Washington, DC, think tanks, we took it to the streets with a ten-foot-high puppet of Iran's leader at the time, Mahmoud Ahmadinejad, holding a giant atomic rocket. Then we sent the puppet, accompanied by street theater performers and cheerleaders blasting loud music, to cavort outside the United Nations. We staged a mock trial and then had the puppet "arrested." Everyone from passersby to diplomats knew exactly what our message was.

We hit the kind of home run that PR people can only dream about. Early the next morning I drowsily opened the *New York Times* to discover that our puppet had made the front page. A few weeks later, I donned the puppet suit on *The Daily Show with Jon Stewart*, where I talked to Samantha Bee about nontraditional protests. Sure, we could have fired off a strongly worded position paper and influenced a few dozen people. Instead, we approached the problem like a five-year-old would: we threw a big party with puppets and dancers and music.

Austin McChord certainly understands the power of the childlike mind. The man who built his first server using Lego bricks was often called a "man-child" by older executives at Datto. Austin encouraged his employees to paint their offices crazy colors and play with toys at the office. He left the key to his Tesla on his desk and let his employees take it for a spin anytime they wanted. Datto workers even created T-shirts with their fearless leader's silhouette and the caption: "Keep Austin Weird."

Here's another childlike quality that's surprisingly useful as an adult: telling white lies. Even the most devoted parent would agree that children often lie. When my wife and I asked our son, Noah, one of the purest primitives I know, if he had done his math homework, he'd reply, "Yup." When we'd ask if he'd read his book for English class, he'd reply, "Yup," and give us a brief synopsis. Noah, it turns out, never did his homework or read his books, but he was such a confident character that he could fool his teachers (and his parents) into believing he had. I remember thinking at the time: *Noah may struggle a bit in school, but he's going to make a ton of money one day in business.* As it turns out, while he wasn't doing his homework, thirteen-year-old Noah was buying Tesla stock long before most of Wall Street caught on.

When Austin was still running his company out of his father's basement, he knew he would have a hard time being taken seriously. To make the company seem larger and more important, he would answer his phone with a British accent, pretending to be a nonexistent colleague.

Whether it's imitating a secretary, embellishing non-critical details on a résumé, claiming the messenger failed to deliver documents you actually forgot to send, or purporting to be further along on a project than you actually are, to the relentless primitive, white lies are part of doing business. Naturally, it's up to you to measure and limit the seriousness of your lies, and prevent yourself from crossing any lines. For example, with Elizabeth

Holmes, the once-celebrated founder of blood-testing firm Theranos, a few early lies quickly became the very backbone of an enterprise that eventually crumbled under its own fraud.

In some other cases, however, a single white lie has sometimes saved a company. One of my favorite examples involves Rent the Runway, the online business that allows users to rent high-end designer clothing. Today, Rent the Runway is hugely successful, but in 2008 it was merely an idea in the minds of two Jennifers—Jennifer Hyman and Jennifer Fleiss—who were section mates at Harvard Business School. They had secured a meeting with legendary designer Diane von Furstenberg, hoping she could help them break into the notoriously cliquish fashion industry. As they were en route to their dream meeting, Hyman's cell phone rang. It was von Furstenberg's assistant: she was canceling the meeting, and it wouldn't be rescheduled. Fleiss began sobbing, but Hyman, every bit the relentless primitive, knew instinctively what to do: she pretended she had poor cell phone reception and couldn't hear von Furstenberg's assistant. Hyman and Fleiss arrived as planned at the famous designer's office, pled ignorance, and insisted they keep the meeting. The assistant relented. The two Jennifers met with von Furstenberg and emerged with a powerful ally and a couple of priceless introductions.

Another crucial childlike quality? Having playdates.

Grown-ups have meetings. They're endless, frequently leave you drained, and rarely seem to accomplish anything. Kids have playdates, which leave them charged up, excited, and ready to take on the world. Instead of boring meetings, why not have playdates? Relentless primitives constantly crave inspiration to fuel their journey—inspiration that often does not come in the workplace. Austin, for example, competed in BattleBot competitions with his friends and colleagues, crashed drones, and infected his own computers with ransomware to figure out how to beat it. A little creative problem-solving outside of the office helped him approach problems at work with a fresh mindset.

Practice the five-to-one rule: for every five unavoidable meetings in conference rooms with agendas and PowerPoint presentations, have one work playdate. I don't necessarily mean drunken karaoke or catching a dumb movie with a colleague (although these are great ways to get to know your coworkers). Rather, I mean getting together with someone you genuinely, truly like— a friend, a vendor, a partner, a boss, an employee—and bouncing ideas around in an environment that isn't the office and doesn't feel restrictive. Billionaire Yvon Chouinard, the founder and CEO of Patagonia, for example, formed a group called Do Boys with his fellow entrepreneurs and executives to embark on a major outdoor adventure at least once a year.

Back when I was taking 7:00 a.m. CrossFit classes, I became friendly with a group of successful guys who loved having playdates. There was Anthony, who worked as publisher of a music magazine; Brian, an FBI agent who holstered his Glock in the locker room; Kirk, who ran security operations at the United Nations and made a habit of flaunting his stab wounds from his peacekeeping days in the former Yugoslavia; Scott, a successful hotelier; and Tim, a computer engineer. At first I was a bit weirded out by the "Morning Posse," as they called themselves, but we became fast friends. We took vacations together, and I even forged professional connections with each member of the Morning Posse. Years later, when Kirk was dying of colon cancer, the rest of the group dropped everything and flew to his home in Nova Scotia to say goodbye. The once 190-pound chiseled rock had wasted away, but he still found the energy to give me words of encouragement on his deathbed, just as he had for years at the gym. In fact, without Kirk MacLeod, this book wouldn't have happened.

Make a habit of scheduling regular meetups with friends and

colleagues—whether it's coffee, lunch, after-work drinks, or ski trips. You might think that sounds trivial, but old-fashioned social interaction can be as important to your overall health as hitting the gym. And no, that group text thread or the occasional Face-Time on your smartphone isn't good enough. Press some flesh and play in real life. You will be surprised how much it helps; playing around with people you enjoy connecting with is an excellent way to work that childlike muscle and escape whatever professional rut you may be stuck in.

Anyone who spends time with children knows another truth about them: they aren't afraid to throw a tantrum to get what they want. When Indra Nooyi became CEO of PepsiCo in 2006, she sought advice from none other than Apple CEO (and über-primitive) Steve Jobs. "He said, if you really feel strongly about something—if you don't like something people are doing—throw a temper tantrum," Nooyi recalled. "Throw things around, because people have got to know that you feel strongly about it." While Nooyi may not have quite gone to Jobs-ian lengths to get what she wanted, she is not afraid to channel her inner toddler.

Finally, just like our ancestors, relentless primitives do not shy away from self-preservation. To be relentless is to be focused on yourself and your goals; everything else is secondary. My friend John, who works for Fidelity Investments, is a generous person, but he isn't selflessly so. People frequently ask him for help getting a job, so John came up with a selfish-ish rule: he will help out if he can, but he'll never meet for coffee or a beer. Instead, John takes phone calls and limits them to ten minutes. He'll make an introduction for you, but never more than one. And perhaps most important, he is not afraid to ask for a favor in return when he sees an opportunity. John protects his most prized possession: his time. He is generous with his ideas, but selfish with his hours. Does he occasionally rub people the wrong way? Of course. But by being up-front with his rules and expectations, he ensures his relentless energy is focused on his career and his family.

TAKE IT PERSONALLY

One of the most successful financial services firms in the country is one you may not have heard of. You won't find its office on Wall Street, and its employees aren't would-be masters of the universe who orchestrate multibillion-dollar mergers and acquisitions. Rather, you'll find its storefronts in small towns and suburban strip malls across America.

Meet Edward Jones. The nearly century-old firm has some forty-seven thousand employees and more than $8 billion in revenues, but its sales associates don't spend their days screaming into telephones and pounding away at Bloomberg terminals. Instead, they knock on the doors of ordinary people and conduct business in living rooms and kitchens. They try to form genuine, personal bonds with their clients, and it all begins with a handshake. You might see your Edward Jones broker at the grocery store or the bowling alley; he might even be your neighbor. The company has more retail offices than any other brokerage firm for the purpose of forging personal relationships between financial advisers and clients. It also routinely outranks other national full-service brokerage firms in workplace satisfaction, and has a permanent spot near the top of *Fortune* and J.D. Power's lists of the best places to work. One of the primary reasons is because the company nurtures independent thinking, with executives encouraging frontline sales associates to pitch new ideas and rethink sales techniques.

Edward Jones is a throwback organization in a time when most business is conducted over email, texts, and Slack messages. Meetings that once required a dozen people to congregate in the same conference room can now be easily arranged by looping in everyone on the same conference call. While efficiencies like these have certainly made us more productive, this convenience has its downsides. Chief among them is that we're losing our ability to simply connect, in person, shaking hands and looking each other in the eye.

It's a skill that Austin understood well. He struggled to find customers after he launched Datto, so he turned to small IT shops who could sell his backup hardware directly to end users. Austin would drive bleary-eyed to visit the many loyal clients who took a chance on his product, even ones in tiny towns. They were fellow entrepreneurs and so rabidly loyal to Austin that, during the company's annual convention in 2018, he attracted a far larger band of autograph seekers than the keynote speaker, Sir Richard Branson.

And so, here's a simple rule to follow: take a page out of the Edward Jones playbook and think like a door-to-door salesperson, not a Wall Street banker. How do you earn a great reputation? It's not just the quality of the returns, but rather the quality and variety of the conversation that keeps customers coming back. Take your work personally. There are many ways to do this, starting with the line of work you choose to get into.

Another guy who takes his work personally is Dan Mullen. On a cold Thanksgiving evening in 1989, Dan was sitting alone on the sidelines of Gill Stadium in Manchester, New Hampshire. His team had recently been eliminated from the state playoffs and Dan, the senior quarterback, would never again play high school football. His coach found him quietly sobbing. "If someone asked me to describe Dan as an athlete and a person, I would say he was relentless," he later said. "You always got his best effort." Fast-forward thirty years, and Dan is now head football coach at the University of Florida, where he is still taking football every bit as personally as he did as a teenager. He blurs the line between family and football; his wife, Megan, is heavily involved with team events and recruiting, and the two "treat every player on the team like they're our own kids," Dan explained in an interview. In return for his devotion, he insists that his players work just as hard as he does. "You will see a team that plays with relentless effort," Dan promised before the 2018 season. He was right: When he arrived in Gainesville, the Gators were coming off a 4–7 campaign. In his first season, the team went 10–3 and the Associated Press ranked it seventh in the nation. The following year Mullen's Gators jumped to No. 6 with an 11–2 record.

The old cliché goes that you should do what you love. "Follow your bliss and the universe will open doors for you where there were only walls," as Joseph Campbell once said. It's hard making a career out of what you love to do, but some people hit the jackpot: Dan Mullen may love coaching football more than anything else on the planet, and it turns out he's pretty good at it. Stephen King adores writing so much that he aims to churn out a minimum of two thousand words per day; it happens that most of those words end up in bestselling novels. But the painful truth is that a lot of us aren't very good at doing the things we love. For example, I love to sing. But as my family not-so-gently reminds me, I'm terrible at it. It pains me to admit it, but as much as I enjoy crooning, I will probably not be the next Frank Sinatra.

One of my favorite movies is *Thank You for Smoking*, a satirical comedy about Big Tobacco. Aaron Eckhart plays Nick Naylor, a smooth-talking spokesperson who lobbies on behalf of a product that kills people while also trying to be a role model for his twelve-year-old son. After Naylor sagely talks down his bosses as they careen from one scandal to another, he remarks to the audience: "Michael Jordan plays ball. Charles Manson kills people. I talk. Everyone has a talent."

The film hopefully did not spawn a new generation of tobacco lobbyists, but it makes a broader point about choosing a career path: find something you are a natural at and then milk it as much as humanly possible. Relentless primitives often do not have the patience to learn a new skill from scratch; they find something they are good at and then search for a way to monetize it. When I was eight years old, I certainly didn't dream of becoming a PR executive. But it turns out I'm very good at talking, and I'm even better at helping people and businesses talk about themselves.

When I was a kid growing up in Venice, California, my dad had a weekly touch football game on the beach with his friends. They'd drink beer, smoke dope, watch the sunset. One of the regulars was a guy named Jeff Smith. For the first twenty years of his work life, Jeff had a series of odd jobs and hustled to make a living, but nothing stuck. At one point he discovered his passion: writing. He wrote a number of screenplays, but, apparently, he simply wasn't good enough at writing movies. But it turned out he *was* good at editing other people's movies, and he built himself a wildly successful career in the movie trailer industry. He became extremely valued for his skill in producing previews, trailers, and TV spots for blockbusters. Once he made his fortune, Jeff sold his company, Open Road Entertainment, and is once again trying to make a go of it as a writer.

When you focus on what you are good at, work inherently becomes more personal. You are valued for a skill that you possess, and you make money doing that. You might find that you grow to love that skill—or, at the very least, you'll love being valued for it. Or, like Jeff, you'll make a boatload of money doing something else, shift gears, then re-devote yourself to your true passion.

GATHER YOUR CHIPS

Of course, finding something you're a natural at doesn't mean there won't be obstacles standing in your way. Sometimes these obstacles are money, education, or loved ones. When someone is affected by these obstacles, we often say he has "a chip on his shoulder." This phrase has a negative connotation, suggesting that this person is bitter and unable to set aside past grievances. A relentless primitive is always looking forward, but that does not mean he doesn't occasionally glance backward at the zigzagging road he has traveled. And he never forgets just how difficult it may have been—or who may have stood in his way. That's because refusing to let go can be a powerful motivator, as in the case of former NFL defensive tackle John Randle. He grew up during the 1970s in a shack in rural East Texas, sleeping in a bed with his three brothers after his father abandoned the family. Randle and his family didn't have indoor plumbing or even a toilet. They could barely get by on his mother's $23-per-week salary as a maid.

Randle was very, very good at playing football. His position was defensive lineman, and no opposing line could contain his unique combination of strength, speed, and ferocity. But he was considered too small to play at the highest levels. Randle didn't brush this criticism aside—it pissed him off. He ground his way onto his high school team, then the local community college team, and then Texas A&M University–Kingsville. Just like he had in high school, Randle continued to terrorize his opponents, relying on brute force over form. Yet scouts still thought he was undersized, and no team took him in the 1990 NFL draft. He managed to secure a tryout with the Tampa Bay Buccaneers, but the team wanted to switch him to linebacker, a position more suited to his size. Randle refused. Finally, he landed with the Minnesota Vikings, where he won a spot on the practice squad, then special teams, then, finally, the starting lineup. Before every game, he'd smear his face with war paint and memorize obscure facts about the other teams' players to throw his rivals off their game. Randle finished his career with more sacks than any interior lineman in the history of the league.

How did he do it? How did he distill his complex emotions

into a potent brew that made him better? Not by obsessing about his disadvantages or allowing himself to fester with resentment—that's never helpful—but by reframing the experience and learning to see each rejection as nothing but an invitation to work harder, do better, and find another way to channel that relentless energy that's so personal and pure.

Many of the most successful people I've met never stop trying to prove themselves to haters—real or imagined—standing in their way. They don't forget slights, and they aren't quick to forgive. But while some people are consumed by their resentments, relentless primitives are fueled by them. For example, Austin's academic adviser at the Rochester Institute of Technology called his data backup idea "terrible" and insisted he focus on graduating. Austin used that C average and his skeptical adviser to drive him, proving he could succeed against the odds. Yet, after he sold his company at age thirty-two, he immediately donated $50 million to RIT—the single largest donation in the school's history.

There are many ways to make use of those chips on your shoulder without letting them overly burden you. I still keep a folder of my rejection letters from my first job search and I look through it from time to time for motivation. Brad, one of my favorite former clients, is a very successful tech CEO who keeps an old wooden shoeshine box in his closet. Many years ago, he shined shoes in South Boston to make ends meet. He keeps the box to remind himself of where he came from and of all the obstacles he had to overcome.

Rather than being quick to forgive and forget—a very civilized attitude—find some physical object of your own that reminds you of a past setback and look at it at least once a week. Reflect on your hardships. Remember your difficult beginnings and use them to fuel your progression.

SPRINT OFTEN, THEN HIT PAUSE

Each year, the tiny Welsh town of Llanwrtyd Wells holds a curious ritual called the Man Versus Horse Marathon. The twenty-two-mile course is a mixture of roads, farm pasture, forest trails, and rocky streams, and it is open to two- and four-legged competitors with the simple rule that the human or animal who finishes the course fastest wins. You might think horses, which can reach a top speed of 30 mph, always win. They usually do, but humans occasionally prevail despite their obvious physical shortcomings. Humans may not be built to compete at the Kentucky Derby, but we are built to run at a moderate pace for very long stretches. Our approximately three million sweat glands keep us cool, and our springy tendons act like pogo sticks to convert elastic potential energy into kinetic energy.

Anthropologists believe that our great endurance abilities were crucial two to three million years ago, when early humans first began hunting. We may not have been able to run down a gazelle like a cheetah, but we could jog for hours at a time, wearing down our prey until they keeled over from heat exhaustion. This practice, known as persistence hunting, is still practiced by indigenous tribes in Africa's Kalahari Desert and elsewhere in the world.

Fortunately, we now have Trader Joe's, so we can choose our meat in the safety of a climate-controlled building. But many of us can still endure. Generations of sitting at desks and standing on assembly lines has not entirely undone our abilities to keep going through physical challenges. The key is that some evolved primitives know when to stop jogging and start sprinting.

Studies show that endurance athletes who implement high-intensity interval training like sprinting into their routine can actually improve their overall endurance levels. That's great, you're probably thinking, but what does that have to do with my own goals? For civilized people, work is always about the long run. They are structured folks, wedded to their respective routines, and they like to feel like everything they do is part of an ongoing and orderly track that leads them very clearly from point A to point B. When they're relentless, it's about carrying on in their path, like marathon runners slogging through the pain at a steady pace to reach the finish line. Relentless primitives are different. They're just as mindful of that ribbon, but they have a very different idea about running races. Like endurance runners who have also trained as sprinters, they feel more comfortable with a series of mad dashes than with one long slog.

The relentless primitive knows that to summon the energy necessary to bust through the tedium, you often need to act like the house is on fire and drop everything and run. Not long ago I was scheduled to fly and meet an important client. It was a stormy afternoon, and, to my great annoyance, my flight was canceled. A civilized person, even the most relentless one, would likely have called the client, apologized, and offered to fly in the next day or set up a videoconference. But my gut convinced me to make a primitive move: this client was just too important to reschedule, and he expected me to be there for him. I told my colleagues I wouldn't be available for the next day or two, kissed my slightly confused wife goodbye at 8:00 p.m., and drove four hundred miles across four states. I slept in a roadside motel and made my morning meeting on time. I made sure that the message to my clients was clear: I will literally go the extra mile for them. My colleagues back home thought I was a little nuts, but they had to grudgingly give me credit for my devotion.

Moves like these are instinctual for primitives. One of the most important skills of the modern workplace is prioritizing. For instance, deciding which emails must be replied to now and which can wait an extra day, or which meetings need to happen and which are less important. Relentless primitives can immediately recognize what requires their attention, and they have no problem dropping everything else on a moment's notice. Like an ER doctor conducting triage, you have to look at your to-do list and determine what is urgent and what can wait.

Daymond John, founder and CEO of apparel company FUBU and investor on the hit show *Shark Tank,* has a unique way of prioritizing his day. "When you wake up in the morning and look at emails, you're going to be consumed by everyone else's emails of people asking you what *they* need to be done," he told CNBC "Make It." "You don't get an email in the morning that says, 'All those problems I had last week, I solved them, and the check is on the way to you for a million dollars.'" Instead of letting emails shape his day, he arrives at the office with his own agenda in mind. Some of the tasks on his to-do list will advance that agenda and some will not, and John prioritizes them accordingly. "When I walk into the world, I'm concentrating on what *I* want to accomplish," he explains.

Relentless primitives never lose sight of their mission and don't allow less important problems to obscure it. Moves like these are selfish, as we discussed in the previous section, but they are necessary. Like John, I now begin my day by laying out precisely what I want to accomplish. Only then do I open my inbox and determine what can wait a day, a week, or a month. I focus on what can help me meet my big goals for the day. You'll piss some people off with this strategy, but that's the cost of doing business.

One thing to keep in mind is that while relentless primitives might find it easier to prioritize their time than civilized people, who are prone to "people please" and put the priorities of others before their own, they are just as susceptible to burning out. Henri Poincaré, the famed French theoretical physicist and philosopher, devised a math problem so complex—aptly called the Poincaré Conjecture—that it took the world's most brilliant mathematicians nearly a hundred years to solve it. His work laid the basis for chaos theory, which has applications today in everything from cryptology to robotics to weather patterns. Poincaré also wrote extensively about his work habits—especially when he was suffering from the theoretical physicist's version of writer's block. Writing about one of his major mathematical breakthroughs, Poincaré described two miserable weeks of hard work and no results:

> Every day I seated myself at my work table, stayed an hour or two, tried a great number of combinations and reached no results. One evening, contrary to my custom, I drank black coffee and could not sleep. Ideas rose in crowds; I felt them collide until pairs interlocked, so to speak, making a stable combination.

By the next morning, the solution appeared. What Poincaré needed to succeed wasn't his usual routine of working hard at his desk, but just one wakeful night of letting his mind go wander wherever it needed to.

To stay nimble, the relentless primitive's brain must be allowed to roam occasionally without purpose, to wander off without being taxed by conventional tasks, free to make all sorts of discoveries. The civilized mind, on the other hand, abhors nothing more than wasting time. In an age when entire professions are structured around billable hours, is there a more serious transgression than declaring some of those hours "me time"? Ironically, the more apps and experts emerge to provide us with new and efficient ways to manage our time, the more we treat time like a resource that must be used to the fullest, which only increases our anxiety.

So, should you disappear for vast swaths of your day to play Pokémon Go? Not exactly—the economy does have to function, after all, and I'd certainly hope the pilot of my red-eye flight or the surgeon performing my knee surgery doesn't suddenly follow my advice. Instead, if your circumstances allow it, channel your inner Ferris Bueller and give yourself short breaks during the workday dedicated to nothing but recharging. If possible: take a thirty-minute walk, bike around the park, or, if you're like me, take a midday yoga class or catch a matinee.

What is some regular downtime during your day that you could take advantage of? When my eldest daughter turned twelve, she insisted on getting a dog. "No way," I said. "How could I possibly make time to walk him?" I was working long hours and often got up before sunrise to catch up on email and prepare my calendar among other busy-bee tasks that civilized relentless people insist on doing. But a child's plea is hard to turn down, and soon a charming mutt entered our home and our hearts. It didn't take me longer than a few weeks to understand that I could barely afford *not* to take the time to walk Winston. Not only was it fun, but the daily respite gave me the time to clear my head. I'd leave my phone powered off, or better yet, at home. I was still thinking about work and trying to creatively solve problems in my head— relentless primitives are almost always thinking about work—but stepping away from the office and being alone (or with Winston), helped me focus. I've lost count of the number of epiphanies that came to me as I scooped up poop.

Research bears this out: in his book *Deep Work: Rules for Focused Success in a Distracted World*, Cal Newport, a professor of computer science at Georgetown University, explains that tasks like answering email, chat messages, meetings, notifications, and social media can destroy our productivity. Instead, he explains that regularly dropping out to focus on a single goal is far more effective. As an example, he offers the tale of the renowned psychiatrist Carl Jung, who routinely escaped to his cabin in the woods for weeks at a time to read, write, and simply sit in perfect stillness. Yes, that form of primitive relentlessness allowed Jung to successfully challenge his erstwhile mentor, Sigmund Freud, whose very name at the time was synonymous with psychology. My friend Alan Lightman (whom we'll learn more about in the

Agnostic chapter) is a physicist, writer, and social entrepreneur who wrote an entire book—*In Praise of Wasting Time*—on the virtues of taking breaks. He even boldly proposes that "half our waking minds be designated and saved for quiet reflection."

How often do you find yourself truly alone—not just away from people, but from your devices? It might be hard at first. If you're like I was, you get that brief pit in your stomach when you can't find your smartphone, or when you haven't checked your notifications for a while. I've slowly trained myself to spend time away from my phone and laptop, and I crave these moments so I can think through my biggest problems at work. (Of course my inability to be reached can drive my wife crazy, so, as always, there are compromises to be made.)

CHANGE LANES

One day in October 2018, I was driving along Manhattan's West Side Highway when I received a call from Austin. About a year had passed since he had sold Datto to Vista Equity Partners. "Do you have time to speak?" he asked. We had just spoken a few hours earlier, and I sensed that something serious was on his mind.

"Sure, what's up?"

"I'm leaving Datto," he said flatly. There was no hesitance in his voice. He wasn't consulting me about his decision—he was informing me.

"Wow…," was all I could say.

And just like that, Austin walked away from the company he had built from the ground up, the company into which he had invested nearly every waking hour of his adult life. I sat in my car, stunned. Relentless primitives don't suddenly abandon their missions. I thought of former Uber CEO Travis Kalanick, who had to be dragged kicking and screaming from the company he founded, and Steve Jobs, who was shown the door from Apple in the early 1980s and spent the next dozen years plotting his return. But Austin? He simply got bored after Datto was sold and wanted to try something new.

I realized that Datto itself was never Austin's purpose in life. He loved his company, but he loved his employees even more. Once he received a suitable offer for his business that would reward the people who had been by his side for years, Austin was ready to refocus on what he thought was his true mission in life: helping the little guy. Having come from a small town in Connecticut and attended college in a struggling city in upstate New York, he never fit the mold of your typical tech entrepreneur. That was the chip on his shoulder that we discussed earlier in this chapter. One of his proudest achievements was building Connecticut's first unicorn—tech industry slang for a billion-dollar company.

Austin is now working at General Catalyst, a venture capital firm that makes early-stage investments in promising companies. The bio he wrote for the firm's website beautifully sums up his broader goal in life:

> During that amazing run [at Datto], my reason for coming to work totally changed. At first it was coding, creating, pushing the technology of the time to enable new possibilities. Over time I realized that I was coming for my employees, to empower them to break through walls and do great things. Becoming a leader was an evolution, with endless ups and downs, but it made one thing clear: If you want an exceptional result, it takes extraordinary effort.

Austin's latest primitive move encapsulates the final ingredient of being relentless: changing lanes. Austin's mission—helping people—has not changed. At Datto he wanted to help small businesses gain access to backup solutions. Now, at General Catalyst, he wants to assist entrepreneurs with big ideas who are trying to grow them into something special, just like he did.

We've all been taught to plow ahead, focus, and stay the course. That is the way of relentless civilized people who craft their careers by staying in their lanes. Think of the employee who worked his way up from the mail room to become head of the company, or the engineer who worked forty years at the same place and retired with a pension and a gold watch. They are relentless, but they never left their lane. Primitives are different: sometimes they make the easy right turn, sometimes they make sharp left turns, and they go backward just as easily as forward. With the growth of the gig economy and the financial insecurity that accompanies it, it's never been more important to change lanes comfortably and nimbly.

Author Troy Anderson understands this principle well. In his wonderful book *The Way of Go*, he shares insights from the traditional Chinese game Go. Here's one I love: don't get too attached to your first moves. If you're up against a good opponent, she'll snuff out your strategy and you'll have to reassess. The same is true in virtually every career path. Novelists and screenwriters, for example, often begin their project wedded to a cherished character or plot twist only to find that it must be jettisoned. Many civilized people will climb their own career ladder, but the relentless primitive is eager to shift lanes, whether it means making a lateral move to a new company or even switching careers entirely. Even if they occasionally sidestep or zigzag, they are always looking for the opportunity to take an enormous leap forward.

As we'll discuss in more depth in the Agnostic chapter, not only does changing lanes keep you fresh, but it's sometimes necessary for your very survival, not to mention satisfaction, in today's workplace. Being a typewriter repairperson may have once been a lucrative job, but the forward-thinking primitives among them also learned how to take apart a computer. For some, that might mean stumbling onto a totally different path, as it did for the two scientists who rejected the directives of their big pharmaceutical company and accidentally discovered the molecule that led to the creation of the antidepressant Zoloft. For others, it might mean making a U-turn and returning to a former employer or career; many of us would consider that a shameful defeat, but as someone who completed three separate tours of duty with the same large multinational public relations firm, I can tell you that each time was different, instructive, and fulfilling in its own way. You can still be moving forward if you take a step back.

Even if you spent twenty years mastering a particular occupation, it doesn't mean that you can't make a sharp turn and try another. Jeff Bezos was once an unhappy thirty-year-old who had spent years working in the financial services industry. He took a coast-to-coast drive and decided to quit his job and launch an online bookstore from his garage.

Hitting pause does not just mean taking a breather during lunch. It can also mean stopping to reassess the weeks, months, and years ahead. What are the alternate lanes you envision your career taking? Do some include possible U-turns back to past employers or occupations? Or perhaps there are on-ramps to entirely new careers. Take frequent breaks to reexamine your situation. Whether it's leaving work in the middle of the day or leaving your job in the middle of your career, never stop reassessing, and never be afraid to sprint to someplace new.

CHAPTER TWO

OPPOSITIONAL

The most formidable person I've ever known was a man named Danny Lewin. We met while I was taking summer classes at The Hebrew University of Jerusalem. Danny was a stocky and rebellious high schooler who'd taken a part-time job at a local gym. We were both fish out of water: me a semester-abroad student and he a Denver-born teen whose parents dragged him kicking and screaming halfway across the world to fulfill a dream of living in Israel. Thrust into a strange place devoid of skiing and football, Danny barely bothered to attend high school, largely because the classes were too easy for him. A math savant, Danny took the SATs "for fun," he said. He'd clean the gym floors and disinfect the locker room and tell anyone within earshot about his plan to join Sayeret Matkal, the most elite unit of the Israel Defense Forces. This was an especially audacious goal considering the unit almost never accepted non-native-born Israelis, let alone cocky Americans who spoke heavily accented Hebrew.

Many people rolled their eyes at Danny, but I was drawn to him. The secretive unit admitted about a dozen young men each year. The Israeli equivalent of the US Army's Delta Force, its commandos do the kind of stuff you see in movies: creep deep into enemy territory to gather strategic intelligence, conduct counterterrorism operations, and rescue hostages. Sayeret Matkal alumni go on to illustrious careers in business and politics. Several have become prime minister, including Benjamin Netanyahu and Ehud Barak. And here was Danny, with his mop and his bravado, claiming he would soon join them. We quickly became friends, and I told the plucky kid with big dreams and an even bigger mouth that I believed in him.

About two years later I found Danny wearing a mischievous smile: he had been accepted into Sayeret Matkal. He devoted himself to his training and quickly became one of the best soldiers in his unit. When the grueling ten-mile marches didn't feel tough enough, he'd strap on twice the amount of gear just to heighten the challenge. In 1995, after four years in the army and a promotion to captain, Danny went on to graduate summa cum laude from the prestigious Technion–Israel Institute of Technology. In 1996, he earned a scholarship to MIT, where, as he had before, he sought out impossible challenges. Danny was especially fascinated with the internet and finding new ways to optimize web traffic. He teamed up with his faculty adviser, F. Thomson Leighton, to create a revolutionary new algorithm called consistent hashing, which became the basis of a system that significantly improved the delivery of web content to computers. Instead of moving on to a civilized career as a university professor or in big tech, he started his own company, Akamai Technologies, with Leighton, MIT Sloan School of Management student Jonathan Seelig, and Randall Kaplan, an executive from SunAmerica. Using the algorithm Danny helped develop, Akamai eventually managed more than 30 percent of all online traffic.

Danny was the living embodiment of a primitive. He would grow obsessed with a vast array of ideas, from knot theory to the concept of infinity, and would not let go until he was satisfied that he understood enough. This often meant staying up until three or four in the morning, giving up sleep to read one more book, learn one more fact, come up with one more idea. He took everything personally, which meant that he sometimes got upset about trivial disagreements. It also meant he was dedicated to his friends and maniacally committed to every task he took on. He had little patience for small talk or polite chitchat; if he perceived something or someone as not being worth his time, Danny was known to just get up and walk away. While this approach could be off-putting, it propelled him to take risks and make decisions that others may have deemed too daunting or impractical. When friends of mine called him a mad genius, I'd smile and say that was the point.

On September 11, 2001, Danny boarded a flight from Boston to Los Angeles. Seated in 9B aboard American Airlines Flight 11, he watched as Mohamed Atta and Abdulaziz al-Omari, sitting directly in front of him, jumped to their feet and charged the cockpit. According to airfone calls from flight attendants to authorities on the ground, which were documented in the 9/11 Commission's report, Danny attempted to tackle the terrorists. But the hijacker in 10B, Satam al-Suqami, moved as well, slitting his throat with a knife. At thirty-one years old, Danny was the attack's first victim. Less than thirty minutes later, at 8:46 a.m., Flight 11 crashed into the World Trade Center's North Tower.

And yet, Danny should not be remembered as a victim. He should be remembered as a business visionary who let his oppositional nature guide him to greatness. The instinct to be oppositional is at the core of the primitive mind. Civilized people place a premium on nonconfrontation—the N in HOMING—which might seem logical on the face of things, but easily devolves into passive aggression and petty office politics. Oppositional primitives, wild and refractory, know that sometimes a little bit of resistance is the best source of energy. They are crusaders against groupthink, the banes of yes-men, the square pegs in the round holes. As my father used to say when explaining his lack of promotions during his time in the US Air Force Reserves:

"Make me a general, or leave me a private, but I refuse to pass on silly orders."

There is of course a civilized way to be oppositional. Healthy differences are part of human nature; you may like potatoes and I may like potahtoes, as the Gershwin brothers put it. As my grandmother from Omaha used to say, "That's why there is chocolate *and* vanilla ice cream." Healthy opposition is enshrined in our Constitution, with the checks and balances that protect us against the "tyranny of the majority." Civilized opposition and dissent are a hallmark of democracy; think of the important role whistle-blowers play in both politics and business.

But it is also easy to see the big-picture shortcomings of our most civilized forms of opposition. Even in a democracy, bucking the system and standing up against political power is not as easy or common as we often tell ourselves. The reluctance of Americans to challenge prevailing political sentiments or the most powerful among us led the country to the McCarthy Hearings and Watergate, the second Iraq War, and blind loyalty to President Donald Trump. Consensus can quickly become groupthink when well-intentioned people make irrational decisions spurred by the urge to conform or stamp out dissent. The stakes may be lower in the corporate world, but I see this all the time. Organizations, especially large ones, often seem to prize consensus building above all else, believing a chorus of "I agree" equates to a "good idea."

Oppositional primitives aren't merely contrarians; above all else, they believe in making progress. They hate being told problems are too large or intractable. I had a client many years ago named Jay Amato, who was a business fixer. People called him the Ty-D-Bol Man, after the popular toilet cleaning product from the 1970s and '80s. Company executives hired Jay to clean up the messy problems that no one else wanted to handle. He was like the corporate version of The Wolf, played by Harvey Keitel in

Pulp Fiction. Jay would present proposals to management teams and invariably hear one of two responses: "We tried that and it didn't work" and "We couldn't possibly do that." An oppositional at heart, Jay would smile and nod and say: "Well, then I've found my solution." Despite the insistence of the executives, he'd focus solely on those supposedly impossible goals. He shook up the status quo and forced companies to consider bigger, more painful, and more creative solutions to their problems. For Jay, changing the mindset of these execs and getting them to do what they previously thought was impossible was key to engineering a turnaround.

Oppositional primitives like Jay and Danny can sometimes be sand in the gears of a large, slow-moving machine. They aren't always team players, and they don't resort to business jargon to mask their true feelings. This doesn't always jibe well with corporate culture. Take, for example, the process by which companies generate ideas. In 1942, BBDO ad executive Alex Osborn—dubbed "The Real Don Draper" by *Inc.* magazine—coined the term *brainstorming.* Two of his major rules: focus on quantity over quality, and withhold criticism. This process persisted well into my stint at BBDO, and during creative sessions, no matter what someone suggested, we had to say, "Great idea, Bob!" or "Excellent thought, Hanna!" But when Danny hired me to do marketing and PR for his company in the late '90s, he'd routinely say: "Marco, that idea sucks. In fact, it might be the stupidest idea I've ever heard," or "Marco, that guy has no idea what the hell he's talking about." His style was abrasive, rude, laughing, and loving—all at the same time. By constantly challenging the people around him to be better, just as he constantly challenged himself to be better, Danny built something that others thought could never be pulled off.

An oppositional primitive is fueled by a constructive form of conflict that sparks innovative breakthroughs. Conversely, a contrarian is like your uncle who's had a few too many at Thanksgiving dinner: he just wants to stir the pot for the sake of it, not to advocate creatively and courageously for an idea or opinion that others may not support. Oppositional primitives innately understand the difference. Thankfully there are some tactics you can employ so that your opposition leads to productive results.

FIGHT EVERY DAY

A few years ago, my family and I were staying at a beautiful B&B in Newport, Rhode Island, that was owned by a couple named Bryan and Fran. Bryan was a former professional football player and Vietnam War veteran; Fran was a feisty Italian American who was a full head shorter than her husband. They had been married for fifty years. Over breakfast one morning, my wife and I asked them to share the secret to making their marriage last.

"Fight every day," they said in unison. We laughed at first, but we quickly realized that they were serious. They fought over little things and big things, money and vacations, politics and music. They didn't fight for the sake of it; they simply held very different opinions about a very wide range of topics and they never felt compelled to agree with each other.

Fran and Bryan's squabbles reminded me of how my kids bickered when they were younger. As adults, we are taught to keep our opinions to ourselves out of politeness. But kids aren't bound by such civilized constraints. They don't have filters and, like Danny Lewin, have no problem yelling about how wrong you are. As we saw in the previous chapter, relentless primitives channel their childlike minds to come up with wildly creative solutions. Oppositional primitives often take this to the next level by approaching every conversation like they're in a playground quarrel.

In his book *The Culture Code*, author Daniel Coyle recounts a competition set up by an engineer to see who could build the tallest structure using uncooked spaghetti, tape, string, and a marshmallow. The combatants: four business school students and a group of kindergarteners. The business students tackled the problem like constructive, civilized people. "They began talking and thinking strategically," Coyle recounts. "They examined the materials. They tossed ideas back and forth and asked thoughtful, savvy questions." The kindergarteners? Well, they acted like kindergarteners. They didn't ask questions or strategize. They grabbed materials from each other and bickered. "When they spoke, they spoke in short bursts: 'Here! No, *here!*' Their entire technique might be described as *trying a bunch of stuff together.*"

Guess which team won? The kindergarteners. In dozens of experiments, they built towers averaging twenty-six inches tall, while the business students averaged barely ten inches. It turns out that the business students were so preoccupied with collaborating and status management that they failed to devote time to actually building their structures. "Their interactions appear smooth, but their underlying behavior is riddled with inefficiency, hesitation, and subtle competition. Instead of focusing on the task, they are navigating their uncertainty about one another," Coyle found. Conversely, the five-year-olds were chaotic in their collaboration, but worked productively and consistently. Instead of competing for status, they devoted 100 percent of their energy to their goal: building a tall tower.

The same can be said about oppositional primitives. Like kindergarteners, oppositional primitives can be uncensored, they can be obnoxious, they can be angry. They come up with brilliant ideas and they come up with terrible ideas. They complain—loudly. An oppositional primitive may initially come across as someone who makes a sport out of conflict—a contrarian—but there are key differences. An oppositional primitive is productive.

She speaks up when she does not think the status quo is functioning, but she has no problem being included in a consensus. Oppositional thinkers don't take an opposing viewpoint out of habit or out of a desire to appear independent; rather, they ask probing questions, evaluate a situation, and come up with a solution that may or may not reflect someone else's.

For the civilized among us, conflict does not come naturally. We have been socialized by our parents, our teachers, and our bosses to believe that conflict is uncomfortable. To succeed, we must be optimistic and cheerful around others—"team players" as managers in large corporations like to say. Indeed, some research does suggest that people want a "No Bad Ideas" culture similar to the one I experienced while brainstorming as a group at the advertising agency BBDO. A Google study of high-performance teams found that what employees crave most is psychological safety— that is, the safety to take risks and make mistakes, and the confidence that "no one on the team will embarrass or punish anyone else for admitting a mistake, asking a question, or offering a new idea." Without a culture of safety, the theory goes, people are afraid to bring up new ideas and challenge established ones.

But does the "No Bad Ideas" system actually produce the best ideas? In 2003, researchers out of the University of California at Berkeley split 265 undergraduates into teams of five. Each team was assigned to find a solution to the same challenge: "How can traffic congestion be reduced in the San Francisco Bay Area?" One-third of the teams were told to brainstorm with no criticism allowed. One-third were told to brainstorm, but to criticize other ideas when necessary. And one-third were given no parameters at all. It turns out the teams instructed to debate and criticize produced the most creative solutions by far. "While the instruction 'do not criticize' is often cited as the important instruction in brainstorming, this appears to be a counterproductive strategy," explained the lead researcher, Charlan Nemeth. "Our findings show that debate and criticism do not inhibit ideas but, rather, stimulate them relative to every other condition."

Research suggests that some of the healthiest companies are those that encourage constructive conflict. For instance, one study of 525 large family-owned businesses found that the healthiest companies handle "conflict appropriately when it arises, encouraging strong family cohesion and communication, and inviting—then resolving—healthy conflict." These organizations succeed by encouraging oppositional viewpoints during shareholder meetings and other gatherings, ensuring that consensus is earned only after spirited debate.

BE OBSTREPEROUS

Early in his life, Danny Lewin was quick to adopt a somewhat infamous Israeli saying: "You are not correct, and I'll explain to you why." He took this brash, at times infuriating demeanor wherever he went. Though he excelled as a soldier, army psychologists nearly booted him from Sayeret Matkal because they worried he was too defiant to follow orders. When he was working part-time at IBM while studying at the Technion–Israel Institute of Technology, he was almost fired several times for butting heads with his bosses. Danny's favorite word was *obstreperous,* which means "noisy and difficult to control." When he met another oppositional person, Danny would call her obstreperous. When he couldn't get a server to work, it was being obstreperous. A difficult-to-solve problem was obstreperous. And, of course, Danny himself was obstreperous.

Today, there is a notable shortage of obstreperous people in business, especially in large organizations. This can have catastrophic consequences. Take the Zurich-based airline Swissair, for instance, which during the latter half of the twentieth century gained a reputation for quality, reliability, and safety. Due to its excellent management and financial stability, it earned the nickname the "Flying Bank." In the 1990s, however, the airline faced stiff competition from low-cost airlines. In a plan known as the "Hunter Strategy," Swissair borrowed enormous sums of money to buy other airlines in an attempt to consolidate market share. By 2000, the Flying Bank was hemorrhaging cash. Following the industry-wide downturn in the wake of September 11, it went bankrupt. The arrogance of Swissair's management in refusing to consider alternatives as it ran into trouble was so profound that its collapse prompted an academic study by The University of Adelaide Business School. The study found that no one in the management hierarchy bothered to question executives' decisions to aggressively expand. Moreover, existing board members were pushed out in favor of "experts" from Credit Suisse and consulting firm McKinsey & Company—people who had practically zero experience in the airline industry. The resulting echo chamber at Swissair's highest levels lacked "leadership and accountability," according to the report. "The decisions relating to the alliances and mergers would suggest that the board's approval was in part a result of group conformity and groupthink. The fact that none of the board members appeared to oppose Swissair's decision to put aside a potentially lucrative alliance opportunity for the 'Hunter Strategy' could be a result of the individual board members' reluctance to display what could be construed by the group as 'disruptive behaviour.'"

The purest oppositional primitives can sniff out a rotten company even when there are no visible signs, even when that company is worth billions of dollars. By the dawn of the new millennium, the energy conglomerate Enron had some twenty-nine thousand employees and was, at least on paper, hauling in $100 billion in revenue. In 1999, Enron was interested in establishing a marketplace for buying and selling internet bandwidth in much the same way it did for oil and natural gas. Enron's CEO, Jeffrey Skilling, reached out to Danny in hopes of doing business with him. Akamai was barely scraping by at the time and desperate for a big client, so Danny and his cofounder Jonathan Seelig flew down to Dallas to meet the Enron executive team in the Admirals Club lounge at Dallas/Fort Worth International Airport. Skilling joined via conference line and tried to woo Danny by explaining how a bandwidth exchange would revolutionize the internet. Everyone in the room nodded along except Danny, who looked increasingly angry and then quickly explained why the concept was flawed. He interrupted Skilling and said: "Jeff, your idea makes absolutely no sense. You've wasted my and Jonathan's time by making us come down here. This is never going to work in a million years." Everyone sat in stunned silence as Danny admonished one of the most powerful CEOs on the planet. Then they shouted at each other for a few minutes before Skilling hung up. Danny quietly left the table and caught the next flight back to Boston. Barely two years later, Skilling was indicted on thirty-five counts of fraud, insider trading, and other crimes related to the Enron scandal. He eventually served eleven years in prison, while Enron's share price collapsed from $90 to pennies. Danny didn't know that Enron would enter the then-largest corporate bankruptcy proceeding of all time, but he had no trouble recognizing an executive team that had no clue what it was doing.

Not everyone's bullshit detector is as finely tuned as Danny's, but it's possible to make yourself more obstreperous in a productive way. First, take note when executives are insulated from criticism. The best way to pierce that veil is to ask too many questions. Don't be afraid to be like the irritating kid in class who constantly challenges the teacher; asking questions lets you confront the status quo without overtly declaring war on it. For many people, asking questions doesn't come naturally. And at organizations that value the appearance of decisiveness and command, some may believe that asking questions makes them look weak or unsure. A recent Harvard Business School study explains:

As we grow older, curiosity tends to be wrung out of us. Parents, schools, and workplaces impose rules and discourage risk. Rather than provoking with inquiry, they insist on correct answers. A child asks 300 questions a day. By middle school, the number is down to practically none. By adulthood, our disposition toward questioning can range from the timid to the hostile.

In short, the study concludes, we need to get better at asking questions. Interestingly, while many of today's workplaces may be deserts of intellectual curiosity, some research shows that managers may not be as averse to being challenged as we assume they are. A study published in the *Journal of Applied Psychology* noted that obsequious employees—those who never ask questions and dutifully follow orders—often fare worse in the long run. These workplace flatterers can be "good actors but bad apples," the study concludes, because the amount of effort required to be a yes-person depletes self-control and makes bad behavior, low productivity, and slacking off much more likely. Politely challenging your boss—either by setting boundaries or suggesting better approaches—sets you apart from others and earns respect.

From "Why did that apple fall on my head?" to "Does the sun truly revolve around the earth?" history's most famous scientists and philosophers never stopped asking questions. And many of the most successful companies operating today insist on questioning the decisions their leaders make. As Eric Schmidt, former CEO of Google, explained, "We run this company on questions, not answers." Danny used to pride himself and praise his employees for asking "nontrivial questions"—in other words, questions that required more than a yes or no answer. Asking nontrivial questions demonstrates intelligence, a drive to learn, and curiosity—all traits that the most successful employees embody.

While asking questions is an effective way to raise some healthy skepticism, be careful not to sound accusatory. For example, when I am reviewing a marketing strategy with my team that was not effective, I don't ask, "Who was responsible for this dumpster fire?" Rather, I say, "Let's learn from our mistakes and think of something better." I pose the hard questions to myself, and then to my team. I'm critical, but I can be oppositional while still being respectful and focused on the answer. When I was a mid-level employee earlier in my career, I asked my superiors to elaborate on their decisions, but I rarely dismissed them outright. I gained a reputation for asking tough questions while still respecting the command structure. But I also learned that if an organization doesn't nurture an environment that is receptive to skepticism, it deserves to become the next Swissair or Enron.

SEE CONSTRAINTS AS CATALYSTS

When Ibtihaj Muhammad was an elementary school student growing up in New Jersey, participating in athletics was difficult. As an observant Muslim, she wore a hijab in public places. A true competitor at heart, Ibtihaj resolved to find a sport that allowed her to remain true to her faith. Then, one day, she and her mother drove past the local high school fencing team practice. The sport was fast-paced, vigorous, and—to Ibtihaj's delight—required gear that covered the entire body. "I don't know what sport that is, but when you get to high school, I want you to try it out," her mother told her. She went on to join the team, and she even became good at fencing—so good, in fact, that she earned herself a spot on the US Olympic team and became the first Muslim woman to bring home a medal for America. And in 2014, Ibtihaj and her siblings launched a clothing company, Louella, that offers a fresh and vibrant take on modest women's apparel.

In many ways, Ibtihaj's success—both in fencing and in the fashion world—was the result of being creatively constrained. Imagine that I asked you to draw a picture of an alien from the fictional planet Minerva. Without any kind of direction, you'd probably grab a crayon and sketch out something that looks like E.T., or a creature out of the *Star Wars* universe, or maybe just an ex of yours. But if I began describing to you in general terms what a Minervan looked like—six eyes, hairy arms, three heads, and feet for ears—your creative juices would start flowing. Instead of relying on alien tropes from '80s movies, you'd be forced to invent something entirely new based on a vague physical description. It might seem paradoxical, but research does suggest that we may be at our most creative when we are constrained. When confronted with a barrier, we find clever ways over, under, and around it. In her book *Creativity from Constraints: The Psychology of Breakthrough*, psychologist Patricia Stokes explains that "the more constrained the solution paths, the more variable, the more creative, the problem solvers." Creatives like Monet, Debussy, Coco Chanel, and Frank Lloyd Wright each encountered what Stokes calls "barriers that lead to breakthroughs."

Sometimes it's important to think inside and reconstruct the box like Ibtihaj did. She accepted the constraints placed on her by her faith, but she stretched those barriers on her own terms. As an oppositional primitive, she refused to accept that she couldn't play sports, so she found a creative loophole. She refused to accept that modest clothing couldn't be fashionable, so she started her own company. In the same vein, if you asked Danny what he thought about the internet in the late '90s, he'd complain about how inefficient and terribly thought out it was. Danny couldn't invent a new internet, but he found a way to make the existing one light-years better.

In 2000, animation company Pixar hired director Brad Bird to direct its next feature film. His idea was to make a superhero movie with next-generation animation that could realistically render minute details like explosions and human hair. Studio execs took one look at Bird's concept and balked. It would cost half a billion dollars, they said. Instead of acquiescing and coming up with a more traditional movie, Bird assembled a motley crew of disgruntled Pixar animators who felt they were too constricted and undervalued. Bird instructed his band of black sheep to find a way, somehow, to produce his movie as cheaply as possible. With their backs against the wall, they figured out ways to create impressive-looking animation with clever hacks and workarounds. They ended up making the film—*The Incredibles*—for under $100 million. It grossed more than six times that.

Instead of finding a way to escape the constraints placed around you, wrestle with them. Be inspired by them. In an attempt to understand the building blocks of greatness, psychiatrist Arnold M. Ludwig spent ten years studying the lives of a thousand people who had reached success in nearly every field, from music to art to business to sports. In his 1995 book, *The Price of Greatness: Resolving the Creativity and Madness Controversy*, Ludwig explained that physical vulnerability and "psychological unease" were the key traits of success. Whether that unease was poverty, a bad job, or a medical condition, people who were forced to navigate within a very unique set of circumstances were the most likely to reach the pinnacle of their field.

Sometimes you have to make your own constraints. Adam Grant, a professor of management and psychology at the Wharton School of the University of Pennsylvania and author of the bestsellers *Give and Take* and *Originals*, explains that he creates constraints by procrastinating. That doesn't come easy to a guy who submitted his college thesis two months early and his graduate school dissertation two *years* early. "Psychologists have coined a term for my condition: pre-crastination," he says. But after a student of his challenged him to try procrastinating,

Grant found that the anxiety of an impending deadline actually helped inspire him: "My natural need to finish early was a way of shutting down complicating thoughts that sent me whirling in new directions. I was avoiding the pain of divergent thinking—but I was also missing out on its rewards."

Instead of—or, at least, in addition to—cursing the constraints foisted upon you, try to draw some inspiration from them. By seeing barriers as opportunities, you just might come up with some truly imaginative ideas.

LIVE BETWEEN YOUR REDLINES

From Nelson Mandela to Rev. Dr. Martin Luther King Jr. to Gandhi to Rosa Parks, the most effective oppositional beacons of our time very publicly created their own redlines—basic principles they would never compromise. For W. E. B. Du Bois, one of the most important oppositional figures of the twentieth century, that redline was full equality. At the turn of the twentieth century, while activists like Booker T. Washington pushed for the Atlanta Compromise, which would guarantee basic education and due process to black people while keeping segregation firmly in place, Du Bois refused. Nothing short of complete equality, integration, and justice would satisfy him. Later in life, in opposition to a Supreme Court ruling that upheld the law requiring communists to register with the government, he joined the Communist Party.

You don't have to be a generational figure like Du Bois to set your own redlines, of course. I work in public relations, a career that requires me to consider my redlines quite literally every day. Often the people or organizations most desperate for good PR have done some very ethically dubious stuff. After Cecil, a beloved lion who lived in Hwange National Park in Zimbabwe, was killed by an American dentist and amateur big game hunter named Walter Palmer, two PR firms tangentially associated with Palmer were accosted by internet activists. While no PR firm took on the disgraced dentist—animal cruelty is, apparently, a PR redline—some firms have no issue with human rights abuses. The multinational PR firm Ketchum seemingly had no qualms with accepting $30 million in fees from the Putin administration between 2006 and 2015. And the well-known PR outfit Bell Pottinger made millions of dollars masterminding fake news campaigns for financial firm Oakbay Investments that were designed to create racial division. When the depth of Bell Pottinger's racist tactics were discovered, the firm saw an exodus of clients, and in 2017 it was ejected from the Public Relations Society of America. Shortly after, it closed its doors for good.

During one of my stints at Burson-Marsteller, my bosses placed me on the account for Philip Morris. I refused, explaining that I couldn't ethically work for a corporation that makes products that kill people. Another time, my own firm was approached by representatives from the government of the Democratic Republic of the Congo, which had experienced a bloody civil war that resulted in the deaths of tens of thousands of civilians. The leader of the DRC, Laurent-Désiré Kabila, ruthlessly violated the rights of the Congolese people by killing, torturing, and "disappearing" anyone who spoke against his regime. I said simply: "Absolutely not." I may lose money by not representing multinational tobacco companies and foreign governments with deplorable human rights records, but I won't lose sleep at night.

Sometimes we lose sight of our redlines, and I'm no exception. Many years ago, while working at Burson-Marsteller, my bosses handed me a brief assignment for the sultan of Brunei, Hassanal Bolkiah. At the time I thought, *Wow, he's one of the richest people on Earth. This will look great on my résumé.* It turns out the Sultan and his brother had been accused of bringing women into their harem and subjecting them to demeaning treatment. The project lasted only a few weeks, and my role was limited to research and reviewing documents, but I regretted it almost immediately. I believed the Sultan had done something wrong and was using his money—and, by extension, me—to bury it. In recent years, Hassanal Bolkiah has been in the news for introducing death by stoning for people convicted of homosexuality and adultery. I've never forgiven myself for the support I gave that government, however small, all those years ago. I neglected my own redlines, and I've spent every day making sure that doesn't happen again.

Of course, most redlines don't involve human rights violations. For my very civilized colleague Bonnie, her redline was having enough time to spend with her family. When she was presented with a big promotion and salary bump at work—something most civilized people would jump on instantly—she made a primitive move and said, "No, thank you." The promotion was a great opportunity to advance her career, but it would also mean less time to spend with her children. No money could ever buy back those lost moments.

The purest oppositional primitives stick to their redlines even when everything is crashing down around them. By 2001, Danny's company, Akamai Technologies, was in trouble. After an initial public offering in 1999 that made him a billionaire on paper, the dot-com bubble burst and Akamai began hemorrhaging customers. Danny was forced to lay off many of his employees to keep the company afloat, which for a relentlessly optimistic person like Danny was incredibly difficult to do. The night before he was murdered, Danny was up late challenging Tom Leighton, his Akamai cofounder, to find a way to retain as many employees as possible.

Sadly, some people never manage to establish their redlines, especially when it comes to family. In May 2005, Eugene O'Kelly received the worst possible news: a brain scan revealed he had glioblastoma multiforme, an inoperable brain tumor. He had barely five months to live. At the time, the fifty-three-year-old

O'Kelly was CEO of KPMG, one of the largest and most successful consulting firms in the United States. He traveled some 150,000 miles every year and almost never took vacations. He missed nearly every school event for his daughter and only had a weekday lunch with his wife twice in the previous decade. Upon receiving his diagnosis, O'Kelly realized how little time he had made for the people who were most important to him. He spent his final months making up for lost time with his wife and kids and writing a book, *Chasing Daylight: How My Forthcoming Death Transformed My Life*, about how his impending death helped him redefine what success meant. O'Kelly's book is beautifully written and delivers a powerful argument for living in the moment and setting effective redlines.

Oppositional primitives have no problem setting and maintaining their redlines. What are yours? Do you hold yourself accountable to them? Or does your red too often fade to pink and then gray? Don't be afraid to reestablish them, even if it means sacrificing short-term goals.

RECOGNIZE YOUR FELLOW TITANS

Being oppositional can be an emotionally fraught experience. What if you don't seem like a team player? What if you miss out on that promotion? Some of these fears are not entirely misplaced, especially for people of color and women.

Pulitzer Prize–winning historian Laurel Thatcher Ulrich coined the phrase "well-behaved women seldom make history." But refusing to bow to the status quo can cause hardship for some. Take for example the African American mathematicians Mary Jackson, Katherine Johnson, and Dorothy Vaughan, whose calculations proved crucial for Project Mercury and other NASA missions. They refused to "behave" even as they endured racist and sexist harassment for daring to do their work. Even then, they were ignored by history books until the 2016 book *Hidden Figures* by Margot Lee Shetterly and the subsequent Oscar-nominated film shed light on their accomplishments.

Eleanor Roosevelt had a unique way to advance women's rights. After her husband won the presidency, Roosevelt was horrified that only male journalists were allowed at presidential news conferences. Her solution was to hold women-only news conferences, which forced major newspapers to hire female reporters. Or ask Joan Jett how difficult oppositional women have it. "There's nothing more threatening than a girl with a guitar," she famously said in 1999. Jett, of course, has never been afraid to speak her mind. "The only reason I have a bad reputation is because I'm a girl and dare to do these things that boys do," she says. For decades Jett has proven that women can rock just as hard—or, in Jett's case, even harder—than men.

Not everyone works at an organization that appreciates oppositional behavior. Despite the challenges I've faced over the years, I've had an easier time than many because I'm white and I'm male. That's one reason why I admire people like Lara Setrakian, an accomplished journalist and chief executive of the digital media outlet News Deeply, which she founded to shed light on the devastating conflict in Syria and evolved into a series of single-issue news sites and topic-driven communities. Earlier in her career she worked at ABC News, where she was the victim of sexual misconduct by star journalist Mark Halperin. She was one of five women who came forward anonymously in a 2017 CNN exposé that led to Halperin losing his post on NBC News and his program on Showtime. Lara courageously revealed her identity in a *Washington Post* op-ed, where she explained how difficult it was to share her story. "I feel compelled to come forward, because we need to understand what went wrong and what it says about television journalism," she wrote. "We can't expect the culture of our newsrooms to get better if we're not honest about what's happening."

As the Me Too movement has revealed, women have been marginalized simply for speaking up about sexual harassment in the workplace—and, sadly, for simply speaking up at all. Studies show that certain oppositional traits, such as being assertive and asking hard questions, are often associated with strong leadership—from men. When women behave assertively, they can suffer consequences that men rarely experience. A 2008 study published in the journal *Psychological Science* found that men received a boost in their perceived status after expressing anger, but "women who expressed anger were consistently accorded lower status and lower wages, and were seen as less competent."

I don't pretend to have a solution to this insidious problem, but what I can do is explain the final ingredient of being an oppositional primitive—delivering frequent praise—which might help soften the unfortunate image many people have of independent thinkers.

Praise is a tricky subject in the workplace. Some crotchety folks grumble that workers nowadays—and especially millennials—are as addicted to praise as they are to their smartphones, and that without constant reassurance, they get angry and look for new jobs. The idea goes that helicopter parents spent too many years doling out participation trophies to promote self-esteem. They say we should look to the Book of Proverbs—"Pride goeth before destruction, and an haughty spirit before a fall"—while stoically going about our jobs and accepting praise in the form of a biweekly paycheck.

This is nonsense, of course. People of all ages appreciate praise, especially when it comes from someone who doles it out sparingly. Research shows that positive reinforcement boosts productivity on the whole. In one study, Harvard researchers invited participants to solve various puzzles. Before the experiment began, the researchers asked half the participants to solicit praise from their friends and family. The other half were told not to. At the end of the experiment, 51 percent of those who had read admiring emails from their loved ones were able to solve a difficult puzzle called Duncker's candle problem, while only 19 percent of the second, unpraised group could. This research corresponds with Gallup workplace polls that routinely find that "top performers need to know their efforts are recognized and valued."

True oppositional primitives are often the fastest to praise, just as they are the fastest to criticize. To the casual observer, Danny Lewin might have come across as brash, arrogant, and self-centered. In reality, Danny was exceptionally warm and fun-loving. He loved calling his friends and coworkers "titans"—a word he picked up from *Titan: The Life of John D. Rockefeller, Sr.* by Ron Chernow. Countless successful entrepreneurs are consumed by ego and have difficulty listening to opposing viewpoints. Not Danny. He'd be the first person to say he hated your idea, but he could also deliver praise with as much sincerity as he delivered a rebuke. When we were working together, Danny would reject many of my ideas. But when one stuck, he would say, "Marco, you're a future zillionaire. A titan. That is an awesome idea. Let's do it." No one else could deliver a compliment like Danny could.

Although he was almost always the smartest guy in the room, Danny knew when he was dealing with an intellectual equal. When he introduced me to his two brothers, Michael and Jonathan, Danny explained that they were the smartest ones in the family, and he meant it. His Akamai cofounder Tom Leighton was a brilliant professor at MIT, and Danny always said he was one of the best computer scientists in the world—a titan. They disagreed frequently, but there was no one Danny respected more than Tom. "If you asked Danny to give you a truly honest assessment of the intellectual horsepower of Akamai Technologies, he would tell you that he was the second smartest person in the company," recalls Jonathan Seelig. "He believed Tom was smarter."

Oppositional primitives ought to be able to let go of ego and accept a good idea no matter its source. George Conrades, the former CEO of Akamai Technologies, serves on the board of directors at Oracle along with the software giant's famously mercurial CEO, Larry Ellison. Although Ellison is a classic oppositional primitive whom few would classify as humble, he listens intensely to his fellow board members. "Larry won't cut you off," George explains. "He won't say, 'That's bullshit.' If he encounters better facts and data, he'll quickly acknowledge a good point or idea."

Sometimes good ideas are the result of consensus, sometimes it's your idea, sometimes it's someone else's. Never be afraid to say, "You're right and I'm wrong." Doing so makes people feel better about themselves, and it makes them feel better about you.

By fighting every day, being obstreperous, seeing constraints as catalysts, living between defined redlines, acting like a titan, and doling out praise, oppositional behavior can become second nature.

As for me, when I'm having difficulty expressing an unpopular opinion, I think about Danny. Just as he was sweeping the floors at Samson's Gym in Jerusalem as a cocky teenager, just as he was as a captain with the elite Sayeret Matkal, just as he was screaming at one of the most powerful CEOs in the world, Danny was an oppositional primitive until the moment he died. Danny, dressed in jeans and a T-shirt, sacrificed everything and took on terrorists armed with knives. He did not watch helplessly as they took control of the aircraft. He was the ultimate oppositional primitive, the ultimate titan, and the ultimate friend.

CHAPTER THREE

AGNOSTIC

Love Whelchel III was on his way to Los Angeles International Airport when the driver turned to him and said: "I've got Sean on the line. He wants to talk to you." The driver thrust a cell phone at Love, who took it hesitantly.

"Hello?"

"Love. It's Sean. I want you to take the job."

"Can I think about it first? This is a big decision for me."

"I'm not going to enjoy my weekend unless I know you took this job, Love. You need to give me an answer right now."

In the span of a second, Love considered the pros and cons of the new role. He was making a very good salary as global chief talent officer at Young & Rubicam, one of the largest advertising firms in the world. After scratching and clawing his way up the corporate ladder, he had finally arrived in the c-suite. He could coast for the next few decades and retire a very wealthy man. Now a guy he had met thirty minutes ago was telling him to upend his life and begin a new career in the entertainment industry.

"Fine. I'll do it," Love said confidently.

And like that, as he had countless times in his life, Love reinvented himself. Except this time his boss wouldn't be some empty suit. "Sean" was Sean John Combs—also known at various points in his life as Puff Daddy, P. Diddy, Puffy, and Diddy—and the job wasn't at a sleepy record label, but at Bad Boy Entertainment, one of the most hard-charging entertainment groups in the business. Love had no idea what he had gotten himself into—and that was exactly how he wanted it.

For many people, this would be a career-defining move. But for Love, it was just another pivot in a lifetime of twists and turns. Born in 1969 in Birmingham, Alabama, Love was the youngest of four siblings. He grew up attending the Christian Methodist Episcopal Church, where his father was a pastor. Love adapted to a life on the move as his father accepted positions at churches in North Carolina, Ohio, and then Los Angeles. During his final semester at Morris Brown College in Atlanta, he had no good job prospects or even unpaid internships. One day he was aimlessly riding the MARTA when he spied a guy trying to decipher the subway map.

"Do you need help?" Love asked him. The man had about a dozen lanyards draped around his neck—VIP passes for some sort of event.

"Do you know how to get to the Atlanta University Center?" he asked Love. "I need to get to this concert ASAP."

Love gave him directions and the man thanked him. The two struck up a conversation, and Love mentioned that he was graduating soon and looking for work.

"Ever heard of the group N.W.A?" the man asked.

"Of course," Love replied. "I love *Straight Outta Compton*."

"I work for them," the man said, pointing to his VIP passes. "We need some roadies for the upcoming tour. You interested?"

Love didn't even think before he responded: "Sure, why not?" And just like that, he was working with one of the biggest groups in hip-hop. That summer, he toured with N.W.A, learning the ins and outs of the music industry as he crisscrossed the country. But soon after the tour ended, Love quit the job that most kids his age would have killed for. Deciding that music wasn't his thing—at least at that point in his life—he veered from the bleeding edge of rap to the mellow world of New Age book publishing. Instead of working sold-out concerts with Dr. Dre and Eazy-E, Love was selling tarot cards and books about spirituality. Working at a small publisher, Love learned to wear many hats and soon found himself in charge of the entire shipping department.

One day, Love was approached by a friend with a new opportunity. The Summer Olympics was coming to Atlanta, and the city was hiring logistics personnel. Love took one of the open jobs. A week later, the executive who ran the department summoned him to his office: "Your boss no longer works here," he said. "I want you to take over his job. You'll be in charge of sending and receiving all mail associated with the Atlanta Olympic Games and you'll need to hire forty people to work under you. Can you handle that?"

Love, who was barely out of college and had never hired, let alone managed, anyone in his life, said: "Sure, why not?" The twenty-four-year-old was in charge of receiving and placing metal detectors, bomb scanners, and other highly technical equipment in preparation for one of the biggest events in the history of the city. Recognizing that he had an eye for spotting talent, Love then pivoted away from shipping to tech, where he recruited programmers to prepare computer systems for the Y2K computer bug. Not long after, Love upended his life once more and moved across country to be a director at a nonprofit. Then he shifted back to IT recruiting, and then to executive recruiting for an advertising firm before he changed gears—and coasts—to become chief talent officer at Young & Rubicam in New York City, where we met.

And after all of that, Love found himself chief of human resources at Sean Combs's Bad Boy Entertainment. There he managed more than three hundred employees, overseeing restaurants, the Sean John clothing and accessory line, the Bad Boy record label, and the Blue Flame Agency, which handled marketing and consulting. The work was thrilling but tiring, and after a few years Love was ready to reinvent himself once again as a talent executive at a PR firm. A few years after that, following a dozen career 180s, pivots, promotions, layoffs, steps forward, and steps back, Love decided it was time to start his own company. Binkable was a new platform that enabled creative talent to connect and work with other agencies, brands, and startups. But before long he sold it, and today he is the head of human resources at Vera Wang. Love has had perhaps the most varied career of anyone I've met. Most of his moves were made on a whim, often to positions in which he had zero experience. "I feel like when I take a new position, I'm dropped in the middle of the jungle with a penknife and a loincloth," Love told me. "I'm looking for the adventure, and I'm trying to survive."

Love is the embodiment of the agnostic primitive. By *agnostic*, I don't mean in the religious sense—that is, someone who believes nothing is known or can be known of the existence of God. Agnostic primitives can be devout Catholics, Jews, Muslims, or atheists. But just as religious agnostics don't believe in any specific creation theory, primitive agnostics don't believe in following any specific career path. They roam from position to position, field to field, rejecting the dogma of the day, guided by opportunity and curiosity. They shun specialization, adapt to happenstance, and embrace uncertainty. Agnostic primitives succeed and they fail, and they do it all over again. They experiment constantly. They fall in and out of love with their jobs. They start and fold companies. They get bit by bugs and follow their whimsy. They are allergic to routine and challenge the notion that you must have a singular focus.

When I was in graduate school in the late '80s, I worked part-time at the Vertical Club on East 61st Street as a personal trainer. One of my clients was a neurologist named Jeff. He often scheduled our sessions for 9:00 p.m., and he'd occasionally take me out for a late dinner afterward. One time he took me to the high-end steakhouse Smith & Wollensky, where he asked about my future.

"Marco," he said. "What are you thinking about doing after you finish up at Columbia?"

"I'm not sure, Jeff," I said. It was an honest response. This was a precarious stage of my life: my father's financial situation was growing ever more uncertain, and I had no savings to speak of. For the first time ever, I wasn't sure how I was going to make ends meet.

"Here's my advice, Marco. You have to specialize. Whatever you do, be an expert."

This seemed like good advice at the time. When you were growing up, think how many times adults asked you, "What do you want to be when you grow up?" Wise minds like Jeff have warned against being a jack-of-all-trades, master of none, for hundreds of years. An ancient Chinese saying translates literally to: "Equipped with knives all over, yet none is sharp." In Estonia, they say: "Nine trades, the tenth one—hunger." Malcolm Gladwell's bestseller *Outliers* further pushed the belief that to truly master any skill, one must devote the proverbial ten thousand hours of practice to it. Jeff had carved out a niche for himself and was encouraging me to do the same thing. But was it actually good advice?

To the contrary, many of today's visionaries don't limit themselves to a single field. Elon Musk has founded or acquired extraordinarily valuable and varied companies, including online bank X.com, which later became PayPal, electric car company Tesla, aerospace manufacturer and space transport company SpaceX, solar energy services company SolarCity, neurotechnology company Neuralink, and infrastructure and tunnel construction firm The Boring Company. Sir Richard Branson has dabbled in everything from magazines to record stores to airlines to telecommunications to space travel. Noam Chomsky, known as the "father of modern linguistics," is also a philosopher, cognitive scientist, historian, social critic, and political activist. Mae Jemison is an engineer and physician who was the first black woman to travel into space. After she resigned from NASA, she founded her own technology company. She is also a dancer who holds nine honorary doctorates in science, engineering, and the humanities. Yoky Matsuoka was a semipro tennis player in Japan before she became a roboticist at Carnegie Mellon, then a MacArthur Fellow (better known as a "genius award" recipient) for her work on next-generation prosthetics, cofounder of the Google X moonshot lab, one of the first employees at the "smart" thermostat company Nest, founder of a tech startup, and the brains behind Apple's HealthKit tracking software. Now she is back at Nest as its chief technology officer.

Mallika Chopra has confidently wandered from career to career for her entire life. The daughter of author Deepak Chopra, Mallika is a mom, media entrepreneur, public speaker, and author in addition to the countless other hats she has worn throughout her life. After graduating from Brown University and the Kellogg School of Management, she founded Intent.com, a social media website focused on personal, social, and global wellness. The company was successful, but Mallika grew restless. She wanted to help people on a more direct, meaningful level. "The business had not been built in a way that I couldn't shift gears," she told me. She had been groomed to run a company like this, but Mallika was ready to move on. With the blessing of her investors, Mallika set aside her management training and went back to school, graduating from Teachers College, Columbia University with a master's degree in clinical psychology and education. She has become an extremely successful author of five books and counting about meditation, inspiration, and living life to the fullest. In the meantime, she's taught meditation to thousands of people and speaks regularly at TEDx events and other major conferences—helping people in a far more intimate way than her company ever could.

Not all of us are showmen like Elon Musk, pioneering technologists like Yoky Matsuoka, or wellness luminaries like Mallika Chopra. We may not be as comfortable jumping from career to career as Love Whelchel III. But there is a lot we can learn from them, particularly in four key areas: agnostic primitives are driven by their curiosity, they find new uses for old skills, they aren't afraid to quit, and they seek out primitive organizations that nurture and adapt to their ever-changing interests.

MAKE CURIOSITY YOUR PRIORITY

If you were a hiring manager looking at Tanya Valle's résumé, you might think she was indecisive or noncommittal—someone who was unable to choose a career and stick it out for the long haul. "In essence, I've just followed my curiosity," she told me cheerfully. In college, she secured a prestigious internship at a boutique PR firm, but after graduation she chose to backpack across Europe for half a year. She eventually wandered back to the United States and convinced the company to hire her for a temporary position. Later she jumped to an entertainment PR firm, where she spent her evenings hobnobbing with celebrities and models. But Tanya grew bored of a lifestyle that most people her age could only dream of. "I always had an interest in working with animals," she explained. "So I left PR to become a zookeeper."

That's right: Tanya went from partying with the glitterati to cleaning out cages at the Queens Zoo in New York City.

She found the change of pace soothing, and despite the modest salary, she was proud to be doing something she loved. Ever restless, however, Tanya soon thought, *What's next? What more can I do for animals?* The logical answer was to become a veterinarian. She signed up for pre-vet classes at Queens College, but the courses were difficult and she swiftly realized she wasn't ready to commit a minimum of four years to becoming a vet. Tanya revisited her list of interests: after animals, she was curious about journalism. As luck would have it, the curator of her zoo mentioned that a local cable program wanted to profile a zookeeper. Tanya was immediately interested and agreed to appear on TV. The segment went well, and, on a whim, Tanya asked the producer if the channel was hiring interns. Sure enough they were—and like that, Tanya had changed careers once again. Within three months she was hired as a full-time associate producer based in the Bronx. But instead of comfortably settling into that role, she decided she wanted to be closer to the news, and convinced her boss to let her be a television reporter.

After reporting for a couple of local news stations for six years, Tanya decided it was time for another career change. "During my last winter reporting, it got so cold I couldn't even move my mouth," she told me. "And I'm like: okay, what's next?" It turns out it was returning to public relations, this time for the Bloomberg administration as press secretary for the Administration for Children's Services, and later the Department of Homeless Services. After Mayor Bloomberg left office, Tanya reentered the world of corporate PR—yet another career that most people would kill to have. But that, too, did not last. As of the printing of this book, she is a career coach who helps everyone from interns to high-powered executives manage the stresses of their jobs. She also teaches mindfulness meditation workshops on the side. Tanya has lived a fabulously varied and interesting life, but you probably won't see a college counselor tell animal-loving students to be

zookeepers by way of corporate PR. We're encouraged to specialize, to find a niche, to make ourselves indispensable in our own
tiny sliver of the world.

But refusing to stay put can also pay off: a piece in *Forbes*
found that employees who stay in companies longer than two
years get paid 50 percent less compared to those who jump
around. Of course, many people who play musical chairs with
their careers often do the same work at different employers and
aren't necessarily learning new skills. Changing jobs *and* job descriptions can be even better: a *Harvard Business Review* analysis
explained that organizations "benefit from employing generalists,
who can challenge the industry's taken-for-granted assumptions
and bring in new ideas." Civilized people who stay with the same
organization and the same specialty lose touch with the outside
world. They might begin to focus on petty office politics, who is
in their rearview mirror, and who can be pushed aside. They may
lose sight of broader trends in their industry and the economy
as a whole, endlessly refining a skill set that might be extinct in
a matter of years. Agnostic primitives like Love and Tanya have
to reestablish their value every time they change careers. They
learn new skills and grow new muscles. They learn to evaluate
their employers in much the same way their employers evaluate
them. They constantly nudge and stretch and inflate their comfort zones. They wear many hats and crave more.

"Routine is the enemy," Greg Glassman, the cofounder of
CrossFit, famously wrote about why his strength and condition-
ing program mixes aerobic exercise with calisthenics, gymnastics,
and weight lifting. To stay in peak shape, the human body
requires a diverse set of exercises; otherwise, some muscles are
overworked while others atrophy. It's not all that different when
it comes to our careers. Even the father of economics himself,
Adam Smith, who hailed the production gains of specialized
labor in his magnum opus, *The Wealth of Nations,* warned against

a too-fine division of labor, explaining that the economy would suffer when an individual's work was reduced to "a few very simple operations." The Harvard law professor Jonathan Zittrain similarly worries that hyper-specialization—such as programmers who only know a single coding language for a single application—can lead to "digital sweatshops" in which workers are exploited for paltry wages. Entrepreneur Andrew Yang was concerned enough about automation to make it the central plank of his 2020 campaign for the Democratic nomination for president, attracting millions of supporters in the process.

Problems with overspecialization aren't limited to our performance at work. By doing the same job, year after year, we get bored. We get lazy. Our minds slip. As we discussed in the introduction to this book, Gallup polls find that barely a third of baby boomers and Gen Xers are engaged by their work. "They show up; they get their paycheck and do the minimum required," explains Jim Harter, Gallup's chief scientist for workplace management. About 20 percent fall into what Harter calls "actively disengaged," which doesn't only sap productivity, but greatly increases the risk of psychological stress, high blood pressure, and depression. As Howard H. Stevenson, a Harvard Business School professor emeritus, observed to *The Atlantic*: "There's a difference between twenty years of experience, and one year of experience twenty times. People do the same thing and they don't grow. They don't face new challenges."

These sort of purposeless feelings at work are quite literally killing us. Researchers at Rush University Medical Center autopsied the brains of 246 elderly people who agreed to donate them to a years-long aging study upon death. They found that people who had a greater purpose in life, as discerned by interviews prior to their death, "had a substantially reduced risk of developing Alzheimer's disease, as well as a reduced risk of the precursor to Alzheimer's, mild cognitive impairment." As one researcher explained: "This finding is exciting because it suggests that engaging in meaningful and purposeful activities promotes cognitive health in old age."

Agnostic primitives crave this sort of purposeful activity. While curiosity leads some primitives to explore as many new and strange jobs as possible, other primitives derive the same satisfaction from jumping to and from positions within a narrower orbit. E. Gordon Gee is currently in his second tour of duty as president of West Virginia University, having previously served from 1981 to 1985. In between these stints, Gordon was president of University of Colorado, The Ohio State University, Brown University, Vanderbilt University, and Ohio State once again. In fact, he has held more university presidencies than anyone else.

Gordon relishes his job as an educator and a leader, but his agnostic spirit pushes him to uproot his life and relocate to a new university every few years. As in the case of The Ohio State University and West Virginia University, he sometimes pivots right back again. By experiencing such a broad swath of American higher education, from the Ivy League to the largest land grant universities, Gordon can understand and adapt to broader trends in academia as well as any of his peers. The problems with specialization are at the top of his mind. "Universities are training people for jobs that are going to be obsolete in ten to fifteen years," he told me. "Any university president worth his or her salt is going to have to ask fundamental questions: What are we doing for the future? And how are we going to educate people for the future?"

Gordon is a champion of the liberal arts in a time when politicians are pushing STEM (science, technology, engineering, mathematics) curricula. "English is a gift in the humanities. Appreciating language is fundamental to being able to read and write and think. For me, that is number one." Like a true primitive, Gordon isn't afraid to rethink the status quo. "The world of disruption is here," he told me. "We need to think carefully in universities about moving away from specialization. There's a tyranny to college that's so specialized. If I were king for a day, I would do away with departments. I would reorganize the universities around the way we think. I'd move from vertical to horizontal, I'd move from colleges and departments to centers, institutes, and working groups in which students could move in and out. Any institution that calls a forty-year-old curriculum a 'new' curriculum needs to reevaluate everything."

As health care has become an ever-larger sector of the economy, Gordon has recruited top medical talent to West Virginia to lead the university's expanding health-sciences division. As the cost of college continues to explode, and with students taking out record sums in student loans, Gordon is proving that the nation's large public universities—WVU's enrollment is nearly thirty-five thousand students across its multiple campuses—can deliver quality, practical education at a fraction of the cost of what private universities charge.

Agnostic primitives jump from job to job, and in many cases career to career, and they stockpile skills along the way. As we'll see in the following section, some of these skills lay dormant for years, only to find surprising and exciting uses later in life.

USE OLD SKILLS IN NEW WAYS

For two decades, my wife, Stacey Nelkin, made a living as a film and TV actress. She got an early break as a teenager auditioning for Woody Allen's *Annie Hall* and had many roles during the 1980s and early '90s. But like so many talented women in Hollywood, the opportunities faded when she passed thirty. Stacey was devastated and rightfully outraged to have to surrender her identity simply because of her age, but she decided to make a primitive move and become an author. Having spent her career around Type A personalities, Stacey understood how emotionally volatile dating and marriage can be during times of financial stress. So she cowrote a book with the psychologist Paul Schienberg, which helped people save their relationships during the very worst of the financial crisis.

After writing the book, Stacey realized she could use her acting background to help not just people struggling with their romantic lives, but the truly downtrodden as well. Some people who suffer from addiction do not respond well to traditional talk therapy, but they are able to communicate their vulnerabilities and heal themselves through role-playing and other creative outlets that Stacey mastered as an actress. She went back to school and earned her certificate in creative arts and health sciences, learning to use theatrical techniques to help people achieve catharsis, facilitate personal growth, and restore positive mental health. Today she is employed in a related field as a certified alcohol and substance abuse counselor. Working with a New York nonprofit organization, The Bridge, Stacey helps the formerly incarcerated, the homeless, and other at-risk individuals who suffer from substance abuse and mental illness. For Stacey—whose father died of a drug overdose at age thirty-seven—the job is especially meaningful, and far more important than any film role. She is generally a very grounded and civilized person, but instead of clinging to her old life, she made a primitive move and started a new one. But she did not leave behind her old skill set. Whether it's inventing a new gadget or helping an addict become sober, agnostic primitives never stop finding new uses for their existing knowledge.

Novelist and physicist Alan Lightman is the same way. As a child growing up in the 1950s, Alan was encouraged by his father, a movie theater owner, and his mother, a ballroom dance teacher, to appreciate both the arts and the sciences. In school, Alan won both statewide science fairs *and* creative writing contents. He eventually chose to pursue a career as a scientist, earning his PhD in theoretical physics from the California Institute of Technology. He went on to make significant contributions to astrophysics and gravitational theory. Alan taught astronomy and physics at Harvard University and the Massachusetts Institute of Technology.

But when Alan reached his midthirties, he decided it was time to shift careers. "I became aware that my powers as a theoretical physicist were diminishing," he told me. "Theoretical physicists do their best work at a young age." He points to Albert Einstein, who was just twenty-six when he published three papers that formed the foundation of modern physics and fundamentally altered our ideas about space, time, mass, and energy.

Despite his parents' gentle objections, Alan summoned his dormant literary skills and made a go of it as a writer. He began publishing essays about science in the early '80s, writing for the *Atlantic Monthly, Harper's Magazine,* the *New York Times,* and the *New Yorker* among many others. Then he moved to fiction and published the novel *Einstein's Dreams* in 1993, which follows a young Albert Einstein as he imagines new worlds in his dreams and formulates his theory of relativity. The book, which beautifully describes various ideas of time that Einstein might have had while working on the theory of relativity and illustrates each dream world with a human story, was a massive bestseller. It has been translated into thirty languages and is required reading for many college freshmen.

Only a mind like Alan's could have produced such a masterpiece. And like a true agnostic primitive, he has again changed careers. During a trip to Cambodia he learned about the horrifying lack of basic accommodations for female university students. While the male students were able to live free in the Buddhist temples and safely rent rooms together, such options were not available to female students. In particular, several women Alan met had to live underneath a university building in a six-foot crawl space between the bottom of the building and the mud. Alan began raising money to launch the Harpswell Foundation, a nonprofit dedicated to advancing a new generation of women leaders in Southeast Asia. His organization operates two dormitories in addition to providing free food, medical care, and specialized leadership classes for women.

Alan is very much a polymath in an era of hyper-specialization. He began in the furthest reaches of the analytical left brain—astrophysics—then veered into the creative ether of the right brain—fiction writing—and then created one of the most promising nonprofits in the developing world. He achieved this by harnessing very different skills. When I marvel at Alan's career, I can't help but think back to that steak dinner with Jeff the neurologist all those years ago. "Marco, you have to specialize," he insisted. What would he have thought about Alan the theoretical physicist who became a bestselling novelist and social entrepreneur, and the first professor at MIT to receive a joint appointment in the sciences and the humanities?

Recent studies suggest that creative breakthroughs are often the result of combining very different skills much like Alan did. After analyzing more than twenty million scientific papers going back centuries, Brian Uzzi from Northwestern University's Kellogg School of Management found that the most groundbreaking research was conducted by teams with diverse, nontraditional backgrounds. Moreover, the most commonly cited studies were much more likely to draw on research from seemingly unrelated fields.

Many of the most notable scientists in history were polymaths, including Newton, Galileo, Kepler, and Darwin. Some of the most important inventions were the result of combining insights from disparate fields. For example, Charles Babbage, who is credited with inventing the first punch card mechanical computer, was inspired by his extensive understanding of the silk-weaving industry, which used cards with holes to create patterns in fabric. Henry Ford, who helped pioneer the automobile assembly line, drew on his knowledge of meatpacking plants and the manufacture of Singer sewing machines.

Recently, I spoke with a young woman named Amanda Gutterman. A book lover, she interned at the publisher W. W. Norton, the *New Yorker*, and various literary magazines. But instead of becoming a book editor, she jumped to the *Huffington Post*, where she adapted her literary skills to a fast-paced news environment. Less than two years later she became editorial director at a new company, Slant News, where she learned how to run a business. Fast forward a few years, and she was chief marketing officer at ConsenSys, a blockchain software company helping to build a decentralized world on the Ethereum platform, the second largest cryptocurrency by market cap after Bitcoin. While so many of her peers painstakingly establish proper credentials and "domain expertise," Amanda has made these unconventional jumps without asking for permission. There may not be a straight line between the highly civilized industry of book publishing and the bleeding edge of crypto, but she has blazed that path by finding new and creative uses for her skills.

It isn't always immediately apparent how skills from an old career can serve a new one. When I bought my apartment in New York, my real estate agents were a dapper couple named Tom Postilio and Mickey Conlon. Impeccably dressed with the crisp manners and wit of bygone Hollywood leading men, Tom and Mickey are perched at the apex of the ruthless New York real estate market, responsible for over $2 billion in residential sales. They haven't always been in real estate, though: When Tom was twenty he landed his dream gig singing Frank Sinatra tunes with the Glenn Miller Orchestra. Mickey, meanwhile, got his start producing theater.

But show business was hit especially hard by the 2008 recession, and by the time they began dating, Tom and Mickey
both needed to pivot. Like Stacey, the two agonized over leaving
their former identities behind. But rather than settle for a life of
singing in dusty cabaret bars and cold-calling theater investors,
Tom and Mickey made a primitive move and jumped full-time
into real estate. Selling luxury apartments, they soon realized,
was every bit a showbiz production as Broadway. Whether
they're breaking into a song-and-dance routine or delivering a
perfectly timed joke, no one is better than Tom and Mickey at
helping people feel comfortable making the biggest purchase of
their lives. The duo became so successful that they even received
the reality TV show treatment, starring for several years in the
hit HGTV show *Selling New York*. Tom and Mickey remember
their showbiz lives fondly, but when it was time to move on, they
never looked back.

The rest of the economy may not be as volatile as show
business, but in today's ever-changing world, many workers
need an array of skills to stay relevant. As we saw earlier in the
book, 25 percent of American jobs are at a "high risk" of being
lost due to automation. Some of these jobs are in the manu-
facturing sector, which has long witnessed the steady creep of
robots. Yet even highly skilled, knowledge-based jobs such as investing, accounting, and legal could go the way of the typewriter.
Consulting firm Deloitte estimates that nearly 40 percent of jobs
in the legal sector could be automated by the 2030s, while some
University of Oxford research suggests a whopping 95 percent
of accountants might eventually need to update their CVs as
AI continues to take over number crunching. Even physicians
aren't immune to the winds of change: computer algorithms are
increasingly able to spot tiny abnormalities in MRIs and CT
scans that radiologists occasionally miss. And many hospitals
outsource the reading of radiology scans for interpretation to

other parts of the country to save money. Doctors may not be losing their jobs en masse anytime soon, but previously "safe" careers are becoming obsolete faster than ever before.

In truth, no one has any idea what jobs may or may not be around in twenty, ten, or even five years. But that uncertainty alone might be reason enough to avoid investing too much of your time in any one specialty. Agnostic primitives understand this innately, which is why they so effortlessly glide from career to career just as primitive nomads once wandered from place to place. As we'll see next, it also means they have no problem throwing in the towel when it's time to move on.

BE A QUITTER

Like many Americans, I was not in a good place in the months following September 11, 2001. My friend Danny Lewin, the primitive we encountered in Oppositional, was murdered as he tried to thwart the hijacking of American Airlines Flight 11. His death made me rethink my priorities, and I wanted to use my background to capture stories about amazing people like him. On a whim, I decided to create a business producing mini-documentaries about inspiring everyday people.

I called my new company Reel Biography. We would hire Emmy-winning producers from the likes of CNN, ABC's *Nightline*, and the History Channel to create short biographical films about intriguing people, from ordinary grandparents to Wall Street executives. We'd bring in media coaches for the camera shy and even genealogists who could track down everything from birth records to immigrant ship manifests. I ran Reel Biography for about four years, and it was some of the most difficult and rewarding work of my life. I learned about complex equipment and web videos in the pre-YouTube era. I learned to attract

clients and scratch and claw for publicity. It was an exhilarating experience—and the only problem was I lost a ton of money. I was hemorrhaging tens of thousands of dollars a month, and my accountant eventually asked me: "Marco, is this a hobby or is this a business?" While it was personally fulfilling, Reel Biography was an abject failure from a business standpoint. When I finally pulled the plug in 2007, the venture had cost me nearly two million dollars.

I made a primitive move when I started that company, and it blew up in my face. Unfortunately, failure is a theme agnostic primitives are often familiar with. Sometimes a step forward ends up being a step backward, a good idea becomes a bad one with the benefit of hindsight. I moved on from my failure, and it allowed me to refocus on what came naturally to me: the communications biz. I wish I could say my experience was uncommon, that all primitive moves result in fame and fortune. Most don't end up as financially burdensome as mine, but a failed primitive move can be an emotionally crippling experience.

Around when I was coming to terms with my failure, I was running on the Santa Monica College track with my friend Dave Schwartz. We were joined by Willie McGinest, a former NFL linebacker who played for the New England Patriots and the Cleveland Browns. They began chatting about their friend Johnnie Morton, another former football player who had been trying to break into mixed martial arts after retiring from the NFL at age thirty-five. A few weeks earlier, Johnnie had debuted in the ring at Los Angeles Memorial Coliseum on nationwide TV. He started the fight strong and landed a few big hits, but thirty-eight seconds in he got clocked in the face and fell to the ground. As quickly as it had started, Johnnie's MMA career was over.

"He got out of his lane, man...," Willie said, shaking his head as we jogged around the track. "He got out of his lane." I thought

about my own failure, how I had gotten out of my lane and tried to become a filmmaker. It may have hurt less, but I was knocked down just like Johnnie was. I'm glad I followed my heart and tried to build something new with Reel Biography, but I am especially glad that I realized I needed to stop trying when it wasn't working out.

When you experience a failure, the old saying goes, you have to learn from it and try again. Think how many times you've heard that Michael Jordan quote about failure, "I've lost almost three hundred games. Twenty-six times, I've been trusted to take the game winning shot and missed. I've failed over and over and over again in my life. And that is why I succeed." And there's that old Wayne Gretzky quote, "You miss 100 percent of the shots you don't take." It's the stuff of our best-loved clichés: pull yourself up by your bootstraps; build your successes on your failures; learn from your defeats; if at first you don't succeed, try, try again; whatever doesn't kill you makes you stronger. You can probably fill an entire book with just Winston Churchill quotes about returning from the brink. From an early age we are taught to take failure in stride, pick ourselves up, and keep at it. But this is not always a useful strategy. As I learned from my experience with Reel Biography, sometimes instead of try, try, trying again, you should try something else. Trying harder wasn't going to get me more clients, or make Johnnie a mixed martial arts champion. Reading Michael Jordan quotes wasn't going to make me a better filmmaker or fill that hole in my savings account.

Instead I found wisdom in the words of writer Erica Brown. In her beautiful book *Take Your Soul to Work*, she explains that "when we are rejected, the door before us becomes a wall. At that moment—that sad, pensive, crushing moment—we have four choices." Erica writes that we can pretend the wall is a door and hope those who reject us change their mind. We can take pity on ourselves and cry on the wall. We can reject that rejection and try to scale the wall. "Or we can *walk away* and look for another door. Leaders find other doors. Those doors are called resilience."

Agnostic primitives also find other doors. Because they don't become emotionally hitched to any one job or career path, they rarely double down after failure. They shrug, wipe their hands, and move on. When Tanya enrolled in veterinary classes at Queens College, she struggled with the workload and decided to quit—not because she lacked confidence or fortitude, but because the time commitment simply wasn't worth it. Likewise, Stacey didn't care enough about being an actress to audition nonstop. As we saw in Relentless, perseverance is a noble trait, but it can also be a foolish one. How many things in life are truly worth gritting your teeth and jumping in the trenches for? Certainly family, a marriage, your closest friends. But a job? Is that promotion really worth hundred-hour weeks? Is that advanced degree worth six-figure student loans and no social life? Maybe they are, but too often we slog on out of a sense of duty—or, in many cases, fear of shame.

Science tends to support the unfortunate fact that we rarely react well to failure. When an animal achieves a task—whether it's a rat reaching a hunk of cheese or a baseball player slugging a home run—the brain releases testosterone and dopamine, which induces a state of euphoria and establishes a positive feedback loop in which success begets further success through risk-taking. Biologists call this the "winner effect." A bull market on Wall Street, for example, is fueled by the winner effect, as euphoric traders make ever larger and more lucrative bets in much the same way a gambler parlays a winning bet. This sort of emotion-driven rally is what economist John Maynard Keynes called "animal spirits," or "a spontaneous urge to action rather than inaction." Similarly, wildlife studies show that an animal who wins a turf battle is much more likely to gain confidence and win its next fight. Losing, on the other hand, releases the stress hormone cortisol, which makes humans and animals more risk-averse and timid—and therefore less competitive.

In one study led by MIT neuroscientists, monkeys who made a mistake in a trial were more likely to perform worse on the same tasks compared to monkeys who did not make mistakes. "Success has a much greater influence on the brain than failure," the study concluded. The same phenomenon is found in humans too. In another fascinating study at the University of Toronto, participants who were led to believe they had ruined their diet by eating too much pizza subsequently ate 50 percent more cookies immediately afterward compared to participants who believed they had eaten less pizza. In other words, we tend not to learn from our mistakes and successfully right the ship. When we fail at something, we dwell on it, and we often fail again.

Think about how many times you've been told, "Don't be a quitter" or "Winners never quit and quitters never win." From high school sports to college classes to our careers, people who give up are seen as losers. If we're in a job we don't like, we're told to suck it up and stick it out. Pay your dues. But should people who slog through life desperately waiting for their situation to improve truly be admired? As we've seen previously, in nearly all metrics, from the workplace environment to vacation policies to their bosses, many Americans are unhappy at work. Is this the new normal?

As agnostic primitives like Love, Alan, and Tanya have proven, quitting is not giving up; quitting is pivoting. They don't think about what they are walking away *from*, but what they are walking *toward*. Agnostic primitives make conscious, confident decisions to leave situations they no longer find fulfilling and move to new ones. They do not find value in seeing everything out until the end, whether it's a job, a bad relationship, or a boring book. They leave when there is no more value in staying.

When I was growing up in Venice, California, one of my father's closest friends was a guy named Mike Uretz. He was making a decent living as a lawyer, but he was unhappy. Mike struggled with drugs and alcohol, and over time he realized that his dissatisfaction at work was largely driving it. The only thing that truly made him feel fulfilled was hanging out at the gym. In the early 1970s, Venice was the epicenter of the bodybuilding community, and Mike spent his free time with the Muscle Beach crowd. But he had devoted years of his life training to become a lawyer—how could he give up all of that now? Then one day he was approached by the legendary Joe Gold, the owner of the gym where he worked out. The two were friends, and Mike often gave him legal advice.

"Mike," he said. "I want to start a new kind of gym. It won't just be in Venice, but all over the world. I want you to quit your job and help me run it." Mike immediately jumped at the opportunity, even though he was taking an enormous risk. But the new venture, World Gym, paid off. Mike used his legal background to help World Gym negotiate licensing agreements around the world. Frequented by the likes of Arnold Schwarzenegger (who later became a partner), Lou Ferrigno, and Dave Draper, World Gym exploded in popularity and expanded to 220 locations across twenty countries and six continents. Mike made a primitive move by quitting a situation that made him unhappy, and it may have saved his life.

Most people who quit a bad situation end up somewhere between my experience with Reel Biography and Mike's experience with World Gym. Whether you are following your curiosity or adapting to circumstances that are out of your control, you'll have failures and successes. Agnostic primitives take them both in stride, and they're equally likely to quit during the highest highs and the lowest lows. Earlier, we saw how Austin McChord quit the company that made him a near billionaire simply because he was ready to move on to something new. And if Danny Lewin were still alive today, I'm sure he would have founded several other companies, some wildly profitable and some total duds. Primitives see success and failure as temporary phenomena, not end points. Like the ancients who built crude rafts and pointed them toward Australia, hoping for the best, agnostic primitives are always on the lookout for the next adventure.

FIND A PRIMITIVE ORGANIZATION

What's the use of jumping from company to company if you aren't happy with a single job description? Many agnostic primitives have no problem staying loyal to the same employer for their entire careers, but they wear many hats and take on a wide range of responsibilities.

Joe Moscola has spent upwards of two decades with one of my longtime clients, Northwell Health, an integrated health care network that has quietly become New York's largest private employer, with some seventy thousand employees. Today, he is chief people officer and in charge of the company's human resources division, but he began his career as a physician's assistant in cardiothoracic surgery. As he grew more curious about the administrative side of health care, he got his master's degree in business before eventually becoming chief of staff for Northwell's COO, Mark Solazzo, and CEO, Michael Dowling. Joe was still curious to learn more, so Dowling shifted him to an operations role where he oversaw ambulatory operations. Most companies would have insisted Joe stay put in his specialized role, but he still wanted to solve new challenges. During a breakfast with Dowling, Joe mentioned that he didn't believe the company's HR division was effectively serving Northwell's tens of thousands of employees. Dowling nodded and then said: "Well, then I think you should take over HR." Joe had never worked in HR, let alone managed such a large entity before, but Dowling made a primitive move entrusting his jack-of-all-trades employee with such a high-stakes job. Joe has been head of HR at Northwell for more than five years now, and while he's content staying in his current role for the long haul, I suspect his meandering journey there has only just begun.

The jumps Joe made are not typical, but they're par for the course at Northwell. For instance, Michael Dowling may be CEO now, but he grew up poor in Limerick, Ireland, became a cash-starved immigrant in New York, then put himself through college. One of his first acts as CEO was to establish the company's Center for Learning and Innovation, a massive continuous learning program for Northwell employees trying to develop new skills. One of Joe's biggest tasks is helping thousands of employees each year shift to new jobs within the organization. This helps explain why the average Northwell employee stays with the organization for 9.5 years, Joe says, compared to the nationwide average of 4.5 years. By most measures, Northwell is a very civilized organization comprising myriad careers. But as Joe's experience has shown, Northwell isn't afraid to make primitive moves and bet big on talented people. And even though Joe has stayed with the same organization for most of his career, he still embodies the spirit of the agnostic primitive by seeking out new roles and new challenges.

Like Joe, you too can follow your curiosity and wear many different hats while staying within the same ecosystem. One great idea for evaluating potential employers is to research how many times they've been forced to reinvent themselves. Take for instance the Japanese entertainment conglomerate Nintendo. Today everyone associates Nintendo with video games, but the company actually got its start in the late 1800s producing *hanafuda* playing cards. For eighty years, it moved to and from niche businesses including taxi cabs, a TV network, a food company selling instant rice, and hourly "love" hotels—all while teetering on the edge of bankruptcy. It wasn't until the 1960s that Nintendo dabbled in toys, and then in the 1970s it shifted to video arcade games. Throughout these volatile years, Nintendo remained loyal to its employees and encouraged them to take on new responsibilities. Gunpei Yokoi, for instance, started his career at Nintendo as a maintenance worker before his bosses plucked him from the assembly line to help design playthings. He built hugely profitable toys for the company and then pivoted to electronic games, where he designed the iconic Nintendo NES controller and produced numerous critically acclaimed video game franchises. At a company that didn't have a history of reinventing itself and nimbly jumping from industry to industry, Yokoi may never have been allowed to leave the assembly line.

Many of today's most successful companies began life as something completely different. Netflix was originally a mail-order DVD rental service in the late '90s before pioneering the online streaming industry in 2007, destroying its original business model in the process. IBM was once the undisputed king of the computing world before increased competition led it to post a loss of $8 billion in 1993, the then-second-largest loss in a single quarter in the history of corporate America. IBM decided to abandon its business model—building low-cost PCs, printers, and other hardware—and today it is one of the world's most successful IT consulting firms. Like everyone else, you probably grew up playing with Play-Doh, but did you know that the modeling compound was originally meant to clean coal residue from wallpaper? After World War II, as people shifted from coal to oil and natural gas to heat their homes, the company behind the toy, Kutol Products, staved off bankruptcy by reimagining its signature product as an arts-and-crafts material for children.

You can tell a lot about a company's comfort with employees

taking on wide-ranging roles by examining its history. Does it routinely make "unconventional hires," like Northwell did with Joe and like Nintendo did with Gunpei Yokoi? Does it play it safe and hire candidates who project the best "cultural fit," or who have the most "domain expertise?" Or does it pick the best talent, no matter their background?

If you're ready for a change, try applying internally at your company for a job in an entirely different division or team. Inquire with HR about shifting from, say, sales to copywriting, or from finance to marketing. If they are reluctant, ask about training programs. If your HR rep responds, "We don't really do that here," maybe it's time to jump to a new organization that constantly evolves and encourages its employees to constantly evolve too.

Take a look at your résumé or LinkedIn profile. Do you read like a lifelong learner who is always seeking out the next challenge? Or does your background suggest you are following a very specialized, linear career path?

As Alan Lightman told me: "Our educational system and our cultural ethos tell us to stay in our lane and stick to one area. But staying in your lane requires the least amount of self-confidence." It means willfully giving up control in return for a semblance of security, and a blind faith that the skills you rely on today will be relevant tomorrow. Primitives prefer to stay in control of their destiny and maintain independence. They stay hungry for new adventures. "I don't get comfortable," Tanya Valle said. "I don't want to be complacent. I will never be caught off guard. I'm always on my toes by thinking about what comes next." Likewise, Love Whelchel told me: "I don't get comfortable. In my mind, I'm in a position where I have my back up against the wall and I got to fight my way out. That's how I look at everything. That's just the way I'm wired."

Make a primitive move and act on your instinct. Connect the dots of your life while looking backward, not forward. Find unorthodox uses for old skills, but learn new ones too. Never stop being a quitter. Seek out organizations that align with—and adapt to—your ever-changing interests. Roam to new careers, double back to old ones, do it all over again. Build your raft and set sail.

CHAPTER FOUR

MESSIANIC

Ali Rezai was a medical student at the University of Southern California when he met the man who would change his life. Ali didn't know his name, where he came from, or what the young man did for a living. He had been brought to the hospital after a horrific motorcycle accident. A team of residents, nurses, and surgeons were fighting to save him.

After hours of surgery, they finally managed to stabilize him. Ali watched as the patient exited the operating room on a gurney. He would live, yes, but he'd never be the same. He would have trouble retrieving memories and forming new ones. He'd barely recognize his friends. *What else could we have done for him?* The question gnawed at Ali for weeks and months. For years, Ali had dreamed of becoming a surgeon. But that dream wasn't big enough. He also wanted to save future lives by inventing new technologies that could help people with devastating brain injuries like the man being wheeled out of the operating room.

Ali was up for the challenge. His family left Iran prior to the 1979 revolution, and he arrived in the United States at age ten with no English language skills. His father left soon after, and Ali lived with his mother and two brothers in a tiny apartment in Southern California's San Fernando Valley. Due to his poor English, Ali was dropped several grade levels and teased nonstop. But he quickly learned the language and devoted himself to his studies, determined to one day help support his struggling family. He returned to his proper grade level and then skipped ahead. At just fifteen years old, he enrolled at UCLA as a freshman. I was also there at the time, but I was socializing with liberal arts students and avoiding everything related to math and science while Ali was working in a lab that studied HIV at a time when AIDS was still poorly understood and derided as a "gay disease." He worked alongside pioneering researchers and learned about immunology and cell cultures along the way. But while treating AIDS patients, and, later, people with debilitating brain injuries, Ali learned firsthand the deficiencies of modern medicine. What was the point of saving a person's life if they could no longer enjoy it?

To me, neurosurgery represents the zenith of human achievement. I can barely operate my TV remote let alone understand how our more than one hundred billion brain cells communicate. Removing tumors and treating strokes is certainly highly complex work, but to Ali, it's routine. It's like setting a broken bone. For him, the true challenge is *restoring* lost brain function. It's enabling paralyzed veterans to regain movement. It's finding new ways to treat Alzheimer's when all other treatments have failed. It's reversing the uncontrollable shaking from Parkinson's disease with a brain implant. It's not just saving the life of a man in a motorcycle accident, but saving him from pain, from depression, and from the inability to recognize his own family.

After medical school, Ali did his residency in neurosurgery at New York University and his fellowship at the University of Toronto. He was then recruited by the world famous Cleveland Clinic, which is routinely ranked as one of the best medical centers in the world. Ali became a star brain surgeon at the hospital, specializing in the treatment of Parkinson's disease, depression, obsessive-compulsive disorder, and brain injuries, and acquiring more than a dozen patents. Ali helped pioneer the use of deep brain stimulation, which involves using implants to send therapeutic electrical currents deep into the brain. Thanks in part to Ali, deep brain stimulation has been used to treat everything from epilepsy to Tourette's syndrome to addiction. In 2009, Ali arrived at The Ohio State University, where he continued his groundbreaking research, accumulating dozens more patents and becoming director of the university's Neurological Institute. He became known as "the doctor of last resort," the man patients turned to when all other traditional treatments failed.

One of those patients was a college student named Ian Burkhart, one of the most courageous and upbeat people I've ever met. In a freak accident while on vacation, Ian dove into a wave at a North Carolina beach and broke his neck on the sandy ocean floor. He lost all feeling in his hands and legs. Doctor after doctor told him he would remain paralyzed from the chest down until, at last, he met Ali. In 2014, Ali and his team joined forces with the Battelle Memorial Institute to implant a chip in Ian's brain that could transmit his thoughts directly to his hand muscles, bypassing the spinal cord entirely. Ian regained control over his right hand and fingers—the first time in history for a quadriplegic. After extensive rehabilitation, Ian could pick up a bottle, pour liquid into a jar, and even stir it with a straw. The technology is still in its infancy, and for now Ian can only achieve optimal movement while connected to a computer in the lab, but Ali's breakthrough has paved the way for future advances that might one day cure paralysis.

A few years after his seminal success, Ali made a curious move. He departed from his prestigious position in medicine for West Virginia University. Most researchers of his stature would scoff at the idea of decamping from a string of the most prominent universities in the country for Morgantown, West Virginia. "Why not head to Hopkins, Stanford, or back to NYU?" Ali's friends implored him. "You're committing career suicide by heading to West Virginia." But for a primitive like Ali, Appalachia was a logical choice. His mission was to cure the uncurable—and in West Virginia, that was opioid addiction. Ali knew that one of the nation's poorest states was in dire need of his abilities. WVU's president, E. Gordon Gee, whom we met in the chapter on agnostics, spearheaded Ali's hire along with Dr. Clay Marsh, the dean of the university's medical school.

Ali was won over by their words about putting purpose over prestige, and he instantly got to work when he arrived at WVU. Upon his arrival, he was appointed by the university and former senator Jay Rockefeller as the incoming director of neuroscience clinical studies for WVU's Rockefeller Neuroscience Institute. In 2018, the Institute was chosen as the first site in the world to participate in a new clinical trial using focused ultrasound technology to help reverse the effects of Alzheimer's disease. Ali became the first physician to safely penetrate the blood-brain barrier in a phase II clinical trial using a technique called magnetic resonance–guided focused ultrasound, potentially paving a path to pioneering treatment options for a disease affecting nearly six million Americans.

Then, in the fall of 2019, Ali began the nation's first-ever clinical trial to treat opioid addiction using brain implants. While too many people see drug addiction as a series of poor choices, Ali understands that it is a physical condition, one that can be treated in much the same way he treated Ian Burkhart. "Addiction is a brain condition, and in addiction you have to deal with our biology as well as our environment," he explained to me. In his revolutionary study, Ali took several patients with life-threatening addiction issues and implanted chips in the reward centers of their brains. Through electrical stimulation, Ali's chips aim to rewire the brain to help eliminate the brain disorder that causes 130 people to die from opioid overdoses every day.

Ali is only getting started. He has now secured more than fifty patents, and along with addiction, he is using his implants to treat countless other brain disorders while fundamentally changing our understanding of our cognitive functioning. Ali quite literally wrote the textbook on neuromodulation and works directly with US military special forces and elite Division I athletes on brain health and human performance. Like any agnostic primitive, Ali approaches each case with a broad spectrum of knowledge that inspires creative breakthroughs that no other doctors thought possible. To Ali, nothing is insurmountable, and I'm proud of the work my firm does to promote him. Most Sunday evenings, I call Ali and we prepare for the countless speeches and presentations he delivers to share his research and secure funding. Sometimes we are laser-focused, other times our chats are freewheeling. "PR is not ER," I like to say, but assisting this messianic primitive makes me feel like my work is mission critical.

Ali is kind, gracious, and humble, but he is also the most driven person I have ever known. I've met my share of workaholics, people who are so singularly devoted to their work that they barely leave the office. Ali puts them to shame. During our calls, I have to remind Ali to eat, to sleep, and to have fun—my "spin doctor's orders." His idea of free time is occasionally driving to the batting cages to crush baseballs while pondering his next breakthrough. To have achieved Ali's level of success in just one region of neuroscience is monumental. But Ali leverages a range of technology from deep brain stimulation to focused ultrasound to transcranial magnetic stimulation. He is recruiting top scientists to help him cure as many conditions and diseases as possible in his lifetime—and for Ali, every minute not spent toward that end is a waste of time.

In the previous chapter, we met primitives who jump from field to field as easily as they change outfits, refusing to be wedded to a single job or even a single career. Messianic primitives are a different breed. Instead of happenstance and opportunity, messianic primitives are guided by a singular calling, one that transcends titles and job descriptions. Like Ali Rezai, they are on a mission to achieve a monumental goal, fix a daunting problem, change the world. They are forces of nature who work to exhaustion, while occasionally (and sometimes not-so-occasionally) pissing off everyone around them.

If you feel skeptical about the term *messianic*, you're not alone. We're taught to make decisions based on observable reality and logical calculations, not wild leaps of faith. In fact, people who blindly believe in things scare us, and often for a good reason. But messianic primitives like Ali don't become the leaders of a doomsday cult. They aren't false messiahs who claim to have all the answers. Rather, messianic primitives sacrifice in order to save and inspire others. They filter out the noise and answer to a greater calling. They take on immense responsibilities. They are determined to solve the unsolvable. They fail often, but when they do succeed, the world knows about it. They attract like-minded followers like a rock band attracts groupies; picture the late Apple CEO Steve Jobs revealing the newest iPhone to throngs of Apple fanboys and fangirls. Finally, messianic primitives are acutely aware of their own mortality and are obsessed with leaving behind a legacy.

I was first introduced to the term *messianic* when I was twenty-four and in my first job out of graduate school at the World Jewish Congress, then a philanthropic organization tied to the Seagram corporation. I was having lunch with Stephen Herbits, the right-hand man of Edgar Bronfman Sr., the powerful Seagram's CEO. Herbits spent his early career on Capitol Hill and became one of the most influential voices behind ending the military draft. Later, he was hired by Donald Rumsfeld, then chief of staff to President Gerald Ford, before landing at Seagram's in 1977 as *chef de cabinet* to Bronfman Sr., helping him negotiate with world leaders. As we ate, Herbits explained to me his theory on the mindset of the ultra-successful and how it propels them to the top. "Sometimes you have to be messianic about your career," he said. When Herbits uttered "messianic," I thought about Jerusalem Syndrome, a well-known phenomenon in which visitors suffer psychotic delusions upon visiting the holy city. I was also put off by the term for personal reasons: my mother had struggled with mental illness for years. Needless to say, the idea that one needed to act like a messiah to succeed in business seemed unnecessarily grandiose.

Can the same be said for messianic primitives? Are people who believe they are destined to solve a problem, build a company, or cure a disease inherently out of their minds or religious freaks? Some messianic primitives believe a higher power matched them with their mission, but most others simply decided to totally and utterly devote themselves to a cause. Herbits was not telling me to act like an egomaniac, but rather to treat my work as if I had been divinely appointed to carry it out. This was a man who had made a career out of turning around organizations—government, nonprofits, and corporations—by fully devoting himself to every task at hand.

As someone who identifies with agnostic primitives, my passions are intense but fleeting. I've changed careers and jobs many times, and have had more clients than I can count. I've failed, picked myself off the ground, and then tried something else. Simply put, I have too much impatience and self-doubt to do what Ali does. (I'm also terrible at math, which I would like to think is a disqualification for engineering lifesaving brain implants.) Promoting others comes naturally to me, but I'm uncomfortable promoting myself. By working with messianic primitives like Ali, I've learned how intense devotion to one's professional career can help to usher in breakthroughs in a larger cause. More content as a disciple rather than a leader, I decided it was my destiny to help messianic primitives like Ali reach their full potential.

Research suggests that many of us can afford to be more messianic about our work. As the accounting firm Deloitte found in a study, "up to 87.7 percent of America's workforce is not able to contribute to their full potential because they don't have passion for their work. Less than 12.3 percent of America's workforce possesses the attributes of worker passion." The researchers explained that in today's rapidly changing business environment, passionate workers with "the resilience needed to withstand and grow stronger from continuous market challenges and disruptions" are more needed than ever before.

We can become more passionate by being more messianic about even seemingly mundane things. Arianna Huffington, for example, decided to become messianic about sleep when she collapsed and broke her cheekbone. After spending years building her media empire on barely any rest, she realized it was her calling to use her clout to encourage professionals to prioritize sleep. "The success at the *Huffington Post* happened after I started taking care of myself," Arianna told CNBC "Make It." Ever since she collapsed from exhaustion, she has been on a crusade to promote better sleep habits, including penning a book, *The Sleep Revolution*, and founding a new wellness company, Thrive Global, devoted to helping individuals and companies avoid burnout and reduce stress levels. I invited Arianna to speak about the importance of sleep at The Ohio State University's first inaugural Brain Health and Performance Summit. Ali was still at OSU at the time, and the two messianic primitives instantly hit it off; they have since collaborated on brain-health projects.

Working with these two primitives made me rethink my day-to-day outlook. When I wake up in the morning, I ask myself: What can I be more messianic about today? In this chapter, we will peer inside the lives of several messianic primitives, including the visionaries, who imagine new industries and disrupt existing ones; the dragon-slayers, who set extraordinary goals for themselves and never stop charging toward them; the zealots, who refuse to compromise when it comes to turning dreams into reality; and the magicians, who wave a magic wand to change their lives—and those of others—for the better, even when they have no idea how.

ENVISION A NEW REALITY

About a decade ago, my business partner, Liel, told me about a young man named Adam Neumann. You might know Adam today as the former CEO of WeWork, who was deposed by his board of directors after the coworking giant's value plummeted from $47 billion in early 2019 to approximately $8 billion by autumn of the same year. Long before he was accused of engaging in rampant workplace discrimination and other malfeasance, he was a student at Baruch College with a crazy idea to reinvent the traditional workplace. In many ways, both Adam's rise and fall can be attributed to his messianic spirit, and he is proof positive that raw primitive energy, if not properly harnessed, can be as destructive as it is empowering.

When one of Adam's professors announced a business plan competition, he was thrilled. He was always interested in business, and even though his professional experience was limited at the time to helping organize large parties in downtown Manhattan, he knew he had a winning idea for a new company. Adam grew up on a kibbutz in northern Israel, and he thought that this model of shared public spaces would resonate really well with professionals in the information age, many of whom did project-based work that did not require a traditional corporate office. Adam wrote up his proposal, submitted it, and waited impatiently for the results. When they arrived, he was crestfallen: his was one of the few business plans that did not advance to the contest's second round.

Faced with such failure, a civilized person would likely nod their head, carefully read the professor's comments, and revise the plan accordingly. Yet Adam was convinced that his idea was not only good, but that it was vitally important. It was up to him to save fellow entrepreneurs from the balance-sheet-crushing harm of the New York City office lease. He looked at the corporate real estate scene and saw a few entrenched and powerful landlords who control vast swaths of property, aided by a network of brokers who could keep tenants in long-term and expensive leases. Because it was hard to find affordable and inviting office space, he realized, small businesses and creative individuals—the forces behind so much of the information economy—had a tough time setting up shop. If you, say, wanted to get your web design business off the ground and your very first step was negotiating a punitively binding and expensive lease in a dreary Midtown office, you were already in trouble.

Adam had a better idea. He grew convinced that by providing an environment where creative people could congregate and inspire each other, he would change the way we think about work. He had a vision of young professionals waking up in the morning and filing into a bright, cheerful space where they could drink good coffee (and, later in the afternoon, beer) and start serendipitous conversations that led to fruitful collaboration. This true sense of community, Adam believed, was exactly what the modern workplace lacked. Instead of focusing on a particular business or specialization, he stopped and asked himself the two seminal questions all messianic primitives ask: What's wrong with the world? And what can I do to fix it? His answer to the former was that there were too many people with great ideas who were not reaching their full potential simply because they had no place to work and no community in which to thrive. His answer to the latter question was to build precisely such a place.

Adam dropped out of college, found investors, and launched

WeWork, leasing office space and renting it out to individuals and small businesses who wanted to gather in well-designed common areas. He cut a Jesus-like look with his loose-fitting clothing, biblical sandals, and ponytail-length hair; it was symbolism that was understandably off-putting to some, but he managed to pull it off for a time. He wore black pants and black T-shirts emblazoned with slogans like "Do What You Love," a uniform that inspired imitators among his early employees and tenants. WeWork inspired a legion of early followers, and I admit I was one of them: my firm eagerly took on WeWork as a client. My business partner, Liel, conceived of and ran the company's *Creator* magazine, which I contributed to early in its run.

As we know now, of course, Adam also had less flattering messianic traits. Dubbed "Silicon Valley's Donald Trump" by the *Washington Post* columnist Helaine Olen, Adam talked publicly about becoming "president of the world" and the first-ever trillionaire. He obsessed over immortality, and invested heavily in a life-extension startup. When WeWork instituted a stock buyback program during a 2015 investment round, it offered employees "a payout per share worth substantially less than what Mr. Neumann was paid," according to an exposé in the *Wall Street Journal*. Like other primitives, Adam was impulsive: he once reportedly instructed executives to fire 20 percent of all employees each year. Another time, he caught his team off guard by banning all meat in the WeWork headquarters. In the wake of his ouster from WeWork, he was accused of discriminating against pregnant employees and sustaining a significant gender pay gap. Despite these horrendous allegations, Adam walked away from WeWork with $1.7 billion after accepting a buyout from the Japanese holding conglomerate SoftBank.

All told, Adam's extreme, if not manic, energy catapulted him to immense fortune—and subsequently brought him crashing down to earth. But his early success is nonetheless a testament to the power of envisioning and creating a new reality, though it doesn't have to be as ambitious as re-creating the global workplace. For example, Amy Wrzesniewski, a professor at the Yale School of Management, wanted to see how ordinary people who weren't making millions of dollars per year found satisfaction with their career progression. She decided to interview the custodial staff at a hospital—not exactly anyone's idea of a "dream job." After meeting janitors, cleaners, and other people in low-paying jobs, Wrzesniewski came to some striking conclusions. Many of the custodians described their work in "rich relational terms," she explained. Their job was more than making beds and cleaning instruments. It was getting to know the individual patients whose rooms they cleaned, from the epilepsy patient who didn't like loud noises to the cancer patient who wanted to talk football for a few minutes. Some patients had allergies to certain chemicals, so the custodians avoided using them. They paid attention to which patients had few visitors and made sure to spend extra time with them. Wrzesniewski realized these men and women were taking their job descriptions and turning them into something new. They recognized themselves as custodians not just of the physical bedrooms, but of the people who lived in them. They were genuine caregivers, and the warmth they showed their patients was every bit as meaningful as the work done by surgeons and nurses. And their work made them happy.

Wrzesniewski calls this phenomenon "job crafting," or finding ways to thrive and find pleasure in existing roles by connecting with the value of that work. I know that I can't directly save lives like Ali can, but I can make a messianic move by assisting visionaries like him who are changing the world. As was seen earlier in this book, sometimes it's crucial to quit your job or even a career to explore new and exhilarating opportunities. But sometimes opportunity can be found in your current situation. Think about what you are doing now. What is the biggest, grandest thing you can make that job into? What can your role become? What can it grow into? You'll be surprised how much untapped potential exists in the workplace if you know where to look—or how big to dream.

SLAY A DRAGON

A former client of mine, Kevin Tracey, is a brilliant surgeon and inventor who, like Ali, is revolutionizing the way we practice medicine. "I never wake up in the morning and tell myself I'm going to work," he shared with me one afternoon in his office, gesturing to a workbench stacked with his latest medical prototypes. "Instead, I wake up in the morning and tell myself I'm going to slay dragons." Kevin wasn't being poetic; he meant that every morning he wakes filled with a sense of absolute mission, since people's lives depend on him doing the best job he can.

To be messianic does not only mean inventing a lifesaving medical device like Ali and Kevin, or redefining what it means to work in an office. A messianic move can be identifying a major challenge—what Kevin calls a dragon—and devoting yourself to slaying it.

What is your snarling beast? Your dragon may not be as ferocious as cancer or Alzheimer's disease, but I'm willing to bet you have come across something that has always moved you, some challenge that you consider it your destiny to address. Most of us feel the pull of destiny every now and then, but ignore it by saying that it's simply not realistic, that we have to make a living, that slaying dragons is too hard, and that we would do well to remain civilized in every aspect of our lives.

Jessica Jackley used to think like that. As a child growing up in Pittsburgh, she loved going to Sunday school and was deeply moved by the line in Matthew that read, "What you do for the least of these, you do for me." Helping the needy, the young girl thought, was the key to bringing about the better world described in the Lord's Prayer that she recited so often, the one that talks about "Thy kingdom come" and about "Thy will be done on earth as it is in heaven."

But like so many mindful and motivated young people, Jessica's faith was soon tested. She may have dreamed of a life helping the needy and deepening her commitment to her religion, but her parents and her peers expected her to go to college and study something more practical. So after excelling at Bucknell, she was off to Stanford to pursue her MBA. Professors and peers rhapsodized about lucrative careers, but Jessica felt it was her destiny to help the poor. Her dragon was poverty, and she was determined to slay it in revolutionary ways.

She looked into various nonprofit organizations, but none seemed innovative or likely to succeed. Then, one day, she met Muhammad Yunus, the Bangladeshi social entrepreneur who would go on to win the Nobel Peace Prize for pioneering the concept of microloans. His idea was simple: many people around the world had good ideas for businesses that could lift themselves and their communities out of poverty, and all they needed was a tiny boost to get started. Instead of seeking a loan from a bank, which is notoriously difficult for individuals to do with no track record or assets, Yunus developed a system that let anyone loan a small amount of money to people who needed it to launch their enterprises.

Jessica was deeply moved. If only, she thought, there was some easy platform that streamlined the microloan process, people would surely take satisfaction in loaning $20, $40, or even $100 to someone across the world. She traveled to Kenya, Uganda, and Tanzania to learn how far a small loan could truly go. From shoe repair to bicycle repair, Jessica saw the real difference small loans made in the lives of their recipients. Together with her partner and eventual husband, Reza Aslan, she met with lawyers and explained her idea. The first one said it was naive and unrealistic. So did the second, the eighth, and the thirty-fifth.

Undeterred, Jessica managed to launch her company anyway. And she gave it a messianic name, Kiva, which is Swahili for "unity." She wrote an email to her family and friends, asking them to give a no-interest loan to a person in need. She couldn't promise they'd ever get their money back, but she could promise it was the right thing to do. She asked each person to lend $25 to seven strangers across the globe. She hit send and held her breath.

Persuaded by her passion, many opened their hearts and their wallets. Then they shared their decision with more friends and acquaintances, who soon flocked to Kiva, intrigued by Jessica's idea of fighting poverty with microloans. It only took a few months before the original investors were made whole, and within a few years Kiva had facilitated hundreds of millions of dollars in loans to individuals and small businesses in more than eighty countries. For Jessica, this work is only the beginning. Her dragon—global poverty—has only been slightly wounded. But by building a financially inclusive world, Jessica is working toward giving people the power to improve their own worlds, one loan at a time.

Put aside practical considerations and ask yourself a question that may sound crazy: What's your dragon? Follow Jessica's example and try to define it in the broadest of terms. Is it to end poverty? Cure cancer? Bring about world peace? Maybe your goals are less grand, such as becoming a full-time artist, creating your own business, or simply climbing the corporate ladder. Take, for example, my old friend in high school and college, Dov Seidman. When most of us wanted to be Hollywood actors or football stars, Dov had a vision about applying his love of philosophy and ethics to the world of business. My eyes glazed over when he explained what he meant by that, and I somewhat resented his supreme faith in himself. Yet Dov never wavered from his dream, and after Harvard Law School and a stint at the law firm O'Melveny & Myers, he founded LRN, the ethics and management firm that specializes in helping businesses institute ethics and compliance programs, from sexual harassment to antitrust. Today, Dov is an expert in moral philosophy and leadership; Bill Clinton even wrote the foreword to his book, *How: Why How We Do Anything Means Everything*.

Learn from Dov's example and choose to be messianic about something you find inspiring, no matter how small or esoteric it may seem. My sister, for example, is one of the most civilized people I know, but chooses to be messianic about raising her three teenagers, making sure she is fully invested in them during their formative years. Being messianic means putting you and your goals first and saying "no" when necessary to others. It means sacrificing and treating your task as an overriding purpose that supersedes everything else. Allow yourself to set these lofty, even seemingly impossible goals and reflect on them for a minute. Then, start asking other, more practical questions: What skills do I have that can best help me pursue my destiny? Am I using them in my current situation? And, if not, what else should I be doing?

BE A ZEALOT

Don't you just hate how hyperbolic so much of business has become? No one, it seems, is selling anything concrete these days—instead, everyone is trying to disrupt their industry and change the world. Very few actually do, of course. In part, that's because most of us do not have complete, unbending faith in our own ability to transform an intractable situation, whether at work or in the world. It may sound silly to civilized folks observing the adjective-fest, but messianic primitives really do believe the hype. They're not in the game just to make a buck. They're in it because they believe they can change the world.

Carol Meyrowitz sure does. From 2007 until 2016, she was CEO of TJX, which operates more than 3,300 discount retail stores, including T.J. Maxx, HomeGoods, and Marshalls. She became one of the highest-paid executives in America by thinking like a messianic primitive in retail, which, despite its rough-and-tumble reputation, can be one of the most civilized industries around. While her competitors were obsessing over their margins and how to cut costs, Carol stopped and asked herself not how to get her customers to spend more money in her stores but why they were walking into her stores to begin with. It wasn't, she realized, just that the price was right—with e-commerce booming, shoppers have abundant opportunities to save a buck if that's truly the only thing they care about. But Carol had a more profound realization: she felt that the folks who shopped at her stores wanted not only to buy good quality items at affordable prices but also to feel good about themselves, to feel as if they were able to exercise their own taste and buy interesting things that reflected their unique personalities even when browsing through the bins of a moderately priced store.

Why, she thought, should only the ultra-wealthy enjoy the considerable benefits of "retail therapy?" Why not give middle- and working-class shoppers the heady feeling of buying something special that really captures their sensibility and style? Find a way to do that, she believed, and you'll transform not only your business but your customers as well, making them a little bit happier and more fulfilled. To achieve her goals, Carol followed a classic pillar of messianic primitive thought: be a zealot. Zealots don't pore over Excel spreadsheets. They don't run predictive models or torment themselves with small and niggling details. They set a goal—the only goal that matters to them—and they pursue it, even if it means tossing out the rule book.

And Carol didn't just toss out the rule book—she wrote her own. In a business that's notorious for ruthlessly streamlining the supply chain, she decided that the most important thing was stocking her stores with items that made shoppers feel as if they were buying something beautiful and special. This didn't mean that the items had to be expensive, but it did mean that the one-style-fits-all approach that most retail chains take as they stock their stores with the same stuff from the same central warehouse had to be reconsidered.

Thinking like a zealot, Carol gave her team a series of instructions. She told them not to compromise and not to be deterred by the usual roadblocks like price tags or logistical difficulties. Instead, she asked them to focus on their true goals, starting with finding things that were uncommon and inexpensive, the sort of objects that would inspire customers to feel that they mattered. To that end, HomeGoods, for example, began sourcing from more than sixteen thousand vendors across the world.

Carol didn't set out to save a bit of cash. She set out to transform the lives of her shoppers, and she did. Already fond of shopping at HomeGoods, customers soon began displaying an uncommon loyalty to the brand, encouraging each other not only to shop there to the exclusion of other chains but also to stop in and buy something more frequently than they otherwise would have. The company added stores at a furious pace. From when Carol took charge of the company in 2007 to less than a decade later, revenues soared from $17.4 billion to $29.1 billion, with profits more than tripling. She did this by setting a messianic vision—a world where retail chains didn't just prod people into buying more stuff but instead helped them feel better about their lives by providing them with affordable and unique objects—and pursuing it zealously, not compromising even when other executives would've opted for more conservative approaches.

She didn't do it alone. To transform her company, she needed to make other people see things her way. But she'd worked for a lot of very large companies over the years, and she knew that people, as a rule, weren't risk-takers. Most people, not being primitive, didn't embrace precariousness. Even good, smart people too often did the math and figured out that it was far more prudent to just do their work and not rock the boat too much, so that when they had really good ideas they were too often reluctant to share them, because they considered the risk too high. And employees like these, Carol knew, couldn't be counted on to transform anything. To succeed, she needed her team to become zealots too.

So she did something that was both simple and daring: she started a university for her employees. The lesson that was imparted was jarring: forget the bottom line. Instead of caring about their department's monthly performance—previously a source of much agitation for executives eager to prove that they were earning the company more money—employees were now told to care about the company's new goal, which was supplying customers with high-quality and affordable items that would help them feel special. If that meant one department had to spend a lot in a given month to make sure stores were stocked with whimsical holiday decorations, Carol told her team members, then she expected other departments to chip in and help with the budget.

It was a radical departure from the ordinary way of doing things, and a long way from how most large corporations are still run, but it worked. It was, in true primitive fashion, a bit of inspired madness, but instead of leading to chaos and waste, it led Carol's employees to unleash their creative energies and sense of teamwork. Before too long, employees were coming up with their own ideas for new product lines and promotions, and one senior executive even slashed her own budget considerably to help another colleague whose plan for growth, she believed, was crucial to the company's long-term goals.

This kind of unconventional initiative is the sort you only see in companies and organizations that provide a clear mission and then help their employees become zealous about making it a reality. If all you're ever trained to pursue is a financial bottom line, you'll find yourself fearful of and averse to change. But if you're committed to a larger, transformative vision, you may soon find that your messianic faith can free you up to make the kinds of business decisions that you would never have even imagined otherwise.

WAVE A MAGIC WAND

When I was working at BBDO, the late head of training, Bruce Leibowitz, would often tell us: "Wave a magic wand. Envision something that replaces and reinvents your current situation." Doing this clarified our core values and provided a strongly needed reality check for how much progress we were truly making.

For Danny Lewin, waving a magic wand meant reinventing the internet. "The World Wide Wait," as he derisively called it in the pre-broadband days of Web 1.0, infuriated him with its static Web pages and excruciating load times. He insisted that through proper optimization, content could be delivered much faster. He compared his ideal internet with the real one and found a way to bridge that gap.

The magic wand exercise can even help organizations generate entirely new principles that transcend profit. Tayo Oviosu is the CEO of Paga, a mobile payments company he founded in 2009 to help bring access to financial services to all Nigerians. With millions of users, Paga reportedly reaches more people than all of Nigeria's banks combined. In a country where three in ten people don't have easy access to fresh drinking water, Paga uses an open, secure payment platform that allows anyone with a mobile phone to make financial transactions, from sending money to family to paying bills to buying groceries. The platform has enabled entrepreneurs to open businesses in a country that previously did not have a reliable way for its citizens to pay for basic services. Tayo routinely asks his employees what they would do if they could wave a magic wand. "I've been wondering what role our business could play in the world around us. What kind of company do we want to be?" he wrote. "What principles do we want to stand up for? I felt this question could help start teasing the answers to these questions.…I did not know what to expect, and was very impressed by the responses and passion behind them." Specifically, Paga employees brought up equality and ending discrimination, ensuring that all people receive a basic education, and solving broader governance issues in Nigeria. One company can't solve all these issues, but Tayo challenged his employees to integrate these moonshot goals into the broader culture of Paga.

The magic wand exercise is important because it helps put your battles in context. If you could wave a magic wand and make everything you are fighting for become reality, would you be satisfied? If you became CEO of your current company, would you be content? Or is your goal bigger? For Ali Rezai, waving a magic wand means imagining a world where paralysis, Alzheimer's disease, addiction, and countless other brain conditions can be cured. Waving a magic wand is a simple exercise, but it's my first step toward making a solution appear tangible instead of theoretical. No matter how difficult a situation seems, I need to know what my ultimate wish is and do a gut check on how far I've strayed from that principle.

Sometimes waving a magic wand can simply mean removing yourself from a bad situation. This was true for Maurice Reid, a young man I've been mentoring for several years. He was one of eight children, and together with his siblings he was in and out of

New York City foster care and treatment centers for most of his childhood. He got into trouble constantly, and by age thirteen he was firmly entrenched in the "school-to-prison pipeline," where at-risk students are funneled out of public schools and into juvenile and criminal justice systems. His classmates were the victims of abuse and neglect, but instead of receiving additional counseling and education, as the American Civil Liberties Union puts it, "They are isolated, punished, and pushed out."

At age thirteen, Maurice was introduced to gang life. He stole, fought, and got arrested—seven times, in fact, before he turned fourteen. He joined the Bloods street gang, where as a young teen he was introduced to the kind of violence most of us only see on HBO. For a boy who had been cast aside by one of the richest cities in the world, gang life was surprisingly empowering. "It's a violent culture. You survive through hardship, adversity, through opposition," Maurice told me. "But it's also very educational. You build comradery with the people in your gang. You build loyalty. You build respect. I had nothing to lose, and you don't care about the consequences." Paradoxically, life as a Blood is in some respects civilized. The gang is hierarchical. It's regimented. You are expected to follow orders and you are punished if you don't. I was struck by how a street gang could sound almost as structured as a staid corporation.

Maurice's actions eventually caught up with him: he spent his fifteenth, sixteenth, and seventeenth birthdays in a maximum-security juvenile detention center five hours from New York City. "While I was there, I spent so much time fighting that it almost became animalistic." He had to fight to get food, to go to the bathroom, to survive. Other gang members saw this as a badge of honor, but Maurice grew weary of the police cars and the mug shots and the cells and the creeping realization that his life wouldn't get any better without making a change. He had his messianic moment while high with his friends, riding an elevator. Maurice made an offhand comment about how he would always return to the hood, and one of his friends looked at him and said: "No, you won't."

At that moment, Maurice realized he was destined for greater things. Even his friends knew it. He didn't dream of revolutionizing medicine or reducing poverty. If he could wave a magic wand, Maurice wouldn't have built a killer new app or gadget. "I just wanted to go to school," Maurice told me. "I wanted to be a role model for my brothers and sisters." He waved his wand, imagined a new future for himself, and he made the simplest, most important decision of his life.

Maurice began taking classes at a community college and got his associate's degree before he turned twenty-one. He volunteered at foster homes, helping at-risk youth avoid the mistakes he made. Not content with an associate's degree, Maurice applied to colleges, laying bare his arrests and gang history in his essays. He wrote about how he dropped out of high school at fifteen and got his GED while in the detention center. At first the rejections flooded in, but Maurice kept applying. Finally, he received a call from his reach school, NYU, asking him to bring in additional materials to support his application. The admissions officer asked him to hang around for a few minutes, so Maurice took a seat. He watched as smartly dressed NYU students walked by, laughing, preparing to become doctors and lawyers and masters of the universe. They didn't even glance in his direction. Maurice had never known their privilege—not by a long shot. How could a former Blood who spent his formative years in the back seat of a police car hope to sit in the same classroom as these future decision makers? What was a black kid from the streets of Bed-Stuy doing in posh Greenwich Village?

When the admissions offer returned, he beamed at him: "Congratulations, Maurice. You've been accepted to New York University." Maurice's messianic dream had come to fruition. He had finally escaped his old life.

He didn't stop moving forward. He had a 3.7 GPA his first semester, and was later accepted into NYU's Shanghai study abroad program. Around that time, he heard that one of his childhood friends had been killed in a shooting, and another had been incarcerated for a major crime. Before he stepped onto his flight to China, Maurice reflected on how his life had changed in just a few short years. He knew he was destined for greater things, and he made a primitive move to upend his life. Since I began mentoring Maurice, I've witnessed his life blossom. I remember taking him out to lunch shortly before he was accepted to NYU, and he admitted it was the first time he had been in a restaurant with white tablecloths and real silverware. Maurice went on to several successful stints at large, publicly traded tech companies before having a second messianic moment: dedicating himself to helping at risk students avoid the fate that he so nearly missed. I'm so incredibly proud of Maurice, and I can't wait to see where his life takes him next.

Your life may not need changing as dramatically as Maurice's did, but we can all learn from him. Identify something that isn't right, wave a magic wand, and imagine what it can become.

What is your destiny? What are the challenges you feel destined to tackle? Are you rising to meet them? If not, what should you be doing to make sure that changes?

You might be like Ali Rezai, devoting every waking minute to a singular purpose. Do you see yourself as a visionary who eyes crusty industries that are ripe for disruption? Maybe you are a righteous dragon-slayer like Jessica Jackley, or a zealot like Carol Meyrowitz, uncompromising in your mission and prepared to tear down barriers and rewrite rules? Or, perhaps, you are more like Maurice Reid, committed less to a mission than to the simple idea that you are destined to do bigger, better, more daring things, that your impact on others will long outlive you.

Be bold, but also be smart about tapping your talents. I don't expect that the answers to these questions will lead a mild-mannered manager to, say, mortgage his house, tap into his daughter's college fund, and start that toy train business he has always dreamed of. But we all feel like we can do better, and when we do, thinking like a messianic primitive can be exactly the charge you need to reset an existing mission or launch an even more daring one.

Think about your dragons every morning and ask yourself if you're likely to get any closer to slaying them once you've had your coffee. When you're thinking about whether to pitch that idea or launch that product, channel your inner zealot. Tap into the energy we all contain that leads us to believe in something fervently and furiously and against all odds and reason. Then apply just a sprinkle of that energy when making decisions at the office and charting the course of your career. A little messianic energy goes a very long way.

CHAPTER FIVE

INSECURE

In the fall of 1972, my father asked me a question that changed my life: "How would you like to skip the rest of third grade and come live with me on the boat in Baja?"

I was eight years old, but the prospect of having an adventure with my dad—my best friend in the world—was too great to pass up. Yet even at such a young age, I had reservations. "I want to go, but what about school? Won't I fall behind?" I asked him, anxiously.

"Don't worry about school, Marco. I've already spoken with your principal. He thinks you'll learn more at sea than you could ever learn in a classroom." Looking back, I had no idea how my father convinced the school that this was a good idea, but he had indeed made all the necessary arrangements. A few weeks later, I was on a bumpy Aeromexico flight bound for La Paz in Baja California Sur. My dad picked me up and took me to our new home: a thirty-two-foot fiberglass sloop. On our first day at sea, my dad taught me the basics of sailing, handed me the tiller, and told me to keep a steady eye on the compass. Then he got stoned and fell asleep in the cockpit.

Roaming the seas of Baja California awakened the agnostic spirit within me, but it also awakened something else. I watched my father adapt seamlessly from location to location and from peril to peril. When our sailboat broke down, he'd jump into the diesel engine compartment with a wrench between his teeth and somehow get it going again. He could fix a ripped sail, repair a rudder, jury-rig a new tiller in a pinch out of fishing rods—all without any sort of formal training. Everything seemed to come easy to my dad, who was something of a Renaissance man. He was good at almost everything he tried, from sketching to photography to body surfing. He had an encyclopedic knowledge of European art history and obscure tree species. He was free of the reflexive trepidation I felt whenever I tried something new, learned a technical skill, or reacted to the unexpected. Once, when we were sailing near La Paz, he had me take the dinghy to shore for supplies. While I was in the store a massive earthquake hit. I fell to the ground in a fetal position, bracing for the worst. It finally passed and I returned to the boat shaking with fear. Dad was sitting in his hammock, reading a book. He hadn't even noticed the quake.

After we returned to California, my father continued to glide between stages of his life as I struggled with developing my own independent identity. He was the first architect and developer to build tasteful apartments along the beach in Marina del Rey. In Venice, he restored ramshackle buildings to their former glory and designed homes that were later featured in glossy magazines. While my friends' dads drove station wagons, mine drove a Porsche. Sometimes he'd get bored and jump on a plane to some exotic place. Once, *Rolling Stone* chronicled his feat of skiing in Aspen in the morning and swimming in Maui later that afternoon. He seemed to have friends everywhere he went, from sailing buddies to business partners to old flames who never fell out of love with him.

I had a much more difficult time fitting in. As I battled anxiety and school bullies and struggled to make friends, I watched my dad party with celebrities, date an endless parade of beautiful women, and extract every ounce of joy from life. Throughout my teenage years I felt my father's magnificent shadow swallow me whole. My insecurities came to a head in twelfth grade, when I was applying for colleges. My father's girlfriend at the time was the movie star Jill St. John, who played the Bond girl Tiffany Case in *Diamonds Are Forever,* among other roles. I told her one night over dinner that my dream was to attend Yale University. "That's great," she told me. "I'll set you up with my good friend Henry, who has a million connections there."

"Henry," it turns out, was none other than former secretary of state Henry Kissinger. During our subsequent meeting at the Beverly Wilshire Hotel, the world-famous statesman took one look at me and said in his gravelly, German-accented English: "When you get into Yale, it will be on your own merit." Nevertheless, he promised to send a letter to the president of Yale, and a minute later he was swept away by his entourage, bound for more important people and places. With letters from Kissinger and Yale's legendary football coach Carmen Cozza, who apparently got my name from the admissions office as a potential recruit for his team, I thought I was all but assured admission to my dream college.

Except, I didn't get in. No amount of connections or privilege could make up for my low standardized test scores.

I wasn't good enough. All at once, I was reminded of everything I wasn't proficient at growing up, how difficult it was for me to learn things that my father mastered so effortlessly. I ended up attending two fine schools—the University of California, Berkeley and then UCLA—but my insecurities continued to haunt me. Even as I found success, the little voice in the back of my brain never stopped asking: *Am I supposed to be here? Am I really good enough? Do I deserve to be successful?*

To the civilized person, insecurity of any kind is deeply distressful, a condition to cure. We are taught to project confidence, even if we aren't feeling it. Or, as the old English aphorism goes, "Fake it till you make it." As long as you act confident and pretend you already are successful, you will naturally levitate toward success. In the workplace, this translates to dressing above your pay grade, walking with your chest puffed out, talking loudly and firmly, and never second-guessing yourself.

This was not me, and for the longest time I thought my insecurities were something to be ashamed of. But as I jumped from job to job, it dawned on me that self-doubt and other insecurities aren't characteristics to conquer or even subdue. Low self-confidence isn't a vulnerability that needs to be papered over or compensated for. When I moved to Israel shortly before I turned thirty, I still felt like an imposter. I never seemed to muster the confidence to truly excel at what I was doing. I thought people could see right through me and expose me for the fraud I was. But a strange thing happened when I met the former chief rabbi of Ireland, David Rosen. While chatting in his book-lined study in Jerusalem, Rosen jokingly muttered the old adage: "Well, Marco, just because you're paranoid doesn't mean they aren't out to kill you."

I've long since forgotten why Rosen said it, but the line has stuck with me ever since. On one hand I thought about my heritage: throughout our history, Jews have been persecuted, exiled, and nearly annihilated. Yet for thousands of years we have survived, somehow. For many of my ancestors, a constant sense of anxiety and paranoia may quite literally have been the difference between life and death. But I also thought about human evolution, about how anxiety itself is a survival mechanism. The fight-or-flight response is located in the deepest, most ancient regions of the human brain. When you encounter a threat, whether it's a charging grizzly bear or an angry boss, your autonomic nervous system—the same region of the brain that regulates heart rate, digestion, and other fundamental processes—orders your adrenal glands to pump out the stress hormones adrenaline and cortisol, increasing blood flow to your muscles to enable you to run faster or fight harder. The stress response even cranks up the blood clotting function, so you can recover faster from wounds.

The creeping anxiety I've felt for much of my life is my body preparing to fend off a threat. Instead of weakness, I began to think of my insecurities as a strength. Feeling that I wasn't good enough meant that I was constantly improving. I was too anxious and paranoid to rest on my laurels. I was hyperaware of threats that others would not ever see coming. Rather than a liability, when taken in moderation, my insecurity was an advantage.

Of course, calling someone insecure may not sound like a compliment. In previous chapters we met Austin, the relentless primitive who charges like a bull toward his goals. And there was Danny, the oppositional primitive, who confidently and loudly asserted his independence. These sound like the traits of people who are born to lead and be in control. But *insecure*? That sounds a lot less intimidating.

And yet, insecurity is a critical component of nearly all the successful people I've worked with. Many of them have learned to not just acknowledge their own insecurities, but brandish them for the world to see. They are propelled by their insecurities, not held back by them. Walking out of their caves, blinking in the bright sunlight, the original primitives didn't know much except that they weren't really safe. The same is true for us; with our world changing so rapidly, we have to not just come to terms with insecurity, but embrace it as a guidepost to which opportunities to pounce on and which pitfalls to avoid. Insecure primitives like me have, to borrow an old Yiddish phrase, a never-ending case of the *shpilkes*, which means a state of impatience, ants in your pants, anxiety, or any combination thereof.

Insecure primitives are aware of their weaknesses, disabilities, inadequacies, vulnerabilities, and blind spots as much as their strengths. They see good fortune as fleeting. They choose anxiety and paranoia as their longtime companions. They work at a frenetic pace knowing they have limited time to make their mark. Like other primitives, they are singularly aware of their own mortality—and they thrive as a result.

DOUBT YOURSELF

"When I first started teaching," says Tomas Chamorro-Premuzic, a professor of business psychology at University College London and Columbia University, "I was so confident in my ability to *edutain* (educate plus entertain) that I never even bothered preparing. Although the classes were fun, the best students quickly worried about the lack of structure and content....On the other hand, the less ambitious students thought the class was great, because they assumed that there was nothing to be learned or studied. I was so pleased with myself that I dismissed any negative feedback from the students and instead focused on the positive comments: 'Finally someone decided to make the lectures entertaining.'"

Eventually, however, the young professor realized he was failing—badly. His lectures might have been funny, but they did little to prepare his students or teach them in any meaningful way. Before long, most started complaining, causing Chamorro-Premuzic to reevaluate his approach. Given his area of study, he started researching the question of confidence, and what too much of it does to the brain. His findings were startling: most of us, he learned, are unjustifiably overconfident, which means we spend less time and energy than we ought to addressing our shortcomings. Nearly 100 percent of his colleagues that he surveyed, for example, replied that they were well-above-average teachers.

"Although society places a great deal of importance on being confident," he wrote in his book *Confidence: How Much You Really*

Need and How to Get It, "there are no genuine benefits except feeling good. In fact, lower confidence is key to gaining competence, which is the only effective strategy for gaining genuine confidence— confidence that is warranted by one's actual competence."

Chamorro-Premuzic explains that there are three main reasons why lack of confidence often leads to greater success. First, people who have lower self-confidence pay more attention to negative feedback. Instead of becoming trapped in their own optimistic biases, they understand that achievement has more to do with preparation than actual performance. The more you are aware of your weaknesses, the better prepared you are to compensate for them. I can attest to this directly: after I was rejected from Yale University, I momentarily puffed up my confidence level by falling back on football, a sport that was very near to my heart. Having been relentlessly bullied as a child, I worked tirelessly to buff up and smash bigger and meaner kids on the field.

"If I can't go to Yale," I told myself, "I'll play linebacker for the Golden Bears," Cal's Division I football team. But my high school football coach swiftly (and wisely) quashed those dreams: "Marco," he told me, "you'll be holding blocking bags and passing out water for four years because those guys are bigger, faster, stronger, and more pissed off than you are." I was crushed. Football was everything to me, yet, once again, I simply wasn't good enough. But I listened to my coach because I knew he was right. I didn't waste my time trying to make a team I had no business playing on.

Second, lower self-confidence motivates insecure primitives to work and prepare harder. Take the legendary *60 Minutes* journalist Morley Safer, for instance. During his sixty-year career, Safer collected countless awards, including twelve Emmys. Yet despite his successes, Safer never rested on his laurels when pitching a new story. At *60 Minutes,* journalists spend weeks and months chasing a lead before putting together a short screener, much like a TV pilot, and presenting it to the CBS brass. The executive producers then decide whether to continue pursuing the story or discard it entirely. Even after decades of reporting some of the most important events in history, from the Gulf of Tonkin incident to the Arab-Israeli War of 1967, Safer pushed his team to make their *60 Minutes* pitches as perfect as possible. After the executives invariably greenlit his stories, Morley would walk out of the conference room with his team and say with a grin: "Fooled 'em again."

Finally, Chamorro-Premuzic notes that projecting lower self-confidence reduces the chance that you come across as arrogant or deluded. You've probably had a boss or two who fit that description. Workplace polls suggest that one of the most cited reasons for workplace dissatisfaction is an arrogant boss. When managers are doing their jobs, employees have a clearer understanding of their responsibilities and feel comfortable communicating potential problems. But when employees perceive their managers as brash or arrogant, morale plummets, productivity dips, and résumés are updated. Have you ever had a job you would have enjoyed if not for a bad boss?

My former colleague Riki Drori is CMO of YouTube EMEA (Europe, Middle East, and Africa) and head of Google consumer products marketing for the region, but earlier in her career she was, in her own words, "not the world's greatest manager." Before launching events for Google, she would fret that not enough people would attend and she'd blame her team for not making a larger invite list. She'd demand to know why certain tasks hadn't been completed yet. Even though her events were always massive successes, Riki was paranoid that each one—and, by extension, she—would be a failure.

After three years, Riki received the results of an internal performance review. They were not ideal: Some of her direct reports said she was arrogant and didn't listen to them. There wasn't always a healthy line of communication. Worst of all, some felt she didn't care about them.

For an ultra-successful and empathetic person like Riki, the results were devastating. She reflected deeply on her life and her career. Was she good enough? Was she really supposed to be there? She thought back to a pivotal moment from childhood. She had just turned twelve and it was the day of her bat mitzvah. But when she entered her living room for the ceremony, nearly all of the seats were empty. A bully at school had convinced the rest of her class to skip the most important day of Riki's young life. The crippling humiliation, the shame, the anger—this singular moment was burned in her mind even years later when she was planning events for Google as a high-powered executive.

Some bosses would have refused to confront these insecurities. They would have ignored the performance review, or worse, retaliated against their direct reports. Instead, Riki firmly believed that great managers are made, not born. She could learn to be better. She accepted that her team was right and that she was wrong. She apologized to them and opened a dialogue about her insecurities. She told them about the bat mitzvah and other moments from her past that made her feel vulnerable. When she was acting high-strung, she told them, it reflected on her—not on them. The impact was immediate. As Riki and her team members got to know each other on a deeper, more human level, the tension eased dramatically. Two years later, out of six thousand candidates, Riki was voted one of the twenty best managers in the entire company.

Like other primitives, Riki learned to own her insecurities and transform them into a strength. She used them to connect and empathize with her team members. She asks for feedback constantly—something she never used to do for fear of looking weak. "I'm the most insecure person in the world," she told me not with shame, but with pride. Over her career, she has seen many executives fail because they feel the need to project confidence and infallibility. They refuse to acknowledge mistakes. They blame others. As Chamorro-Premuzic explains, "It is therefore time to debunk the myth: high self-confidence isn't a blessing, and low self-confidence is not a curse—in fact, it is the other way around."

If you read enough self-help books, you might get the opposite impression. Many of them come with brash titles like *Confidence: How to Overcome Your Limiting Beliefs and Achieve Your Goals* or *You Are a Badass: How to Stop Doubting Your Greatness and Start Living an Awesome Life*. But are you really a badass? Do you really want to extinguish all limiting beliefs? The investment bankers who brought us the greatest financial crisis since the Great Depression were once incredibly confident about their multibillion-dollar bets. The shipbuilders and crew of the *Titanic* were so confident in the indestructibility of their vessel that they barreled through treacherous waters hoping to beat a transatlantic speed record. More recently, a performance review of physicians noted that the most common error was premature cloture of an initial diagnosis. Once a patient was diagnosed with, say, fibromyalgia, a doctor was very unlikely to rethink that conclusion, or consider other diseases with similar symptoms. This overconfidence can obviously lead to disastrous results.

Several business school professors decided to test how important perceived confidence levels were in a corporate setting. They assembled several hundred undergraduate participants and asked them to rate how likely they were to work with a candidate who was outwardly confident as compared to a candidate who was less self-assured. Confidence was beneficial to a candidate initially, the authors noted, but if the candidate's performance did not live up to expectations, their advantage crumbled. "The results replicated our previous studies, in that confidence, no matter how it was expressed, was beneficial *until* it became clear that performance fell short," the study concluded.

Insecure primitives don't take their or others' knowledge for granted. They listen to that nagging voice in their head: "What if I'm wrong? What if *they* are wrong?" Insecure primitives never stop doubting themselves, and, like Riki, they become better people for it. As Neil Armstrong once said about NASA's tireless work in the '60s to land a man on the moon: "Well, I think we tried very hard not to be overconfident, because when you get overconfident, that's when something snaps up and bites you."

BE AN IMPOSTER

Imposter syndrome is the psychological pattern in which people doubt their accomplishments and have a persistent internalized fear of being exposed as a "fraud." The term was coined by the clinical psychologists Pauline Clance and Suzanne Imes in 1978 after they discovered that their study subjects, despite having ample external evidence of their accomplishments, were convinced they weren't worthy of their success.

Imposter syndrome is a very real phenomenon, one that afflicts even the most successful people. Maya Angelou, the late American poet, writer, and civil rights activist, attained fifty honorary degrees and earned Pulitzer Prize and Tony Award nominations over her storied career. Nevertheless, she worried she was pulling a fast one: "I have written eleven books," she reflected late in her life, "but each time I think, 'Uh oh, they're going to find out now. I've run a game on everybody, and they're going to find me out.'" What do Oscar-winning actor Tom Hanks and Supreme Court justice Sonia Sotomayor have in common? They admit to having struggled with imposter syndrome, agonizing over whether they were smart or good enough even at the pinnacle of their careers.

"I am always looking over my shoulder wondering if I measure up," the first Hispanic Supreme Court justice, who grew up in a working-class family in the Bronx, said in a 2009 speech.

Hanks admitted: "No matter what we've done, there comes a point where you think, 'How did I get here? When are they going to discover that I am, in fact, a fraud and take everything away from me?'"

Sheryl Sandberg, the high-powered COO of Facebook said: "Every time I was called on in class, I was sure that I was about to embarrass myself. Every time I took a test, I was sure that it had gone badly. And every time I didn't embarrass myself—or even excelled—I believed that I had fooled everyone yet again. One day soon, the jig would be up."

Academy Award–winning actress Natalie Portman, while delivering the 2015 commencement address at her alma mater, Harvard University, said: "I have to admit that today, even twelve years after graduation, I'm still insecure about my own worthiness. I have to remind myself today, *You are here for a reason.*"

Even the famed writer John Steinbeck was crippled with self-doubt: "I am not a writer," he wrote in a 1938 journal entry. "I've been fooling myself and other people." While writing his magnum opus, *The Grapes of Wrath,* Steinbeck agonized over what he felt was his lack of talent: "I am assailed by my own ignorance and inability....Sometimes, I seem to do a little good piece of work, but when it is done it slides into mediocrity."

Studies suggest that as many as 70 percent of individuals may experience imposter syndrome at some point in their lives. I've certainly been afflicted by variations of it over the years, especially when I started my own companies. I was fairly confident in my abilities, but I worried no one else was. In 1998, two days before I married Stacey, who was six months pregnant, I lost two of my five clients at my new firm, which I'd only opened at the start of the year. Just like that, all my childhood anxiety flooded back. *I truly am not good enough. My clients finally figured out I'm not supposed to be here. How can I provide for my wife and child?* Even my mother piled on: "You gave it your best, Marco, but maybe it's time to go back to Burson-Marsteller," referring to the corporate PR firm I had worked at twice before. In my bravado, I replied: "I'll hand out fliers to topless bars on 42nd Street before I go back there." But on the inside, I was panicking. *How will I pay for the wedding? How will I pay the monthly mortgage? Or the hospital bills? Will Stacey stay with me?*

In its most extreme form, imposter syndrome is debilitating and prevents smart, competent people from reaching their goals. But sometimes a small dose of imposter syndrome is a positive force. Experiencing self-doubt indicates that you are challenging yourself. You are venturing outside your comfort zone. You are growing and experiencing new and exciting things. It keeps you from confidently blundering into a colossal mistake. When I started my current firm, Thunder11, I had nightmares about losing my biggest clients. I worked around the clock to keep them happy and convince them I was worthy of that five-figure monthly retainer. Insecure primitives are prepared for the occasional catastrophe because they always expect it.

I like to think of myself as part of a long and distinguished line of imposters. My grandfather J.B. and his brothers Ike and Dan started with nothing in a tiny San Francisco apartment during the outbreak of World War I. They made fortunes and they lost fortunes, as my cousin likes to say, and it all began with beans. As teenagers, they'd buy beans from farmers north of the city and then resell them for a profit. Hoping to expand their business, they attained a meeting with Amadeo Giannini, the famed banker who founded the Bank of Italy, which later became Bank of America. Giannini took one look at the "Greenberg boys" and laughed. "You're all under eighteen," he said. "Your signature isn't worth anything." But the banker was impressed with their spunk, and he gave them the loan anyway.

When the war ended, J.B. and his brothers bought up cheap

army surplus and opened a store in San Francisco's Mission District. But the Greenberg boys knew nothing about running a retail store, and in July 1922, thieves broke in and stole much of their stock. Their troubles didn't end there: after a few dubious auctions involving a lucrative contract to sell army surplus goods at a military base near San Diego, the brothers were indicted in a price-fixing scheme after some shady dealings by their business partner. Fortunately, the charges were eventually dropped. The boys continued to veer to new industries they knew nothing about, including insurance liquidation, a liquor distillery, and a Hollywood costumer called Western Costume Company (which is still one of the most prominent suppliers to movie studios). Toward the end of the 1930s, they purchased a bankrupt paint outfit and reorganized it into the Standard Brands Paint Company.

Of course, they knew absolutely nothing about paint. "They knew that they knew nothing," my grandmother used to quip. "And that's so important in business." The Greenberg boys also understood that they were imposters in every industry they wandered into, and they didn't pretend to be paint barons. My grandfather insisted on retaining the paint company's original owner to help them expand the business. Together, they grew Standard Brands Paint into an empire of 120 stores, across all the Western states, with thousands of employees. By 1972, the company's stock was such a sure bet that it was named to the vaunted Nifty Fifty list.

As an insecure primitive, I've learned to embrace my weaknesses and ask for help, just like my grandfather and his brothers. When I was helping to guide Akamai Technologies toward its IPO in 1999, I could barely program my VCR let alone understand how Akamai managed internet traffic. I know next to nothing about neuroscience, but I've been able to help my client Ali Rezai be recognized for his groundbreaking use of brain chip implants to treat everything from Parkinson's disease to traumatic brain injury. To help visionaries like these, I freely admit when I am in over my head. I am honest about my weaknesses. I proudly ask for help when I do not understand a topic that may be trivial to others.

Some of the biggest names in business are proud imposters. Take Richard Branson, for instance, the founder of the Virgin Group. You might expect that the billionaire owner of a music empire and an airline had mastered the most esoteric of business concepts. Except, on his fiftieth birthday, when the magnate was in a meeting with Virgin executives, he was presented with a list of figures. Branson looked at the numbers and frowned.

"Is this good news or bad news?" he asked.

The executives in the room looked at each other awkwardly. It dawned on them that their billionaire boss didn't understand the difference between "net" and "gross"—concepts that high school students learn in introductory economics. Without an ounce of shame, Branson politely asked one of his executives to walk him through the basics, complete with brightly colored diagrams.

"He colored in this piece of paper blue, and then he put a net—a fishing net—amongst it. And he put little fish in the fishing net," Branson told *Freakonomics Radio*.

"The fish in the net are your profit," the executive explained. "And all the fish that are not [in] the net are your gross turnover."

How could one of the most successful entrepreneurs in history not understand such a basic business concept? Branson is dyslexic, and he had trouble understanding math in school and decided it was not worth his time. As a businessman, he simply assigned the tasks to others. "If you have a learning disability, you become a very good delegator," he told *Bloomberg* in 2015. "Because you know what your weaknesses are and you know what your strengths are, and you make sure that you find great people to step in and deal with your weaknesses."

Many much less successful businessmen and women would be mortified to admit not understanding basic economic principles. They would be afraid to ask for help. Insecure primitives understand that a little bit of imposter syndrome is a motivating force. When the anxiety is too overwhelming, insecure primitives are comfortable reaching out to others for support. When self-doubt is inhibiting their progress, they surround themselves with friends and family who believe in them. When I lost a client—or when I fretted about writing this book—my wife, Stacey, was there to comfort me.

Sometimes your doubts are unfounded, and sometimes they are prescient. No matter what happens, have a well-cultivated support system to guide you through it. Proudly accept when you are an imposter, and never be afraid to sing it to the world.

STAY PARANOID

Years ago, I had an employee named Debbie. She brought an incredibly upbeat and positive attitude to the office, I was impressed by—and even a bit jealous of—her confidence. Debbie was very good at her job, but she began making mistakes that would discombobulate insecure primitives like me. For one, she was constantly late—for work, for client events, for new business meetings. "*Debbie, where are you?*" I'd say into my phone, exasperated.

"It's all good," she'd reply. "The subways were messed up."

Debbie relied solely on her smartphone's estimated travel time; she was so relentlessly optimistic and confident that she couldn't foresee delays that most seasoned New Yorkers take for granted. She wouldn't double-check the address for a meeting she added to my calendar, and I'd show up embarrassingly late. When she set up video calls, she rarely came up with a plan B in case the Wi-Fi cut out or a server went down. "It's all good," was Debbie's constant refrain, even when everything was falling apart. Sometimes her optimism helped calm me down, but just as often it terrified me. Unlike Riki, who was paranoid that no one would show up for her events at Google and worked over-time to prepare for the worst, Debbie believed that nothing bad could ever happen. It was a case of the Dunning–Kruger effect, in which individuals believe they are far more capable than they actually are. (The classic example is drivers, the vast majority of whom consider themselves "above average.")

One day I took her aside and explained that anxiety is a very underrated personality trait. I repeated the old Jewish saying that Rabbi Rosen told me all those years ago: "Just because you're paranoid, Debbie, doesn't mean they're not trying to kill you. I want you to internalize that."

"It's all good," she said cheerfully.

But the behavior continued. I needed her to plan for things to go wrong. I needed her to be at least a little paranoid. Instead, Debbie's swagger was becoming detrimental to my business. Despite my affection and admiration for her, I had no choice but to let her go.

As my friend Tarik Sedky likes to say, "I suck, you suck," which sums up what it means to be an insecure primitive. Insecure primitives instinctually believe they don't have all the answers, and they soon realize that neither does anyone else. In 2002, I remember meeting filmmaker Woody Allen and complimenting him on his latest movie. Woody rolled his eyes, lifted his hands, and said: "I'm actually embarrassed. I don't think it's very good." I mentioned this to my wife, who had known him for decades, and she explained that it wasn't a shtick; he really didn't think his films were that good. He had an aversion to people who are secure and confident, and it motivated him to keep refining his craft.

Not long after I met Woody, I was producing a film for New York University for the fiftieth anniversary of *Brown v. Board of Education*. Actor James Earl Jones very graciously agreed to lend his voice to the narration. I was intimidated to work with a man whose basso profundo voice was the stuff of legend. But Jones was incredibly kind, charming, and deferential. "I'm dyslexic and I sometimes stutter," he explained to me. "So please let me know if I mess up the script and I'll do it again." Here was a man who had uttered some of the most famous lines in American cinematic history opening up about his vulnerabilities. I immediately relaxed in his presence, and we ended up producing a wonderful documentary. (In contrast, I once produced a video featuring Donald Trump in his gold-plated office at the top of Trump Tower. He insisted that we only film him from one angle and refused to do second takes. I left the interview unsure if Trump registered that I was in the room, let alone remembered my name.)

Woody Allen and James Earl Jones aren't unique in proudly broadcasting their insecurities. Take Troy Carter, for instance, the prominent music manager who helped launch the careers of Eve, Lady Gaga, and Meghan Trainor among many other stars. The son of a single mother and a father who was jailed for murder, Carter agonized over how to afford food and clothing at an age when most kids are blissfully unaware of the real world. As Carter related on Guy Raz's podcast, he is still plagued by his "financial PTSD." While it initially impaired his ability to understand and manage his own money as an adult, this extreme anxiety also set him up to be a careful steward of his finances and a shrewd startup investor.

As Shakespeare wrote in his pastoral comedy *As You Like It,* "The fool doth think he is wise, but the wise man knows himself to be a fool." Insecure primitives may not think of themselves as fools—at least not all the time—but they instinctively understand that nothing is ever certain, there is always room for improvement, and it could all end in the worst possible way. This inherent paranoia is incredibly useful in business, especially at the very beginning of an entrepreneur's journey. When I started my businesses, I was paranoid about getting clients, making payroll, hiring and retaining employees, and surviving in an ever-changing economy. At times this paranoia was overwhelming, from sleepless nights to midday anxiety, but constant unease ultimately catapulted me forward. As an insecure primitive, I was hyperattuned to my clients' needs and could smell trouble when few others did.

"The paranoid person does not project onto the sky, so to speak," wrote Sigmund Freud, "but onto something that is already there." Likewise, insecure primitives may be a neurotic lot, but their anxiety is often warranted. "The best way to maintain a company's success is to always be paranoid," explains Ratmir Timashev, founder and CEO of data management firm Veeam Software. Timashev operates in an especially cutthroat field, where new players with seemingly killer apps appear practically daily. "Despite having a good product and a solid customer base, if you're not constantly looking over your shoulder for the next upcoming technology, you'll most likely be displaced," he wrote in *Fortune.* The founder and former CEO of Intel, Andrew Grove, even penned a book about the subject: *Only the Paranoid Survive.* Despite creating one of the most successful tech companies in history, Grove was constantly afraid that he'd wake up one day to find a company had introduced new tech that destroyed Intel's business model. For this reason, he pushed his company to constantly innovate and stay ahead of the industry.

Reading about these titans of industry relying on a healthy dose of paranoia reminded me of a sukkah, a temporary hut constructed for use during the weeklong Jewish festival of Sukkot. The sukkah is a beautiful structure adorned with branches and other harvest themes meant to commemorate the time God provided for the Israelites in the wilderness after they fled from slavery in Egypt. The sukkah symbolizes the frailty and transience of life. It's not a solid foundation. It can blow away in the wind or be trampled by a wild animal. Insecure primitives, I realized, see their lives in much the same way Jews see a sukkah: as fleeting as much as it is beautiful. Anything can go wrong at any moment, and the best we can do is prepare for the unexpected. Insecure primitives operate best in the most precarious situations, when they are relying on their most ancient fight-or-flight reflexes.

"Prudent paranoia," Stanford Business School professor Roderick Kramer wrote in the *Harvard Business Review*, is a "constructive suspicion regarding the intentions and actions of people and organizations....They are aware that those around them harbor powerful—and often conflicting—motives for the things they do....In many cases, the paranoia serves as a healthy defense against a genuine outside threat." The paranoia Kramer is talking about isn't the same as the kind you see in the movies. It's not the paranoid schizophrenia that genius mathematician John Nash suffered from in *A Beautiful Mind*. It's not the paranoia that led Joseph Stalin to purge his own government, or Richard Nixon to obsessively record White House conversations. The insecure primitive's paranoia is not representative of an underlying clinical condition, but rather a hyperawareness and constant reevaluation of everyone and everything around her.

For example, not long ago, I began feeling uneasy about one of my favorite clients. He was floating the idea of me acting on his advisory board, which I interpreted to mean he wanted to eliminate my firm's retainer. My business partner, Liel, thought I was crazy.

"You're being paranoid, Marco," he told me. "Don't worry about the retainer. I just spoke with him. Everything is fine. He hasn't given any indication that he wants to do that." I was still worried—Liel, a classic oppositional primitive, is much more carefree and confident than I am and not nearly as paranoid. He did have a point, but the warning signs were there. In the previous weeks, our client had been having trouble locking down investors for a fresh round of funding. He sounded different on the phone, and he hadn't been throwing us new assignments like he used to. In my gut, that handsome retainer was not safe, and I had to prepare for it. Finally, I called my client and asked him directly: "Is everything okay? Do you want to keep working with us going forward?" There was a pause, and, sure enough, he admitted that he had to axe the retainer and move us to project work. Fortunately, I had already made the necessary arrangements.

Kramer's research indicates that in business, we often are right to feel paranoid. After speaking with hundreds of managers and executives over two decades, Kramer found that eight out of ten "reported having made a major mistake with respect to trusting the wrong person at least once in their careers." They believed that power is benevolent, that as long as everyone acts civilized with each other, nothing bad can happen. In the absence of prudent paranoia is complacency. In one famous example, energy conglomerate Enron once instructed seventy low-level employees to spend the day in an empty trading room and pretend they were wheeling and dealing. Company executives were bringing a group of Wall Street analysts by later that day and wanted to impress them. The fake traders brought in fake phones and fake computers and, in a George Costanza moment straight out of *Seinfeld*, "looked" busy and successful. The analysts were fooled, and they gave the massive corporation another stellar rating. Enron, of course, went bankrupt a few years later.

How can you be more paranoid in your day-to-day life? What do you constantly worry about? What *don't* you constantly worry about? What is "all good," when, in fact, it might not be? What are you taking for granted? Maybe that coworker really *is* trying to undermine you. Perhaps your boss's off-the-cuff remark after your presentation *was* indicative of a deeper problem.

Act on your prudent paranoia. Ask your coworkers hard questions when you suspect something is wrong. Be honest with your boss and ask her to be honest with you. Acting a little paranoid doesn't just keep you aware of your blind spots, it keeps the channels of communication with your coworkers and clients open and truthful.

"Your family is broke."

I heard these words when I was twenty-eight years old, making $35,000 a year and tending to a fifty-five-year-old father who was dying of stage IV lung cancer. Our attorneys told my younger sister and me that the financial tides had turned for our father, who had been a self-made millionaire. We all watched as the real estate market, where he had all his wealth invested, suddenly tanked. All at once, there were more liabilities than assets. I was scared.

Gone was the man who effortlessly picked up new skills, who partied with movie stars and designed multimillion-dollar beachfront homes. Gone was the carefree man who could not fail at anything if he tried. As I combed through his ledger, I realized that his finances had long been precarious. I spotted his mistakes one after the other. I saw where my father dug his fine-tipped drafting pencil into the paper, harder and harder, angry and confused that he could not make the numbers add up. In his elegant architect's script, he'd write in all caps: THIS DOES NOT MAKE SENSE or THESE NUMBERS DON'T WORK. My heart broke as I pictured his handsome face reddening, his lips pursing, his exterior cracking in ways he repressed so effectively when in public. It suddenly dawned on me that, if I were in his position, I would have instantly delegated to an accountant or financial adviser. I would have no problem admitting that I wasn't good enough, that I wasn't an expert. But my father had a hard time asking for help, and instead always sought to help others.

For his entire life, my father insisted he had everything under control. "I'm not like them," he'd say, referring to his friends who succumbed to their various addictions. My dad believed he could smoke twenty joints and focus at a high level. Once, my father was pulled over for reckless driving while high on drugs. As part of his plea agreement, the judge ordered him to get substance abuse counseling. Angry and determined to prove the judge wrong, my father gave up drugs altogether—but soon thereafter turned to drinking to cope. It wasn't until he attended AA meetings that my father finally realized he had a problem. He couldn't do everything himself. It wasn't all good. He needed help and he finally got it. He was sober the last decade of his life and was at his best.

Since my father died, I've been given "the news" and received the dreaded thirty-day notice dozens of times in my career in client services, as it's the nature of the business. I've had my professional life repeatedly torn apart and I've managed to survive every time in part because I no longer have any illusions about "job security." Each of these calls, emails, and texts is almost as gut-wrenching as the first time. I know I will be fired many more times in my career for a variety of reasons usually not within my control, and each one will hurt almost as much as it did when I was younger and much less financially prepared. But I'm ready. I may not be as confident or carefree as my father. I may not be as brilliant or magnetic. But I embrace my insecurities, where for much of his life he self-medicated to repress them. He was terrified of his self-doubt, where I've finally learned to accept it, use it to my advantage, and actually enjoy the roller coaster ride.

Be proud of your insecurities. Own them. Turn them to your advantage. Weaponize them. Know what you don't know, as my grandmother used to say. Take a page out of the insecure primitive playbook and avoid overconfidence, accept when you are an imposter, and be prudently paranoid. By practicing these precepts and operating on the bleeding edge of uncertainty, you will be more successful.

CHAPTER SIX

NUTS

In some tiny town in Louisiana, Dorian Paskowitz pulled his twenty-four-foot camper van to the side of the road and turned to his nine children, who were crammed onto the couches and along the floor.

"Guys, there it is," Dorian said, producing a coin from his pocket. "We're down to our last dime."

For most children, such an experience would be deeply traumatic. But for the Paskowitz kids—Moses, Joshua, David, Jonathan, Abraham, Israel, Adam, Salvador, and Navah—it was just another day. By that point, they had spent almost their entire lives living with their parents in a succession of dilapidated campers, journeying from one beach to the next. They surfed the West Coast, the East Coast, Baja California, and the Gulf of Mexico, all in pursuit of the perfect wave and a simple life. Dorian did not believe in traditional education and insisted on homeschooling his children. As Salvador explained in the 2007 film *Surfwise*, a documentary about the Paskowitz family (executive produced by another über-primitive, Mark Cuban): "Your parents would have said, 'You can go to school because it's safe, but don't go swimming with the sharks because it's dangerous.' Our parents said, 'No, you can go swimming with the sharks, but you're not going to school because *that's* dangerous.'"

For a man who spent most of his life on a surfboard, the first thirty years of Dorian's life were comparatively civilized. Born in 1921 in Galveston, Texas, he was hampered by childhood asthma until a lifeguard taught him to surf at age ten. Convinced that the waves were improving her son's health, Dorian's mother moved the family to Mission Beach in San Diego. He surfed regularly while attending San Diego State University and then Stanford Medical School, and later set up a lucrative practice in Honolulu. It was around that time that he met my father, who came to see the headstrong Dorian as a role model. By most measures Dorian was extremely successful: he was married, had become the head of the American Medical Association in Hawaii, and was even asked to run for governorship of the islands.

Except Dorian didn't see it that way. "It was the lowest point of my life," he admitted.

He suffered from panic attacks. He felt like a fraud. His marriage was ending in divorce. He was uncomfortable taking money from sick people. He wasn't having fun. Most important, he had no time to surf. Then, one day, he made a decision that everyone around him thought was crazy: he gave up his medical practice to go surfing.

"Surfing re-creates you," Dorian explained. "I have gone into the water literally ready to blow my brains out and come back a warrior." He fell in love with a Mexican American opera singer named Juliette, remarried, had a child, and the family moved into the back seat of his 1949 Studebaker and took to the road.

My father initially disapproved of his friend's lifestyle, confused as to why a respected doctor with a young family would spend all his time surfing. In Dorian's book, *Surfing and Health*, he wrote that my father "was worried about my way of life as a surfing doctor—or a doctoring surfer. Now he was flabbergasted that into this, in his eyes, marginal existence I had taken a wife and had a child." My dad was frustrated that Dorian refused money he did not explicitly need, even returning a $50,000 inheritance because he feared it would somehow constrain his lifestyle. Dorian brought my father with him when he mailed back the check. "Tony," Dorian said, "you're a rich man's son. Some day you are going to be a rich man yourself. For a reason that I cannot easily explain, I want you to know what I've done here and why I've done it. I have a feeling that one day it will have some special meaning in your life." When my father pulled me out of school a dozen years later to join him on our sailing adventure around Baja California, it was with his old friend's words still in mind.

Before long, Dorian and Juliette's family had grown exponentially. They purchased a rickety camper and settled into their bohemian surfer lifestyle. What little money Dorian made came from providing medical services on Native American reservations, in migrant labor camps, and at other places of need. But he usually preferred to treat injured surfers on the beach and dispense nutritional advice. When the Paskowitz children entered surfing contests, the other contestants groaned; the motley, hippie kids who lived in their dad's camper hardly ever lost. Four sons turned professional—one even became a world champion longboard surfer—winning endorsements from the likes of Nike and other major brands.

What inspired Dorian to give up his medical practice, ignore his friends' protestations, buy a broken-down camper, and surf the world? As he later wrote, "We were simply *messhugge* [*sic*], a Yiddish word for nuts."

At first glance, *nuts* seems like a perfectly appropriate word to describe Dorian. Somewhere between a survivalist and a surf bum with a midlife crisis, Dorian tossed convention aside and upended his life in a way that would almost suggest a psychological breakdown. The word *nuts* has, unfortunately, come to be associated with genuine mental illness—but that is a very different thing. Those who have loved ones suffering from mental illness tend not to appreciate the use of *nuts, crazy, mad,* and other common terms for people living with very complicated medical conditions. I was raised by a mother who, while incredibly loving and supportive of me, has suffered from mental health setbacks, and I continue to deal with her issues to this day. All this to say, I use the word *nuts* very carefully in this chapter.

It wasn't until the late 1700s that *nuts* became a British slang term, wherein a very enthusiastic person was said to be "nuts upon" a particular topic. By the 1850s, *nut* became slang for "a person's head," and a mentally ill person was said to be "off their nut." Soon, *nuts* was immortalized in the *Oxford English Dictionary,* meaning "out of one's mind." I prefer the older definition. Nuts primitives like Dorian Paskowitz may appear out of their minds to others, but they are making a rational and deliberate decision to follow their primal instincts and pursue their passions, often in unorthodox ways.

If you've seen the Academy Award–wining documentary *Free Solo,* you might think its subject, rock climber Alex Honnold, is out of his mind. Honnold is famous for climbing without ropes on some of the most challenging routes in the world, including the three-thousand-foot El Capitan in Yosemite National Park. One tiny mistake, one slip, and Honnold would plummet to his death. But he fears death just like the rest of us, and he doesn't climb thousands of feet in the air without exhaustive preparation. He spends months and even years climbing the same route with ropes, memorizing every crack and crevice. By the time he is ready to scale the rock face without ropes, he is fully confident in his abilities. Some people still think he's crazy, but I would call him a fine example of a nuts primitive—someone who will blow aside convention and ignore danger in the passionate pursuit of a goal.

Nuts primitives may also have a tendency to be a little, well, weird. While interviewing potential hires, Tony Hsieh, CEO of online shoe retailer Zappos, asks candidates how weird they are on a one-to-ten scale. (Tony ranks himself an eight.) Despite running a footwear company, he doesn't especially care for shoes. "I'm actually not passionate about shoes at all," he has said. After he sold his first company, LinkExchange, to Microsoft, he was so miserable that he walked away from millions of dollars rather than continue working until his stock vested after a year and a half. As Dorian once did, Tony lives in a trailer (albeit a much nicer one), along with a herd of free-roaming alpacas.

It should be said that nuts primitives are not always model citizens. Dorian, for one, denied his children the same high-quality education that he received himself. He did not believe in privacy. He was not a good listener. His relationship with his children deteriorated, ripping apart the family for long periods of time. Fortunately, Dorian made peace with his children before his death in 2014. But humility, selflessness, and self-reflection are not qualities for which most nuts primitives are known.

You might recall Bikram Choudhury as the disgraced founder of Bikram Yoga, a popular form of hot yoga. But in the 1970s, Bikram was a poor immigrant teaching his groundbreaking new yoga style to young Californians. I remember tagging along with my dad as we drove in heavy traffic from Venice to Beverly Hills just to exhaust ourselves in Bikram's 105-degree studio. When Bikram was struggling financially, my father at one point paid his rent in return for free classes. He went on to found studios in California and Hawaii and made millions by licensing his brand to studios across the world. However, he later faced numerous lawsuits. As espnW reported, "Choudhury had allegedly violated women under his tutelage, the accusations ranging from racial discrimination to gay slurs to harassment to rape." After he was ordered to pay $6.8 million to his former attorney, he reportedly packed his bags and fled to India. Bikram was a nuts primitive, but

I believe a lack of integrity caused him to career off the rails. He appears to have been intoxicated by money and fame, and to have thought that treating people cruelly would beget yet more money and fame.

Bikram is an extreme example, but one we can learn from. Evolved nuts primitives allow civilization to rein in their worst impulses and transform their eccentricities into a positive force. They are the ultimate risk-takers who make impulsive decisions without warning. They can be mercurial and taxing, but they inspire others to tackle challenges big and small. Sometimes they succeed and sometimes they crash and burn and gleefully try again.

LIVE LIKE YOU AREN'T SUPPOSED TO

"The best part about going through hell is that you come out on fire!" Bea Arthur wrote in *Forbes* in June 2016. Five weeks earlier, Bea had made the most painful decision of her life: she shuttered her five-year-old company, In Your Corner. Now she was mired in debt, about to be evicted from her apartment, and spelling out exactly how she screwed up with brutal honesty.

Things had started out promisingly enough: as a Columbia University–trained psychotherapist, Bea realized that traditional talk therapy was increasingly becoming a luxury for the well-off. Barely half of insurance providers covered mental health care, and an hour-long session could cost upwards of $300. Bea had the simple idea to bring therapy online in a way that would enable people to receive the help they needed without leaving home. She became the first-ever black woman founder at Y Combinator, the elite funding group that helped launch the likes of Reddit, Airbnb, and Twitch. Before long, In Your Corner was serving thousands of clients in thirty-nine states and thirty countries, arranging affordable, internet-based therapy sessions. She appeared on TV and delivered a TEDx talk. In Your Corner was raising money and it was profitable.

"So how did I end up in debt, crying on my keyboard, and eating burritos in bed a short five years later?" Bea wrote. "The answer is simple. Love." The young CEO made heartfelt decisions instead of prudent ones. She trusted the wrong people. She delegated tasks without understanding how long they would take. She spent too much money on office space and didn't focus enough on sales. And when everything was falling apart, Bea took out predatory business loans to keep her beloved company afloat. And then, just like that, the company she had poured her heart and soul into was gone.

To cheer her up, a friend took her to see the hit Broadway show *Hamilton*. "I had exactly $2.45, and I'm ready to go see this play," Bea told me. "I guess *Hamilton* tickets were going for $2,000 or $3,000, and I didn't have $3 to get on the subway." Here she was seeing the most exclusive show in town with a negative net worth—two familiar and opposite New York City experiences occurring at the same time. The jarring experience made her think about her own anxiety, her insecurities. How could she be a successful therapist and a failed businessperson at the same time?

Bea emerged from the theater with a new perspective. So what if her company failed? As her mother told her, "Just because it didn't work out, doesn't mean it didn't work." Another founder may have dusted herself off and moved on to the next idea; as we saw earlier in the book, agnostic primitives do this all the time. But Bea is a different sort of primitive, and she refused to give up on her mission to help others. She took a long, hard look at her mistakes and learned to be truer to herself instead of bowing to outside forces. "Now I always trust my gut," she said in an interview. "Before, I'd go back and forth and overanalyze, but when I look back, every time I had to make a tough decision, I always wish I'd just made it sooner. Humans are the only animals that deny their instincts. I consult my advisers always, but I can only trust myself to defend my decisions."

Bea poured her energy into a new company, The Difference, which allows people to instantly connect with a therapist using the Amazon Alexa virtual assistant. There is no scheduling, just help when you need it most. Bea is harnessing one of the best things the internet has to offer—the ability to connect anyone, anywhere at a moment's notice—and turning it into a force for good. And she has no patience for people who are skeptical of her idea. "I can act entitled," she told me. "I do what I want. Sometimes I offend people. I'm black and I'm a woman—I'm technically supposed to be at the bottom of the pole, but I don't live my life like that. *That* is nuts—living in a way that I'm not supposed to."

Living in a way you're not supposed to is the essence of nuts primitives. They can be irrational. They make gut decisions based on what feels right. Their behavior makes little sense to the civilized world. They insist on abandoning safety for the unknown. They gleefully take risks. Most important, they don't waste time overthinking their decisions.

Take Ed Mitchell, for example. In 1958, he was riding the commuter train from New York City to his home in Westport, Connecticut, when he decided he was going to do something exciting—some said "crazy"—and open a clothing store. Every day for most of his business life, Ed had slogged to and from work with other bleary-eyed businessmen. He'd climbed up and down the corporate ladder and held many jobs in marketing and advertising, but he never quite felt completely comfortable. By his fifties, the stress was taking its toll on his health; Ed suffered from terrible ulcers and had undergone numerous operations. Finally, he decided he couldn't take another commute, another ulcer, another day of corporate life.

"When my father decided to go into the retail men's and boy's clothing business in 1958, I thought he was nuts!" his son Bill explained in a short film I made about the company, which helped inspire a case study at Harvard Business School.

Nothing about the decision made sense on the outside. The closest that Ed and his lovely wife, Norma, had ever come to selling clothes was doing a little retail consulting earlier in his career. He tapped into their savings and opened up an eight-hundred-square-foot store in a former plumbing supply shop in Westport. The store—Mitchells—sold $50,000 in merchandise in its first year, and the business gradually expanded to women's clothing. Ed and Norma's son Bill joined the company in 1965, followed by their son Jack a few years later. Before long they expanded to a much larger location. Now, more than sixty years later, they have eight other stores, from Huntington, New York, to Seattle, Washington. In a time when brick-and-mortar retail stores are hemorrhaging red ink, Mitchells is only getting stronger. Today the company boasts tens of millions of dollars in revenue and is one of the country's top luxury retailers for men's and women's clothing and jewelry, and a third generation of Mitchells now leads the business. As for Ed, who felt like an old man by age fifty, he died at ninety-eight after making the seemingly irrational choice to change his life.

PLAY HOCKEY, NOT GOLF

What would have happened if Bea gave up on her dream of democratizing mental health, or if Ed Mitchell stuck it out on the commuter train instead of opening his store? Those certainly would have been rational decisions, but not the right ones. "Rationality has to be defined according to how well you accomplish some goals," explains Hugo Mercier, a researcher at the

Institut Jean Nicod in France and coauthor of *The Enigma of Reason*. "You can't be rational in a vacuum, it doesn't mean anything. The problem is there's so much flexibility in defining what you want." In other words, if you really want to do something, perhaps the most rational choice is to just do it. Will spending days, weeks, or years contemplating your decision truly impact your chances of success?

These days, it's even more difficult to make big decisions. This is true thanks in part to the near-infinite amount of data available. We can google the pros and cons of everything including which fridge to buy, which neighborhood to rent in, and which astrological sign to date. This abundance of data stymied my dear friend Olivia. She is a brilliant woman who attended Harvard Business School and was brimming with exciting, innovative ideas for companies. But when it came to actually executing her vision and taking a risk, she froze up. First she had to assess the ROIs (return on investment), the KOLs (key opinion leaders), the SOWs (statement of work), SWOT analyses (strengths, weaknesses, opportunities, and threats), and SOPs (standard operating procedures), and perform countless other busywork that she used to assess her risk. There were always more business plans to write, analyses to perform, data to mine, best practices to emulate, and acronyms to discover. Olivia was terrified of making a stupid decision, so she chose what she believed to be the most rational path. Like so many people at the far end of the civilized spectrum, she worshipped at the altar of process. Despite her impeccable credentials and intelligence, she was never able to get her ventures off the ground.

Olivia's experience is known as "analysis paralysis," and it's an epidemic not just among entrepreneurs, but rank-and-file employees. A LexisNexis survey found that, on average, employees spend more than 50 percent of their workday receiving and managing information, not actually performing their jobs.

George Conrades, the former CEO of Akamai Technologies, likes to say that in today's fast-paced business environment we are playing hockey, not golf. He means that while it's important to make informed decisions, they must be made quickly, like a hockey winger on a fast break.

Now, compare Olivia's experience to Audra Fordin, the owner of Great Bear Auto Repair in Queens, New York. Think for a moment: How many female auto mechanics have you met in your life? One? Zero? Auto repair is one of those stubborn fields where you expect your mechanic to be a bearded dude with a beer belly. The stereotype that they aren't suited to this sort of work has prevented countless women from being taken seriously in the garage. Not Audra. She grew up working in her family's shop and went on to graduate from an automotive technical training program in New York before returning to the family business as a full-fledged mechanic. Even her own father was concerned about her skills when he reluctantly handed over the reins of the fifty-five-year-old family business to her two years later. "There was some skepticism about my ability to handle the challenges of running a business," she explained.

Her first major challenge came in 2008, when the Great Recession caused a drop in business. Her solution wasn't to play it safe, but to go bold and go female: she hired more female mechanics, hosted free weekly workshops to teach women to perform their own car maintenance, and founded an organization, Women Auto Know, whose proceeds fund car repairs for single mothers. As her classes exploded in popularity, she began booking speaking engagements and television appearances. Audra didn't overthink her decision to bet on women; she attacked deeply entrenched sexism head-on and empowered women to turn their own wrenches—all while quadrupling her garage's revenues in a matter of years.

Our species has long been heralded as the "rational animal,"

able to avoid impulsive decisions and problem-solve in a methodical manner. But research suggests we don't function at our
best when working this way. "Of all the definitions of man," the
French journalist Anatole France once wrote, "the worst is that
he is a rational animal." France may have been onto something.
In a behavioral experiment out of Tel Aviv University's School
of Psychological Sciences, researchers designed an experiment
in which participants were shown new sets of numbers every
second. The numbers were divided into two groups, one on each
side of a computer screen, and the participants were told to use
"intuitive arithmetic" to estimate at the end of the experiment
which group had the highest numerical average. Interestingly,
the more numbers the study subjects were shown—and therefore the less able they were to count in their head—the more
accurate they were. When shown six pairs of numbers, the participants were right 65 percent of the time. Yet, when shown
twenty-four pairs, their accuracy rate jumped to 90 percent. In
short, the study suggested, our best decisions are often made
when we don't have time to overthink them.

Michael Bruno, the serial entrepreneur who founded 1stdibs,
the online marketplace for antiques, furniture, jewelry, and fine
art, doesn't have much patience for analysis. "I have never put
much weight on focus groups outside of a small circle of friends,"
he wrote to me. "I have a tendency to get an idea and go for it
once I let it settle in." Michael's way of brainstorming is a bit
more creative than what you'll find in the typical boardroom:
"We used to call it 'going Roman,'" he said. "We would have too
much to drink, smoke a little pot, think up ideas and solutions
to problems, then decide to meet again completely sober and
review all the outrageous things we came up with to see if anything good came of it." And, despite his success, Michael actually
regrets his other, more civilized impulses: "I wish I was more
nuts!" he lamented.

If there is one guy who doesn't have any regrets about his impulsive behavior, it's my friend Roger Abramson. He started his career as a commercial real estate broker in New York before honing his skills as a salesman at a commercial furniture company. He quickly emerged as one of the top salespeople in the country and, at just twenty-five, started his own furniture outfit called the Atlantic Group. Within five years it had passed $100 million in revenue with industry-leading profit margins. These days, Roger advises CEOs on impactful business models, mergers and acquisitions, and organizational design, and he is a major investor in the fast-growing cannabis market.

Roger is also a classic nuts primitive. "Speed is the ultimate competitive advantage," his website proudly boasts, and for good reason. "I pretty much always go with my gut no matter what," he explained to me. "Whether you apply it to investing, to business, to life—my gut decisions have been right probably 98 percent of the time. For me to dwell and overthink every decision, that would add eight hours to my day that I don't have." For most investors, deciding to put money into a new company in a new industry would take months of due diligence. But when a portfolio manager at a dinner party told Roger about a promising cannabis company that was closing a new round of investment, he acted completely on instinct. The only problem was the investment fund was about to stop taking new money. If he wanted in, he had to wire a big sum overseas first thing the next morning. Roger woke up his accountant and lawyer in the middle of the night, performed crash due diligence, put together all the relevant paperwork, and sent the money off within hours.

"That was the craziest thing I've ever done," Roger explained. Indeed, sending off a sizeable investment to an unknown overseas company in the dead of night might seem incredibly stupid. But to Roger, the risk wasn't as big as it seemed. He understood the market, he understood the financials, and he had trusted contacts in the industry who vouched for the company. Roger was fully prepared to make his investment, and he was also fully prepared to make a snap decision. He made a daring choice, but thanks to hard work and preparation, it wasn't a reckless one. The cannabis company has since blossomed into one of Roger's most successful investments.

Roger especially trusts his gut when it comes to hiring employees. "Whether you have a formal education, or how good it was, has nothing to do with if you'll be good in the job," he explained. "You have to be good with change and good with the unexpected. The first thing I do when you give me your résumé during an interview is look you in the eye and rip up the résumé. If you freak out or confront me, I excuse myself to the bathroom and the interview is over. If you laugh, say nothing, or act calm and collected, the interview goes on."

What's the last purely gut idea you had? Did you go through with it? Or was your nutty scheme doomed by your attempts to justify it? As I've learned over the years, a stupid idea is not always a bad one. You may succeed, you may fail, you may try again, and you are guaranteed to learn something about yourself along the way.

NEVER GROW UP

When I think of the word *nuts*, I think of the freak show that was Venice, California, in the 1970s and '80s. The cast of characters I grew up around included Dave Schwartz, who built an extremely successful company called Rent-A-Wreck. For rock-bottom prices, Dave would rent you a fifteen-year-old Ford Mustang or Volkswagen Beetle with chipped paint and a dented bumper. The only caveat was that Dave wouldn't rent to you if he didn't like you. His idea of having fun was sneaking into sporting events and, in the more innocent years before 9/11, onto airplanes.

Then there were the Webster brothers, Guy and Roger. In addition to being the legendary album cover photographer for the likes of The Doors, The Rolling Stones, and Simon & Garfunkel, Guy paid the bills by shooting weddings and parties. My parents paid him to shoot my bar mitzvah; we soon found out he was so high during the ceremony that he forgot to take off the lens cap. Roger, meanwhile, drove around in his Volkswagen Bus with a surfboard perpetually strapped to the roof. He'd walk around bare-chested with wetsuit bottoms during the day and women's dresses at night. His fingernails were six inches long and he told anyone who wanted to know about his marriage to a dominatrix. Later, Roger asked that we call him Mona, and we didn't bat an eye. And, as it turned out, throughout all of this, Mona shrewdly bought up property and today is one of the richest landlords in Venice.

These characters, whom we charitably called eccentric, were all primitives in their own right. They were obsessive, intense, and thoroughly unfiltered. They didn't play by civilized rules. They were like a young Steve Jobs, who was notorious for rarely bathing early in his career, much to the dismay of his coworkers. Or Dean Kamen, inventor of the Segway among other devices, who enjoys claiming that the island he owns off the coast of Connecticut has "seceded" from the United States and dispensing his own currency in units of pi. There is a common thread uniting these nuts primitives: they all acted like children. They didn't let civilization stand in their way of their passion. They wanted to make their mark and have as much joy as humanly possible. This sort of behavior is considered normal for children, but not for adults. But why? Is it because we naturally mature and lose that childlike spirit as we age? Or do institutions like schools and companies inculcate us with civilized manners and routines?

Once again, just as we touched on in Relentless, research suggests we might be better off acting like five-year-olds. In the 1960s, NASA officials asked professor George Land to develop a creativity test to help the agency identify innovative engineers and scientists for the space program. Land was so impressed with the results of the study that he created a version to test how creativity changes as children age. The results were astounding: of the 1,600 four- and five-year-olds tested, 98 percent scored in the "genius" category of imagination, meaning they were able to formulate innovative ways to solve problems. In comparison, when the test was given to adults, a mere 2 percent scored at this level.

But that's not the full story. Land tested the same children again five years later, but this time only 30 percent fell in the genius category. After another five years, that figure fell to 12 percent. Land credited this dramatic fall to the education system, which emphasizes convergent thinking, the ability to focus thoughts and develop simple answers to problems that do not require inventiveness. Divergent thought—the ability to generate creative ideas by exploring many possible solutions—suffers as a result. According to Land, children are forced to suppress their creative impulses to excel in school. "When you look at what's happening inside the brain you see the neurons are fighting each other and diminishing the power of the brain," he explained at TEDxTucson in 2011. "This isn't going to work, folks. You need to find the five-year-old."

In 2014, University of California, Berkeley psychologist Alison Gopnik explored this idea. She invited 100 preschoolers to her lab and asked them to solve a complex puzzle involving fitting clay discs into slots to activate a music box. She also recruited 170 college students and asked them to do the same thing. "What we discovered, to our surprise, was not only were four-year-olds amazingly good at doing this, but they were actually better at it than grown-ups were," she said. "The noisiness, unpredictability, and variability that we see in young children, which we tend to think of as something we need to get under control, is actually one of the things that enables new generations of human beings to think differently."

As research from the University of Minnesota's Developmental Social Cognitive Neuroscience Lab reveals, this phenomenon is largely because children spend up to two-thirds of their time engaging in imaginative play. Rather than learn and internalize the difficulties and restrictions that curb adults, children entertain a wide range of ideas and possibilities, helping them pursue paths that may not have occurred to you and me. Unfortunately, the modern workplace often does not lend itself to original thinking: many businesses still have rigid hierarchies and are set up with traditional offices and cubicles lit by buzzing fluorescent lighting. Creativity can exist in such bland environments, but it certainly lacks the rainbow carpeting and art-strewn walls of your typical kindergarten classroom.

Think back to when you were a child. What naive goals did you have that made adults smile and pat you on the back before gently telling you they couldn't be done? For the tech entrepreneur (and über-primitive) Elon Musk, it was going to Mars. As an escape from the relentless bullying he experienced, Musk retreated deep into his science fiction novels. Before long, he was convinced mankind had to colonize another planet before Earth became uninhabitable. Unlike most people, Musk's dream didn't fade away with age—it only got stronger. After he made his fortune selling PayPal, Musk turned back to his childhood idea: build rockets, turn the interiors into a greenhouse, stuff them with plant seeds, and use them to fertilize Mars. When the adults in the room told him it was too expensive, Musk had another naive childlike idea: make space travel less expensive, *then* go to Mars.

He founded a company, SpaceX, hounded the top astrophysicists until they broke down and agreed to work for him, and managed to build a prototype rocket in just over a year. With NASA phasing out its space shuttle program, SpaceX was determined to win lucrative contracts as the business of spaceflight shifted from the government to private companies. But NASA ignored SpaceX and gave a $227 million contract to another commercial space company named Kistler Aerospace. Musk was furious. Why wasn't he—or anyone else, for that matter—allowed to bid on it? Kistler was a well-connected company with many friends inside NASA, and Musk saw the arrangement as a sweetheart deal. So, he did what any determined child armed with a phalanx of high-priced lawyers would do: he sued NASA. Musk's colleagues pleaded with him to rethink his decision. "I was told by everyone that you do not sue NASA," Musk later said. "I was told the odds of winning a protest were less than 10 percent, and you don't sue your potential future customer." It was arguably reckless, even childish, to think this gambit could actually work. Yet Musk was both oppositional and relentless. He plowed forth with his lawsuit, and eventually the Government Accountability Office agreed with Musk and forced NASA to withdraw its contract with Kistler Aerospace. Musk had staked his company and his fortune on a childlike idea, and it paid off enormously. Kistler eventually went bankrupt, while SpaceX won billions of dollars' worth of NASA contracts.

Another nuts primitive, Marc Benioff, cofounder and CEO of the cloud computing giant Salesforce, has long understood the power of childlike marketing techniques that border on petulant. After launching Salesforce.com, Benioff hired actors to "protest" a conference of his then-biggest rival, Siebel Systems, and chant, "The internet is really neat....Software is obsolete!" He even hired fake TV crews to cover the protest. In another stunt, he targeted a Siebel event held in Cannes, France. Most of the attendees were flying into nearby Nice, so Salesforce rented out every airport taxi, decked them out with Salesforce logos, and delivered a sales pitch for every attendee during the forty-five minute ride to the conference.

Naturally, not all of us possess Musk or Benioff's brains—or their bank accounts. But harnessing some childlike creativity is a great way to get noticed and remembered. Philippe Krakowsky is the chief operating officer of the advertising conglomerate Interpublic, as well as chairman of IPG Mediabrands. Managing some fifty thousand employees, it's safe to say Philippe has pretty much seen it all when it comes to creative pitches. He loves telling the story of "a very unusual cat" named Philippe Michel, whom he worked with at the ad agency BBDO. After Michel won the Apple Computer account for the CLM BBDO agency in France, BBDO in the US had the opportunity to compete for the tech company's domestic business as well. The BBDO brass asked Michel to come to New York to help them prepare for the pitch. He walked off the plane with no materials, no slides, no notes. When he arrived at the board room, Michel removed his jacket to reveal a T-shirt on which he had printed all of the pertinent insights for the Apple pitch. For hours, Michel stood in front of his fellow BBDO's executives, gesturing to various graphics plastered on white cotton that illustrated the key consumer and brands insights he felt were key to understanding and connecting with the Apple brand. Instead of a boring slide show, the US executives were treated to an offbeat performance by a charismatic iconoclast who oozed confidence and ensured a highly memorable presentation.

I've had hundreds of employees over the years, from one end of the primitive-civilized spectrum to the other, and many in between. Some of the more primitive among them have gone on to start their own businesses or rise up the ranks at the likes of Google and Amazon. Others have been quite civilized, with more predictable paths like in-house marketing positions at big organizations, but I like to think they benefited the most from a ride with Liel and me on the more primitive side of business life.

We once, for example, had a very straitlaced and cerebral employee who was a civilizing foil to our more primitive instincts. He was one of the brightest employees I ever had and a consummate diplomat—so diplomatic, in fact, that he dreamed of being a diplomat himself. He joined my firm after being rejected by the State Department. He hung around for more than five years until he aced the foreign service exam and was finally invited to join Foggy Bottom. I like to think his acceptance was in part due to the more wacky and nonconventional work he did for us, from launching startups and new mobile apps to overseeing guerilla marketing and street events. Score another point for the value of making a few primitive moves, especially if the goal is to work your way up in the most civilized of organizations.

Take a moment and think: What would be your childish response to a recent complication? If there weren't any rules, how would you go about solving it? Now consider: What exactly is holding you back?

BE THE CRAZIEST DOG IN THE FIGHT

"Listen—I'm going to ask the fucking questions here," Todd Dagres joked when I called him on the phone for an interview. Todd is the cofounder and general partner of Spark Capital, which has led investments in the likes of Twitter, Warby Parker, Wayfair, Foursquare, Tumblr, 1stdibs, Medium, and Slack. When he's not preparing billion-dollar companies for their IPOs, Todd serves on the advisory board of Brigham and Women's Hospital in Boston and even produces Hollywood films. As you might have guessed, he's also a pure primitive who has little patience for pesky PR guys like me.

"You've got to be the craziest dog in the fight," Todd replied when I asked him what makes a successful entrepreneur. "If you're faced with an obstacle, you do whatever it takes to get over it. If two dogs are in a fight, they don't consult their local parishioner on how to fight the other dogs. They do whatever's necessary to survive."

As an investor, Todd doesn't always choose the "smartest" entrepreneurs or the best credentialed ones. He picks the ones who are going to win. "You want to invest in people that are going to be lucky. And by the way, there is no such thing as luck. You're going to be in the right place at the right time, and you have to work to beat the competition. It takes certain kinds of people to do that. They have to be relentless and persistent while remaining ethical. They have to be creative. They have to motivate people and get people to do things they didn't think they were capable of."

When it comes to politics, there are a lot of fights and a lot of mean dogs. And veteran operative Lis Smith is one of the craziest of all. As David Freedlander wrote in *Politico*, "She puts the word *fuck* through every part of speech the word can be bent into: noun, pronoun, gerund, verb, term of endearment, sobriquet, epithet, honorific. She is practically shaking with excess energy." When strategists were elbowing each other out of the way to sign on with the big name candidates vying to defeat Donald Trump, Lis hitched her star to Pete Buttigieg, the unknown thirty-seven-year-old mayor of South Bend, Indiana, with an unpronounceable last name. She dropped nearly all her other clients. Her colleagues thought she was nuts for going all-in on a guy nobody had heard of. But she didn't sit around and hope that the *New York Times* wrote a piece about Buttigieg's stance on consumer protections. Rather, Lis launched a manic assault on the media as she cajoled, coerced, and sweet-talked everyone from producers to interns to get her candidate on every outlet imaginable. She got him on the *Late Show with Stephen Colbert* and a podcast recapping episodes of *The West Wing*. She got him on NPR and the crass sports blog Barstool Sports. "I want him on everything," she told *Politico*. "It's about hustling for opportunities."

Nuts primitives like Lis Smith have no patience for procedure and hierarchy, and they are poor fits for certain environments. Airline pilots don't decide to impulsively fly to Hawaii instead of Anchorage, and trauma surgeons can't choose to operate when they get around to it. Nuts primitives can make poor managers, but when given the opportunity to do their own thing, they are invaluable.

Most of us aren't nuts primitives, but we can learn from them and make a crazy move now and then. If Todd Dagres is a Rottweiler, then Vibhav Prasad is a golden retriever. He is mild-mannered and polite to a fault, and for many years he was an executive at both startups and large companies, including MasterCard. His parents immigrated to the United States from India and were very strict, always insisting that work comes before play. His hard work paid off, and he had a beautiful family and a well-paying job. But Vib still felt unfulfilled. Work had become particularly stressful and monotonous, and he felt an impulse to try something new—something his parents would have admonished him for even thinking about. One day, Vib woke up and decided he needed to climb an active volcano. Specifically, he needed to climb the 19,347-foot Cotopaxi, located in the Andes Mountains about thirty miles from Quito, Ecuador. The volcano had been closed for several years after a major eruption rendered it dangerous, but in 2017 the Ecuadorian government reopened it. Vib was not going to miss his chance. His wife thought his impulse to climb an active volcano was crazy, but she gave him her blessing.

He found a guide who could take him up the volcano…and then he did it. Vib hopped on a plane and flew eight hours to Ecuador, successfully climbed Cotopaxi, and flew back that evening. He returned exhilarated, and he jumped back into his civilized routine with vigor. The entire trip took thirty-six hours. "I had never done anything like it before," Vib explained to me. "It was impulsive and fun!" That simple nuts move gave Vib a new perspective on his career, and he eventually realized his work wasn't getting any less stressful or stifling, so he made another primitive move and quit. Today he's following his passion, coaching New York City–based tech startups. He can pick and choose his clients, allowing him to spend more time with his family and, if the impulse returns, climb another volcano.

One of the best decisions of my life was thoroughly weird—and, according to almost everyone around me, insane. In 1997, I was emerging out of a depression. I'd had a string of casual relationships, I didn't like my job, and I was living in an apartment I couldn't afford. A month after I took a leap of faith and quit my job to start my own firm, I met an actress named Stacey Nelkin. We immediately fell in love, and we had the crazy impulse to do everything in reverse. Not two months after we met, Stacey was pregnant, and it was not a mistake. We didn't get engaged or have a wedding shower or do any of the other civilized customs. First we went on our honeymoon, then we invited a few close friends to our Upper West Side apartment for Sunday brunch and a wedding. I didn't even know what I was going to wear until an hour before the ceremony. Everyone thought Stacey and I were rushing into things, that we were completely nuts. But we were both ready. We were ready for a long-term relationship and we were ready to start a family despite not having a nest egg. Our romance may have moved unusually fast, but that doesn't mean it wasn't purposeful. That ability to plan and still do something insane—

whether it's Alex Honnold plotting his next death-defying climb or Dorian Paskowitz deciding to go surfing for the rest of his life—is the hallmark of a nuts primitive. As for Stacey and me, we're still together more than twenty-two years later with three beautiful grown children. The best moments of my life never would have happened without that weird, impulsive, thoroughly nuts decision.

How can you make your life a little weirder? What are some positive impulsive decisions you can make? What are some ways you can set aside your civilized instincts and act like a child? Or, more simply, how can you act weirder at work? Maybe it's not censoring yourself before blurting out a crazy, uncivilized idea, or cultivating a reputation as the office oddball who doesn't care much about what others think. For some people, acting nuts means starting a new company or app, building a rocket, or going surfing. For others, it's getting away for thirty-six hours to climb a volcano, or scaling El Capitan without ropes. Fantastic opportunities are waiting, but you must be willing to take a risk first, no matter how small. As Franz Kafka once said, "God gives the nuts, but he does not crack them."

CHAPTER SEVEN

GALLANT

"I would say around 120 kids would claim me as mom," India Howell told me on the phone from halfway across the world.

India proudly calls Tanzania home. "I most definitely, absolutely plan to stay in Tanzania until my last breath," she said. It is one of the most beautiful places on earth, from the pristine lakes to the world-famous Serengeti National Park, yet the East African country of fifty-five million people is as economically troubled as it is lush. Nearly half the population is under the age of fourteen, many of them abused and homeless. A lucky few of them manage to find their way to India Howell and Peter Mmassy. Together they run the Rift Valley Children's Village, a safe haven for marginalized children of all ages, many of whom have nowhere else to go.

"My kids aren't orphans," India told *60 Minutes'* Bill Whitaker in 2016. "They're not up for adoption. They never have been and never will be because they're home now." The village is located on about nine acres of land and is supported by social workers, counselors, and dozens of volunteers. The children have regular routines. They wake up in the morning, have breakfast, and go to school. They have structured playtime. They grow up to have fascinating and successful careers. And India is there to support them every step of the way.

Yet little about her background suggested she was a candidate to open a refuge for homeless children, especially in Africa. She grew up in an affluent community on the North Shore of Long Island, New York. She was loved by her family and afforded a top-flight education. She moved to Boston to join a commercial bakery startup, first as a consultant and then as CEO. The business exploded in popularity. Burned out after several years of nonstop work, India longed for a quieter life, maybe someplace where she could run a bed-and-breakfast. She was scouting potential locations in Vermont when a friend invited her to climb Mount Kilimanjaro to celebrate her fortieth birthday. "When I set foot on the tarmac in Tanzania, I just knew that I'd come home," India told me. "I could just feel it in my soul. The whole time I was here, it felt like I was turning into my parents' driveway returning from college. Every day felt like a homecoming."

After finishing the climb, India made a primitive move by quitting her lucrative job and joining a safari company based in Tanzania. "My mother and father said, 'Are you crazy? You can't move to Africa.' But I was too dumb to be scared. I just met every day as it came."

As India settled into her job running a tented lodge overlooking Lake Manyara National Park, she explored some of the most beautiful landscapes on the planet. She gazed upon Serengeti sunsets and relaxed on the pristine beaches of Unguja. Yet she couldn't help but notice Tanzania's less idyllic parts: the grating poverty, the malnutrition, the lack of fresh water—and most of all, the homeless children. "There were kids living on the streets all over the cities, like Arusha, where I went every week. They were kids who had been orphaned in rural areas and no one wanted to care for them properly, so they ran away."

One day, a security guard at the safari company quit his job and left behind a three-year-old son. Instinctively, India adopted him—and then adopted three more children. Before she knew it, India left the safari business and rented a house in the countryside on a former coffee plantation. Her family continued to grow as village and church leaders dropped off children, many of whom were abandoned or whose parents died of AIDS. The family grew to seventeen, then fifty, then ninety as India continued to expand the home into Rift Valley Children's Village.

In 2012, my wife, Stacey, and I visited the Children's Village, where we witnessed the overflowing passion India has for her beautiful family. Two years later, Stacey returned with our oldest daughter for a month to volunteer. They met kids like Nala, who suffered from crippling learning issues relating to post-traumatic stress disorder. "If not for joining our family, by the age of twelve she would probably have been pregnant, just trying to survive day to day," India said. But Nala went on to graduate from a design college and is now starting a career in fashion. Another child they met, Jonathan, had been forced by his family to beg on the streets for change. Without India, he would have likely ended up working at a brothel near a mine. Instead he is now a college graduate with a degree in business, dreaming of starting his own company.

Taking an enormous risk to commit her life to helping others is what makes India Howell a gallant primitive. At first glance, gallant primitives share many traits in common with messianic primitives, who act as if they were divinely appointed to achieve a mission. I wrote earlier about Ali Rezai, who believes it is his singular purpose to cure the world of as many neurological diseases as possible, and his exhaustive work schedule reflects that. Through the nature of Ali's work, however, he is often forced to see human lives through an MRI scanner, and as a scientist he maintains a professional distance from his patients so that he remains objective. Even the most benevolent researcher must run clinical trials knowing that some sick patients are given a potentially lifesaving drug while others are given a placebo, doomed to end up a statistic in a spreadsheet.

Gallant primitives are different. They measure their impact by how much good they do for other individuals. For her part, India has no plans to found an international nonprofit that tackles the gravest challenges facing the world. Her mission is simple and deeply personal: to be a mother to homeless children in Tanzania. "In the nonprofit world, there are many people who think it's not worth doing something unless it's going to affect the entire planet," India told me. "That is what prevents so many from doing good things. But if you think about it, in any management course, what do they say? Start small and chip away at it. I'm not going to singlehandedly change the world, but if people like me keep plugging away at a problem here and a problem there, they will start to melt together and you'll see a worldwide impact."

Humans have long wondered whether we are preprogrammed to be kind to others. The eighteenth-century philosopher Jean-Jacques Rousseau famously posited that we are born "noble savages" who are fundamentally well-intentioned; it's only after we are corrupted by civilization that our selfish instincts emerge. The English philosopher Thomas Hobbes countered that we are all innately selfish brutes who need civilization to subdue our worst impulses. So who's right?

A 2006 study of toddlers found that nearly every eighteen-month-old was willing to hand an object to a researcher who "accidently" knocked it off a table, suggesting that humans are innately altruistic by nature. In another study, UCLA researchers administered to one group of volunteers a theta-burst transcranial magnetic stimulation, which temporarily blocked activity in regions of the brain associated with impulse control. These areas were left untouched in the other group. Then the researchers gave both groups of people a certain amount of money to keep for themselves or to give away to strangers. With less control of their impulses, would people be more or less generous? Would they act more like Hobbes's selfish brutes or Rousseau's noble savages?

Score one for Rousseau: the group who had less ability to control their impulses were 50 percent more generous than members of the control group. "Knocking out these areas appears to free your ability to feel for others," explained the lead researcher. "By dampening this area, we believe we laid bare how altruistic each study participant naturally was."

What this suggests is that one of our most primal instincts, contrary to what you might expect, is to be kind toward each other. Obviously, some people are kinder than others. I met enough bullies as a kid, and as an adult, to know that some humans can be pretty rotten. But what is it about civilization—a concept that ostensibly curbs our worst traits and forces us to work together—that has the opposite effect on people? This is what makes India Howell such a primitive; she has resisted the civilized world's attempts to wring out purely selfless behavior. She has chosen to define her life in service of others.

Until now we've mostly looked at primitives as distinct archetypes, but as we discussed in the introduction to this book, this is not always the case. Some are purebred primitives; others are mutts like me. Oppositional primitives can be agnostic. A relentless primitive can make a messianic move. A nuts primitive can be a little insecure now and then. Primitives may strongly identify with one group or another, but what makes them unique is their ability to harness the instincts civilization has taught us to repress. Science now suggests that perhaps the most human instinct of all is to be gallant. Or, as the psychologist Judith Rich Harris wrote in *The Nurture Assumption,* "Life in the jungle may be bloody, but it is not devoid of love and loyalty."

Gallant is an old-fashioned word. Men were called "gallant" back when showing basic respect for women was considered a virtue, even a rare one. I prefer to think of it as being noble to others without expecting reciprocation. There is a Hebrew word *achrayut*, which translates to "responsibility" in English. The word is derived from another Hebrew word, *acher*, which means "other." Thus, *achrayut* means not only being accountable for your actions, but a moral responsibility to make others' needs and concerns your own. Gallant primitives embody *achrayut* at their very core.

Even the toughest and hardest-charging primitives are capable of gallant behavior. Gallant is when Austin McChord, the relentless primitive, returned to the Rochester Institute of Technology after taking six years to graduate and announced he was giving the school $50 million—its largest-ever donation. Gallant is when Danny Lewin, the noisy and difficult-to-control oppositional primitive, tried to thwart terrorists from storming the cockpit on American Airlines Flight 11. Gallant is Alan Lightman, the agnostic primitive, who has been a physicist, a novelist, and now a social entrepreneur empowering a new generation of women leaders in Southeast Asia. Gallant is even Dorian Paskowitz, the doctor turned nuts surfer, who hated to take money from people in need of medical care.

I strongly believe that being gallant is our most primal instinct of all, one that every human—primitive and civilized alike—embodies at their core.

BUY YOUR DAD A CAR

Kirk McDonald is chief business officer at Xandr, the advertising and analytics division of AT&T. He is one of the foremost experts in the business, with more than twenty-five years' experience in sales and marketing for some of the biggest media, advertising, and technology brands in the world. But, at the zenith of his career, he nearly died.

It happened when he and his family went on vacation with friends to St. John, in the US Virgin Islands. After dozing on the beach with his newborn baby for several hours, Kirk decided to go snorkeling with a friend late in the afternoon. He had grown up in Jamaica and was comfortable in the water despite never really learning how to swim well. The lifeguard had left the beach, but Kirk was confident he would be fine as long as he stayed in shallow water.

Kirk ventured fifty yards offshore, where the water was still a manageable depth. He and his friend snorkeled with their heads submerged in the crystal blue sea, watching angelfish and sea-horses dart through the coral—blissfully unaware that the tide was sweeping them ever farther from the beach. Finally, they popped their heads up and realized what had happened. Now, more than a football field away from shore, they turned around and moved toward the sand, but Kirk quickly exhausted himself trying to keep up with his friend, who was wearing fins. Reality hit as the shallow water gave way to black emptiness.

"Then I suddenly remembered," Kirk recounted to me, "I didn't know how to swim."

Kirk panicked and flailed his legs futilely, searching for the sandy floor far below him. He ripped the snorkel out of his mouth and gasped for air. Instead, he sucked in a mouthful of water. He began to sink.

As anyone in that situation would be, Kirk was scared—more scared than he had ever been in his life. Yet the only thought that crossed his mind as he sank deeper was his family. "I had a wife, a month-old baby, and a two-year-old son back on the beach. I became more afraid of the impact on my family than the depths of the water. I was afraid of what would happen to my kids." He was terrified of leaving his family alone for the rest of their lives. For their sake, he wasn't going to let himself die.

Kirk forced himself to calm down—no small feat for a guy

sinking into the abyss with two lungs full of water and no real swimming skills. "I made myself put the snorkel back in my mouth, get back to the surface, and blow the water out." He made it back to the beach relying on the deepest, most ancient parts of his brain to keep him alive. It was the impulse to protect others, not himself, that saved his life. It was an instinct that has long driven him to succeed. "Somewhere at around age eleven, when I saw what my parents sacrificed to come to this country, I knew I owed them something." Kirk was determined to buy his father his dream car: a red BMW. He threw himself into his work as he slowly climbed the corporate ladder. As an African American in corporate sales and marketing, a notoriously white industry, Kirk was always looking over his shoulder and suffering from the ever-present imposter syndrome. "I'm never going to claim to be the brightest person in the room, but I will outwork everybody," Kirk said. "Perseverance is how I compete. That's what imposter syndrome can be good for." Finally, when he was hired as a vice president at CNET Networks, Kirk had made enough money to surprise his father with that less-than-practical new car.

Gallant primitives like Kirk see every job, every promotion, every career change in relation to how it helps others more than how it helps them. For Kirk, every hour he works is a step toward making his family happy. When he accomplishes a goal, he finds new other-focused goals. For instance, when Kirk is looking to hire employees—a time when you are quite literally looking for candidates who can best serve the company's needs—Kirk remains other-focused. He needs competent workers, yes, but he also needs people he can mentor. Kirk routinely has one-on-one meetings with members of his team to understand what makes them excited. As a primitive, he knows that the most successful people are driven by infectious passion. "What is the thing that creates for you so much excitement, so much pride, that it's addictive?" Kirk asks them. He sees it as his responsibility to create a fulfilling work environment, and that compassion reaches down to his very core. Knowing firsthand the struggles young people of color face trying to enter majority white industries, Kirk also serves as cochair on the board of directors at Mouse, a nonprofit that is helping to break the poverty cycle of inner-city youth by providing access to technology training.

You might be thinking, "That's great, but most 'good guys' get left behind in life." In some cases, you would be right. For instance, in one study, 160 engineers in California rated each other on how willing they were to help others. These results were correlated with job performance measures such as errors made, deadlines missed, and money wasted. Lo and behold, the nice-guy engineers were some of the least-productive employees. In another study of six hundred medical students in Belgium, the worst-performing students tended to score high on statements like "I love to help others" and "I anticipate the needs of others," and were more likely to help colleagues with assignments. Adam Grant, a psychologist and professor at the Wharton School of the University of Pennsylvania, has devoted his career to studying what he calls givers—people who prioritize helping others over helping themselves—and takers—people who, well, do the opposite. After studying salespeople in North Carolina, Grant found that, like the engineers and doctors, the givers brought in 2.5 times less annual sales revenue. "They were so concerned about what was best for their customers that they weren't willing to sell aggressively," Grant explained in his bestselling book *Give and Take*.

So, case closed? Are the most successful primitives merely takers who see helping others as tantamount to burning money? Not so fast. Grant acknowledges that while some givers stumble to the bottom of the success ladder, they are also clustered at the very top. The very worst engineers may have been givers, but so too, it turns out, were the very best. The worst medical students may have been givers, but the most gifted minds were also willing to lend a helping hand. And in North Carolina, the most bumbling salespeople may have been givers, but so too were the rock stars. "Givers dominate the bottom *and* the top of the success ladder," Grant concluded.

Gallant primitives are the givers at the top. They don't merely serve on the boards of charities and take a write-off on their taxes; they insert themselves on the front lines of places in need. They are capitalists and socialists, bankers and artists, Republicans and Democrats. In many cases, givers at the top of the corporate ladder can attract and retain the best talent with simple, heart-felt actions. Look no further than Ronald Meyer, currently the vice chairman of NBCUniversal. In the mid-1970s, he cofounded Creative Artists Agency (CAA), which he grew into one of the most dominant and influential talent agencies in the world. Ron thrived in one of the most cutthroat industries around, and, as such, may not be the first person who comes to mind when you think "gallant." Yet he is hailed as "Hollywood's Mr. Nice Guy." When my father died, broke, at age fifty-five, Ron was there to help. My sister was one in a long line of entry-level assistants he'd had over the years, but, of his own volition, Ron instinctively sprang into action when our father passed away. Ron paid for the catering at the shiva for hundreds of mourners, and he was one of the first to pay his respects for a man he had never met. When my cousin Jonah, then a teenager, went to work as an agent for CAA years later, he stayed for thirteen years—long after he had lost interest in the talent business. When I asked Jonah why he deferred his dream of becoming a filmmaker for so long, he replied that he respected the culture at CAA and he wanted to honor Ron's loyalty to our family.

Sometimes gallant behavior is rewarded with profit, but many times there is a price to pay. I experienced this firsthand not long ago. I had labored for nearly two years cultivating a connection with a promising biotech company, hoping to win its PR business. After I spent countless hours in meetings and drafted proposal after proposal, they were ready to sign on the dotted line. It was a big achievement for my firm, and we were rewarded with a handsome retainer. But immediately after we began working together, I noticed a level of intensity and criticism I'd never experienced before. We'd emerge from meetings sweating as if we'd been cross-examined in the courtroom. Yet we hung in there, even as their behavior toward us became disrespectful. We worked hard to win that retainer, so we took our licks and soldiered on for several more weeks.

Then, one day, the account supervisor at my firm, Alyssa, showed me a furious email from one of the company's executives, lambasting her for drafting a tweet they weren't happy with. The tone was aggressive and mean-spirited, as if they were trying to humiliate her. If this firm was willing to berate one of my employees over an unpublished tweet, I thought, how were they going to treat us when something truly important came up? Would they scream at Alyssa when the *New York Times* decided not to cover an event? Would they demand she be fired if they didn't reach a hundred thousand Instagram followers? The following business day I called up the chief marketing officer of the biotech firm and, to his shock, resigned the account. Alyssa was one of my most dedicated employees, and no retainer was worth seeing her treated poorly by a client.

No matter what situation you find yourself in, consider the following: How other-focused are you being right now? The average adult makes thousands of decisions each day—how many of them are made with the best interests of someone else in mind? Sometimes we need to look out for ourselves, of course, and being other-focused should never mean sacrificing your own health and well-being. But what are some other-focused goals you can devote yourself to? Is it a shiny red BMW for Mom or Dad? Or maybe it's simply calling them on the phone more often?

By making a gallant move each day, you can train yourself to be a better coworker, a better friend, and a better person. A recent study by California State University researchers even suggested that being gallant may improve your own psychological well-being. "People striving for happiness may be tempted to treat themselves," the study concluded. "Our results, however, suggest that they may be more successful if they opt to treat someone else instead."

FEEL THE FEAR AND SAVE SOMEONE

One day in 2017, I had the distinct honor of meeting a man named Stephen Valyou. I was at the batting cages with my son in Connecticut when I spotted Stephen, a paraplegic, who was gliding around effortlessly in his manual wheelchair. He had a well-built physique and I had a hunch he might be a veteran, so I struck up a conversation. His story nearly brought me to tears.

Before he was paralyzed, Stephen was in the army during the height of the Iraq War. By the time he deployed, more than one hundred thousand Iraqi civilians had already perished along with thousands of American troops. More were dying every month, long after Saddam Hussein's government had been toppled. Approximately 63 percent of all American deaths were caused by improvised explosive devices (IEDs) planted along roads. These roadside bombs were hidden in inconspicuous places like soda cans, boxes, signs, and roadkill. Some were designed to take out armored Humvees, others were built to kill passing infantry and civilians. Most of the IEDs were extremely unstable and could detonate at any moment, and it was Stephen's job to defuse them before they could injure or kill others.

"That job wasn't for everyone," Stephen explained to me. "But the way I saw it, if I could go up there and render safe that IED and save ten or twelve lives, that was worth it. Even if I didn't survive—even if it took me out but saved ten other guys. That's what I wanted to do, and I was okay with that." By early 2007, Stephen had deactivated more roadside bombs than he could count. Hundreds upon hundreds. On any given day, Stephen was shot at by insurgents, witnessed suicide bombings, and saw his friends die. When you and I were eating lunch or seeing a movie, Stephen was squatting over a device he knew could blow him to bits, prepared to give his life to keep others safe.

It wasn't a bomb that nearly killed Stephen. It was a sniper positioned hundreds of feet away, watching Stephen in his crosshairs as he deactivated the bomb and then searched the area for others. The bullet ripped through Stephen's abdomen, liver, and lung, then shattered his T9 vertebra, instantly paralyzing him. But the last thing he wants is for you to feel bad for him. "You should feel bad for the families whose loved ones came home with a flag draped over their coffin," Stephen told me. The way he sees it, that bullet probably saved his life. If he hadn't been paralyzed, he would have gone out there the next day, and the day after that, until he was killed. The only thing he feels badly about is that he couldn't help more people along the way.

When Stephen woke up in the VA hospital, he gazed down at his legs. He took in that he would never walk again. Then he looked at the nurse beside his bed and asked: "All right, what do I need to do to get out of here?" For Stephen, paralysis was just another life event. Just another obstacle he had to overcome. It may have been bigger and more physically crippling than most, but he had no intention of letting it stop him. Even today, more than a dozen years after his injury, Stephen still suffers from stabbing neuropathic pain—a cruel irony for those whose limbs never move but still may cause excruciating discomfort.

In the years since he was wounded, Stephen has been elected to the board of fire commissioners in his hometown. He's taken up skydiving, scuba diving, and downhill skiing; now he's a ski instructor, helping paralyzed vets reassert control over their lives through sports. He coaches high school basketball and baseball. He operates heavy machinery for a paving company. In his spare time, he mans a hotline for vets contemplating suicide. "I tell them that I've been there," Stephen explained to me. "I know it sucks. But you know what? You can get through it. Take a knee, drink some water. We're going to get through this and we're going to do it together."

Pete Paxton is another gallant primitive who, like Stephen Valyou, seems to have been put on earth to help other people— or, in his case, animals. "Pete" is his pseudonym; I don't know his actual name. As the world's most prolific undercover animal investigator, he needs to keep his identity secret. Though you don't know him, Pete has done more for animals than just about anyone. As he chronicled in his gripping book, *Rescue Dogs,* he's gone undercover at some seven hundred puppy mills, secretly acquiring evidence and footage that prosecutors use to shut them down. He's worked with activists to pass sweeping legislation in California and Pennsylvania that put many of the worst puppy mills out of business. He's helped put animal abusers behind bars while rescuing thousands of dogs who would otherwise have been euthanized. When Pete's not saving puppies, he's going undercover at factory farms and slaughterhouses doing some of the most horrendous and grueling work imaginable, all while wearing a secret camera to record animal cruelty violations and hold the nation's food suppliers accountable. When Pete gives interviews to the media, he wears dark shades and a ball cap so that his identity remains concealed. Many of his friends and family will never know that he has done more good for animals than perhaps anyone else on the planet—and he's just fine with that.

What is it about gallant primitives like Stephen Valyou, Pete Paxton, and India Howell that make them so hardwired to help others? I've tried to make gallant moves in my life, from mentoring at-risk youth to giving connections to job seekers to donating money to worthy charities, but this sort of altruism requires less time and thought. I still sometimes feel inadequate compared to those who so effortlessly and reflexively help others. In fact, for many gallant primitives, the impulse to help others can be greater than the impulse for self-preservation. Scientists have coined a term for this: "extreme altruism." Abigail Marsh, an associate professor of psychology and neuroscience at Georgetown University, set out to understand what makes these people tick. Her journey began when she was nineteen, when her car spun out of control on the highway. Her engine gave out as she skidded to a halt in the middle of oncoming traffic. As cars swerved to avoid her, a stranger across the highway pulled over and ran to her aid. He pushed Abigail into the passenger seat, managed to get the car started, and drove her to safety. Then he disappeared, and she never saw him again.

What prompted that man to stop his car and risk his life for a stranger? In her book *The Fear Factor,* Abigail concludes that an ancient part of the brain known as the amygdala is largely responsible for altruism. First she studied psychopaths, including a boy who lobbed a fake grenade into a crowded room to incite terror. These individuals are quite literally fearless; they have dysfunction in the amygdala that prevents them from feeling fear. Then she studied extreme altruists, like those people who give a kidney to strangers. Unlike the psychopaths, the altruists had large and fully developed amygdalae. "People who are highly altruistic are really good at recognizing other people's fear and that may be one reason they're motivated to help," Abigail explained to *National Geographic.*

The gallant primitives I've spoken with are indeed motivated in part by fear. It was Kirk McDonald's fear for his family that helped him escape drowning. India Howell feared for the lives of orphans living on the streets. Stephen Valyou told me about the fear he felt for his fellow soldiers in Iraq, not to mention the wounded vets he counsels who are at a high risk of suicide. "Fear is normal," he explained. "Being scared is normal. When that fear consumes and starts to control you, that's when bad things happen." Pete Paxton explained that what drives him is "seeing fear in the eyes of animals. They can't talk, but I feel their fear in my very bones, and I have a primal need to help them."

Feel the Fear and Do It Anyway is a legendary mental health book by the late psychologist Susan Jeffers about the crippling effects of fear and how it impacts nearly every decision we make. I like to think that gallant primitives feel the fear and then go save someone anyway. They are not paralyzed by fear, but galvanized by it. They are highly attuned to people in need, and their gut instincts instruct them to help. While this reflex may be stronger in some people than others, you do not need an overly developed amygdala to be gallant. Like most people, you may hesitate before jumping onto the subway tracks to rescue a fallen stranger, but that doesn't mean you can't do your small part to save the world.

Ari and Noah Meyerowitz are doing their part. I met Ari and Noah when they were children; Noah was once a classmate of my daughter, Antonia. Their father, Steve, was a local legend in the town of Great Barrington, Massachusetts. The "Sproutman," as he was affectionately known, pioneered the practice of sprouting, the natural process by which seeds germinate and put out shoots. You may remember sprouting beans in first grade science class, but Steve popularized the nutritional benefits and cost savings of eating sprouted legumes, seeds, and nuts straight from your kitchen. Throughout the 1970s and '80s he taught indoor gardening in New York City, wrote a collection of popular books on sprouting, and built a small mail-order business. Tragically, in 2015, Steve lost his life in an automobile accident while returning from a business trip. All of a sudden it fell to Ari, age twenty-five, and Noah, age sixteen, to continue his hard work and take sprouting mainstream.

The two brothers were understandably trepidatious. They were young and inexperienced, but they threw themselves into marketing a product that few people understood. They refused to let their father's legacy fade, despite the considerable obstacles they faced. Ari and Noah may not have rescued orphans or defused roadside bombs, but their motivation was similarly gallant. "We took over because of the mission," Ari explained to me. "We had a website, we had a legacy, we had a fan base—and we had no real revenue coming in." The brothers developed a product line, from seeds to sprouting bags to juicers, that turned their father's vision into a growing business. More important, they are helping people get healthy by bringing ultra-fresh organic foods to places not fortunate enough to have a Whole Foods. Ari and Noah have donated sprout bags to nonprofits serving countries where fresh produce is difficult to come by. By turning ordinary people into the sustainable farmers of tomorrow, the brothers are doing their part to reduce our dependence on industrial agriculture, one of the biggest contributors to climate change. "We just want to add sprouts in people's lives," the brothers said proudly. "We can all do our small part to save the planet."

I may not have the courage or singular focus of truly gallant primitives, but like Noah and Ari, I find simple ways to be more gallant in my day-to-day life. As someone who connects people for a living, I've acted as an unofficial career counselor for hundreds of family members, friends, friends of friends, and strangers. I've been unemployed and underemployed numerous times in my life, and I understand the anxiety associated with not knowing how to support yourself and a young family. I don't want other people to suffer like that, so I go out of my way to make introductions and give paid internships at my firm to talented young people who need a little help getting started.

What are some small ways you can save someone? Tap into your most basic human instincts and feel the fear around you. Whether it's a struggling coworker, a recent immigrant, or a depressed friend, we are surrounded by people who need us. Now think: What is a simple way you can help?

PLACE YOUR OXYGEN MASK ON FIRST

Meet Beverly Warne, one of the most gentle, humble, and remarkable people I've ever met. Born and raised on the Pine Ridge Native American Reservation in South Dakota, Bev is a proud member of the Oglala Lakota tribe. She earned her undergraduate and master's degrees in nursing at Arizona State University, then served as the school's director of American Indian Students United for Nursing program, before returning home to South Dakota to do what she could to help decrease the tremendous health disparities among the Native people in the Great Plains. Continuing her work in nursing, she serves as an instructor and mentor at the Native American Nursing Education Center at South Dakota State University College of Nursing in Rapid City. Her work is to recruit Native American student nurses and support them academically, financially, socially, and culturally from the beginning of their schooling through licensure as registered nurses. When her husband, Jim, was diagnosed with multiple sclerosis, Bev worked tirelessly as his caregiver while remaining steadfast in her mission to increase the number of Native American nurses on reservations, ensuring that there are competent medical professionals in some of the country's most disadvantaged places.

In the summer of 2019, I met Bev at her office at SDSU in Rapid City, South Dakota, and we spoke at length about her mission. She stresses to her students how important it is to give back to the community, perhaps now more than ever before. A recent study found that the Pine Ridge Reservation has the second lowest life expectancy—forty-eight years for men and fifty-two for women—in the entire western hemisphere. In a place with 70 percent unemployment, with many homes lacking electricity and running water, with a suicide rate quadruple the national average, Pine Ridge is in danger of losing not just its culture, but its people. Up to two-thirds of adults there live with alcoholism, an epidemic that was until recently fueled by a tiny town right across the state line in Nebraska, home to just twelve people, that was selling four million cans of beer per year to people on the reservation. Thanks to the work of activists, the stores were stripped of their liquor licenses and Pine Ridge is walking down the long road to recovery, with Bev and her fellow nurses actively involved and giving back to their communities.

But one of the most important aspects of Bev's job is making sure nurses focus on themselves as much as they do others. "Part of what happens to nurses is they give so much of themselves, not just physically but emotionally," Bev told me. "If you take care of others without taking care of yourself, that is how some nurses burn out and quit the field of nursing. It's called compassion fatigue."

She continued, "During my mentoring sessions with the Lakota students, I always talk about self-care. Once, a student said to me, 'But that seems selfish!' I replied: 'Think of it this way: On an airplane, if there is a problem and the plane is not getting enough oxygen, the masks drop down and you are instructed to put your mask on before you help others. You have to keep yourself strong—physically, mentally, emotionally, and spiritually— to continue being a nurse who cares about his or her patients.'"

Compassion fatigue is a very real phenomenon, and it's particularly common among those who work directly with victims of disaster, illness, and trauma. But anyone, from lawyers to journalists to police officers to PR guys like me, can experience forms of compassion fatigue, which is why practicing self-care is so important. Before you can help others, you have to help yourself. Put your mask on before assisting the person next to you.

As an airline pilot, Diana Higbee quite literally understands the importance of putting on her own oxygen mask first. I met her on a plane while she was off duty and catching a ride home. Diana was in the seat next to me and we struck up a conversation. She proudly recounted that she flew her first glider at age fourteen and immediately fell in love. She took lessons, spent time in the military, and finally landed her dream job as a commercial pilot in 2012. She excelled, and within a few years she made captain. But then tragedy stuck. After finishing a flight, she was descending the aircraft stairs when she became light-headed. Her legs felt like jelly, as if they forgot how to walk. When her brain said to walk straight ahead, her legs instead veered right, left, anywhere but forward. A friend took her to the hospital, and after a battery of tests, Diana was shocked to learn that she, a thirty-three-year-old conditioned athlete, had suffered a stroke. The culprit was her birth control, which in rare cases can cause blood clots. Her recovery was challenging, as the stroke affected her peripheral vision and depth perception—critical requirements for a pilot, as you can imagine. But she ground through and refused to quit.

Within months Diana was fully healthy, but the Federal Aviation Administration (FAA) refused to reinstate her medical certification. Diana passed test after test—MRIs, stress tests, ultrasounds, heart monitors, sleep studies, endless blood work—to prove the stroke was caused by birth control, not a defect in her body. But the FAA didn't budge. Officials wanted her to undergo a highly invasive surgery to install a heart rate monitor.

This time Diana refused. "They would have pushed me and pushed me until I gave up," Diana told me. "Except they pushed the wrong person." She held firm and flooded the FAA with letters from her doctors demanding that her flight status be reinstated. The situation was grossly unfair: male pilots who suffer "normal" strokes, the kind that are the result of an unhealthy lifestyle, are grounded for two years before they are allowed to fly again. Yet Diana, a perfectly healthy young woman who happened to be prescribed the wrong birth control, was grounded for nearly three. Like so many women who struggle in male-dominated fields—roughly 94 percent of commercial pilots are male—nothing she did was ever good enough.

Despite the ongoing sexist treatment from the FAA, Diana's instinct was to help other pilots. After getting herself healthy and subjecting herself to nearly every medical test imaginable, she became an instructor for her airline, guiding students as they learned in simulators. She rose to chief pilot, one of only a handful of women in the world with that title. In her spare time she mentored high school students interested in aviation, helping them secure scholarship money to join a field that seemed intent on shutting her out. Then, one day, a letter arrived from the FAA. She ripped it open and burst into tears. Finally, at long last, she was given clearance to fly. "I was crying and sweating and jumping all at the same time," she told me.

Today Diana is back where she belongs, thousands of feet in the air. "I hope the path of other women in my situation is a little smoother because of me," she said. "For women everywhere, whether dealing with a medical issue or trying to overcome their own battles, I hope they can hear my story and get a sense of the beauty in the struggle. To know that it's okay to get knocked down, it's okay to cry it out, and to let that be the fuel that expands your dreams."

Gallant primitives find ways to help others even during times of immense personal struggle, but they also aren't afraid to fight for themselves. As Diana told me, "Let me prove you wrong. I'll do it with a smile on my face. I'll always fight for what's right." Being gallant means doing the right thing, whether it's for others or for yourself. You can follow your dreams, you can become fabulously rich, you can advance to the pinnacle of your career—but whenever possible, pause and consider how you can help others along the way.

Consider Jane, a gallant primitive who has found personal success through empowering the less fortunate around her. Growing up in a blue-collar family, Jane was determined to find a career path that would mean she never had to worry about money. She graduated from an Ivy League school with an economics degree and secured a position as a junior consultant at a global accounting firm, where she worked in business development. Jane excelled at her job and was squarely on a partnership track when she realized she needed more out of her work than a cushy salary. Like other gallant primitives, the nagging feeling that she should be helping others was too strong.

Jane gave up her lucrative job and joined a charter school in Washington, DC. Despite having no relevant experience, she taught introductory Spanish to disadvantaged students in one of the most troubled school systems in the country. It was the hardest year of her life, but also one that galvanized her need to help people. A year later she returned to New York to teach classes to budding female entrepreneurs. But like many other gallant primitives, Jane remained personally ambitious. She graduated from business school and took a job in private wealth management. Once again, she was making a lot of money. She was sought after and valued for her skills. And yet, as she told me, "My soul was just empty." She craved a career in which she could use her skills for a higher purpose, and she finally found it with an immigrant empowerment nonprofit. As CEO, Jane helped thousands of immigrants and refugees build professional careers in the United States. Every year, millions of talented immigrants are working under their skill level, a phenomenon known as "brain waste." Under Jane's stewardship, the nonprofit helped thousands of immigrants from more than a hundred countries secure professional jobs suited to their skills and education level.

Learn from Jane's example and remember that self-care does not mean being selfish. Focus on you so that you may better focus on others. Whether you devote your days to helping the less fortunate or you make a lot of money and then give it away or you fall somewhere in the middle, take the leap and be gallant in your own unique way.

PUT PRINCIPLES OVER PROFIT

Years ago I was shooting a promotional video for the law firm O'Melveny & Myers. I had the pleasure of interviewing Warren Christopher, a senior partner at the firm who had served as secretary of state under President Bill Clinton. He was the epitome of the elder statesman, courtly, self-effacing, and famously measured with his words. He spoke slowly, enunciating each noun, verb, and preposition as he composed complete sentences. As an expert negotiator who helped arrange the release of American hostages from Iran, he knew the importance of choosing his words carefully. Chris, as he insisted on being called, discussed his work as vice chairman of the governor's commission on the Watts riots in 1965 and head of the Christopher Commission in 1992, which helped create significant reforms in the Los Angeles Police Department following the Rodney King riots. He spoke passionately and proudly about his firm's pro bono civil rights work for African Americans who were unfairly targeted by the police some fifty years before Black Lives Matter.

Then he paused to gather his thoughts. "Those were before the days when we worshipped the almighty dollar." He lamented that his law firm, where he had practiced since 1950 around numerous stints in public office, no longer had time to take on the kind of important pro bono cases it once had. At the end of our interview, he asked me to cut out that potentially explosive line. He had said it on purpose, and he meant it as a message to his colleagues who were in the room at the time, but as a diplomat he did not want to even indirectly criticize his own firm. Curiously, one of the most civilized people I've ever met taught me a great deal about being a primitive.

Chris, who died in 2011, lived a gallant life, regularly using his considerable clout to try to help the least fortunate among us. He believed in placing these principles above profit. My great-grandfather Joseph Krieger was the same way. He was a poor German-speaking immigrant who came to America in 1902. An avid tea drinker, he was frustrated with how people brewed tea using a clumsy strainer called a "tea ball." What if you could simply dip a prepackaged cotton pouch into the hot water? Joseph hired fellow immigrants in the San Francisco Bay Area and in 1920 released the first commercially available tea bags. Much larger than today's tea bags, his were designed for restaurants brewing tea for many people. This being the tail end of the Second Industrial Revolution, Joseph's competitors quickly found ways to mass-produce smaller tea bags that could be sold to individual homes. To compete, my great-grandfather would have had to invest in machinery that automated the jobs he created for his fellow immigrants. He refused. Joseph never sacrificed his core principles and proudly employed immigrants until he sold the company in 1937. Afterward, he began a new business: developing board games to help blind children learn arithmetic. His games became widely used in schools for the blind throughout California.

Joseph was a gallant primitive who cared more about helping

his fellow immigrants than he did about becoming a tea baron. He knew his company would go out of business if he didn't automate production, but if it meant putting money in his employees' pockets for a few years longer, he accepted his fate. But being good to people isn't always bad for business. Consider another gallant factory owner, Aaron Feuerstein. In 1995, Aaron's company, Malden Mills, suffered a devastating fire, the largest Massachusetts had seen for a century. The advisers surveying the disaster's aftermath had no doubt: it was time to shut the company down, collect the $300 million insurance money, and enjoy early retirement.

But Aaron refused. "I have a responsibility to the worker, both blue-collar and white-collar," he told an interviewer at the time. "I have an equal responsibility to the community. It would have been unconscionable to put three thousand people on the streets and deliver a deathblow to the cities of Lawrence and Methuen. Maybe on paper our company is worthless to Wall Street, but I can tell you it's worth more."

Aaron decided to pay all employees their full salaries plus benefits for as long as it took to get the factory back up and working. The decision cost him $25 million, and, within a few years, his company had gone bankrupt. The very cynics he had railed against used his story to argue that gallantry was lethal, that anyone who stood up for what's right was likely to end up ruined. But Aaron didn't give up, nor did his grateful employees. Together they developed new fabric technologies, and one of them was finally bought by the Department of Defense, making Malden Mills profitable once more. Despite its ups and down, the company lives on to this day.

You may have heard of a duo of gallant primitives named Ben Cohen and Jerry Greenfield, cofounders of Ben & Jerry's ice cream. "Thirty-plus years ago, most people thought you couldn't be caring and still make a profit," David Evenchick, president of Greater Talent Network, told me. David's agency books engagements for Ben and Jerry along with some of the top names in politics and entertainment, from Anderson Cooper to Michael J. Fox. When the ice cream company went public in 1985, Ben and Jerry made the unprecedented decision to commit 7.5 percent of its annual pretax profits to philanthropy while also pledging that no executive would make five times that of entry-level employees. "They went up against the major players in the ice cream world with nothing more than a never-take-no-for-an-answer attitude and an entrepreneurial spirit," David told me. "They never, ever budged on any of their beliefs. It is why today, more than twenty-five years later, they are still hugely in demand on the lecture circuit. They are the go-to entrepreneurial success story that all start-up companies aspire to. They are folk heroes at this point, and they never gave in from their beliefs."

These examples might strike you as anomalies, the rare exceptions to the rule that profit must always come before principles. But consider the surprise announcement in August 2019 by more than two hundred chief executives, including the heads of Walmart, Apple, JPMorgan Chase, and Amazon, that shareholder value is no longer paramount when it comes to corporate responsibility. The group of CEOs, who collectively comprise the Business Roundtable, stated that corporations must also compensate their employees fairly, be responsible stewards of the environment, and behave ethically with their suppliers. "While each of our individual companies serves its own corporate purpose, we share a fundamental commitment to all of our stakeholders," the group affirmed. "We commit to deliver value to all of them, for the future success of our companies, our communities, and our country." It might seem like a trivial declaration, but keep in mind that for decades boardrooms across the country took their moral guidance from the economist Milton Friedman, who famously wrote that "the social responsibility of business is to increase its profits." While the "greed is good" mentality is certainly alive and well, even Wall Street is coming around to the idea that we're all in this together.

How can you be more gallant in your life? What wrongs can you right? How can you let in a little more sunlight in your corner of the world? You don't need to be a gallant primitive highly attuned to the struggles of others to identify a person in need. You can be acutely focused on your career and still be gallant. You can be for profit or not for profit. You can be relentless, oppositional, agnostic, messianic, insecure, or nuts and still be gallant.

It's rarely easy. In fact, it's painful. You may lose money, friends, or worse. "No gallant action was ever accomplished without danger," the American revolutionary John Paul Jones said. Gallant primitives identify problems to solve when the rest of us choose not to. They feel the fear. They know their mission is too hard, too dangerous, too big, too unpopular, too scary, too crazy. And then they do it anyway.

CONCLUSION

We are surrounded by primitives.

Look around you: from the barista whipping up your morning latte to the bartender pouring your after-work beer, primitives are lurking everywhere. Some are obvious to spot; others are hiding in plain sight. Primitives are gay and straight and everywhere in between. They are male and female and nonbinary. They are captains of industry and captains of their high school basketball teams. They are the 1 percent and the 99 percent, billionaires and socialists, Yankee fans and Red Sox fans. They are not merely outliers, rebels, and mavericks. While the civilized are intent on following the pack, primitives are allergic to convention. It may sometimes be easy to write them off as not the "right cultural fit," but we dismiss these primitives at our own peril.

This discovery did not come readily to me. For much of my career I lacked such insight, and I've engaged in my share of "mustabation"—a term coined by the late behavioral psychologist Albert Ellis about people who incessantly feel they "must" and "should" follow civilized conventions to get along and fit in. Primitives, on the other hand, refuse to let the civilized world inculcate and mold them in its image. They tap into their most primal instincts and see the world differently than everyone else.

That said, one of the purest primitives I know can't see at all.

"I wish I could encourage you to major in English instead of chemistry," one of Matthew Guberman-Pfeffer's professors at

Fairfield University said to him. Chemistry is a highly visual subject that requires an understanding of three-dimensional spatial relationships. Matty was legally blind; how could he peer through a microscope or understand molecular geometry? But then his professor smiled and finished her sentence: "The problem is you're too darn good at it."

The more civilized decision would have been to study English, a field in which accommodations for visually impaired students are widely available. Matty did not need to see in order to appreciate metaphor or to visualize a story. But like a true oppositional primitive, he was stubborn. He didn't care that people with his disability weren't supposed to become chemists. He didn't ask permission. Chemistry was a new and exciting challenge, a dragon to be slayed. The thought of conquering it with his disability was tantalizing. Like a messianic primitive, Matty fell in love with the subject matter. "As a discipline that seeks to understand and utilize the molecular language of nature," he wrote, "chemistry attracted my curiosity—my desire to understand the 'secret motions and causes of things,' to use Sir Francis Bacon's phrase."

The odds were stacked against Matty. Only one in a hundred students in general chemistry go on to graduate in the subject— how much higher were the odds for a blind student? Like a nuts primitive, Matty gladly assumed the risk. "Within months of working together, my professor saw me differently," he said. "I was no longer just a blind student, but a student for whom sight and insight were not synonymous." When it came to seeing the subatomic particles that make up the universe, his peers were just as blind as he was. The visual images that comprise textbooks are merely human conventions for depicting a reality that no human could really see. Matty knew that you didn't need eyes to listen to nature's chemical language.

Once, before a chemistry lecture, he overheard two students

complaining about how difficult the subject matter was to under-stand. "It's not like we can *see* atoms," one complained. Matty turned to them and said, cheerfully, "Neither can I!"

With the help of audio textbooks, he threw himself into his work. Like a relentless primitive, he refused to give up on his dream. Along the way, he helped redefine what is possible for people with disabilities. It would have been an achievement if he simply completed his general chemistry class; instead, he aced it. He was recognized by the American Chemical Society as the best organic chemistry student at Fairfield University, coauthored a paper in the *Journal of Physical Chemistry B*, and graduated from college with a BS in chemistry and a 3.98 GPA. Then it was off to the University of Connecticut's chemistry graduate program on very competitive and prestigious scholarships. In 2016 he was one of two thousand recipients of a National Science Foundation Graduate Research fellowship. He secured his PhD and is now doing his postdoctoral research at Yale.

I was thinking a lot about Matty as I wrote this book. The most obvious or familiar primitives are innovators and company founders like Danny Lewin and Austin McChord, high-flying ex-ecutives like Kirk McDonald and Riki Drori, or medical pioneers like Ali Rezai. They're superstar venture capitalists like Todd Dagres. They're heroes like India Howell and Stephen Valyou. They're the kind of people you find at the pinnacle of their field because they've had to sprint, jump to the front of the line, cut corners, argue, and burst their way through obstacles repeatedly, and often dangerously. But primitives are everywhere. They're middle-school teachers who challenge their students in new and exciting ways. They're stay-at-home parents who prepare their children to become the movers and shakers of tomorrow. They're blind chemists who are quietly reminding the world that disabil-ity is not inability.

I hope that this book has helped you reconsider what makes

some of the world's most successful people tick. They don't rely on credentials and connections, but rather on their mindset and their ability to make primitive moves on their respective journeys. More important, I hope it will help you to better understand what *success* truly means. For me, above all else, it is about collecting passionate and gifted people whom I am lucky enough to call friends. What does it mean for you?

What are some simple primitive moves you can make in your life? Can you be more relentless about that side-hustle you're trying to build? Can you be more oppositional with your boss at work? More agnostic when you think about your career path? More messianic when it comes to devoting time to your professional dreams? Maybe a healthy dose of paranoia and insecurity is necessary to light a fire under your career. What's that crazy, nutty, insanely difficult thing you've always wanted to do but were too civilized try? And while you are thinking about all of these possibilities, think of a simpler one: Who can you help today? Define what gallant means to you and act on it. Who of your friends, family members, and coworkers could use a helping hand?

So get out there and go ROAMING. Visit www.primitivebook .com to take a quiz to learn where your dormant primitive instincts lie. Define your success by your own measures. Is it money? Or is it something more primal, like independence? Find big and small ways to act a little more primitive in your day-to-day life. Wander to new places, shuffle back to old ones, and do it all over again. Go out and live the life humans were meant to, and when you return to civilization, I encourage you to get in touch with me and share your story. If you find yourself failing, try again—or maybe try something new. And, if nothing else works, slow it down and connect to your deeper intuition, your own unique spirit.

Above all else, try to have some fun along the way. English philosopher L. P. Jacks once said, "A master in the art of living draws no sharp distinction between his work and his play, his labor and his leisure, his mind and his body, his education and his recreation. He hardly knows which is which. He simply pursues his vision of excellence through whatever he is doing, and leaves others to determine whether he is working or playing. To himself, he always appears to be doing both."

I sincerely hope you are lucky enough to reach that point where work blends into play and you can no longer tell the difference between the two—for a primitive, that is bliss.

ACKNOWLEDGMENTS

When it comes to writing, I'm much more of a sprinter than a marathon runner, and *Primitive* has certainly tested my endurance abilities.

Through the ups and downs, I recall a handful of people without whom this book would not be possible. It starts with a wise woman, Erica Brown, an author and scholar who, unlike many of her colleagues, not only has a well-developed sense of humor but a finely tuned ear that allows her to truly listen and figure out what makes other people tick. She spotted something in me that I didn't see in myself and made this defining moment possible.

Most writers are not "huggers," in the metaphorical sense, of course, as in going above and beyond to extend a helping hand, but Erica is an exception to that rule. Of her own volition, she introduced me to her agent, Michael Palgon. Michael ended up taking a shot on me, an over-fifty first-time author. He wasn't just an agent extraordinaire, but a key figure in shaping the premise of this book and making me realize that what I had to say had more value than the advice I usually dispense in my day job. Michael always pushed me to go deeper, to be more original, and to keep the reader top of mind. Along the way he reminded me to take some of my primitive medicine, including the need to be more messianic about my writing. On many occasions he kicked the shit out of me when that same writing fell short of his high standards, and I couldn't be more grateful for it.

Michael also connected me to Nick Bromley, who became a true collaborator and cowriter. A thirty-one-year-old steady hand with a few *New York Times* bestsellers to his credit, Nick's effortless and polished writing captured my voice and smoothed my words, taking the narrative to a new level. His knowledge, patience, and professionalism wove the words together and made them sing. Nick sits on the civilized side of the spectrum and is grounded and measured in the best way, while adopting an oppositional-primitive mindset to give me needed constructive pushback (including the occasional millennial reality check). I introduced Nick to my friend Jonathan Schienberg to round out the team. Jon is a mensch and an award-winning journalist and documentary filmmaker who led the *Primitive* research efforts. Jonathan took his *60 Minutes* sensibilities and forced us to interview sources tirelessly, unearth original content that you won't find on Google, and make sure that every sentence was interesting. The three of us, each representing three different decades, met faithfully on Tuesday afternoons at the City Diner on West 90th and Broadway. With its friendly staff and solid comfort food, it rekindled my childhood love for Jell-O with whipped cream. Highly recommended.

While Michael landed several offers from publishing houses, we ended up signing with Mauro DiPreta at Hachette. During our first phone conversation, Mauro instinctively got the primitive premise and saw the potential. He then dissected the proposal and got us to make several crucial adjustments. While he ended up leaving the company after I signed with Hachette, my hope is that this book meets and exceeds his expectations and justifies the trust he put in me.

Dan Ambrosio at Hachette quickly adopted this project as his own. He kept me on track and made necessary tweaks to ensure *Primitive* made the intended impact and lived up to the concept. My heartfelt thanks to him and his talented team, who also lit a necessary fire under me, especially toward the end. I'm beyond honored and humbled to be listed as a writer published by Hachette. Thank you to Michelle Aielli, Michael Barrs, Michael Clark, Alison Dalafave, Amanda Kain, Emily Lavelle, Kenrya Rankin, and Lisa Rivlin, and my publicity team, Sarah Russo and Robin Wane.

That winning proposal, and the concept of primitive, along with a chunk of the content, would not be possible without Liel Leibovitz. I met Liel in 1996 while serving in the Israeli Defense Forces Spokesman's Office. I was a thirty-two-year-old agnostic primitive experiencing a new adventure when an IDF officer introduced Liel, nineteen, to me as a "genius." It wasn't that officer's personal opinion, mind you, but an objective measure determined by the IDF's rigorous testing. I'm proud to report that his genius has only grown more towering over the years. Liel's brilliant mind, primitive ways, oppositional spirit, and terrific writing played a huge part in laying the foundation for this book and is forever appreciated.

Primitive couldn't have happened without all of these wonderful people, but it starts and finishes with another wise woman: my wife, Stacey Nelkin. "Write the book," she's been telling me, in tender whispers and loud shouts, for twenty-two years. She's showered me with unwavering belief, she's been my strongest supporter, and she's been my most constructive critic. I'm an immeasurably better man for all of it. Stacey enthusiastically read countless iterations of proposals and chapter drafts and provided crucial insight. She gave me the faith to soldier on. Her book is next!

I'm a collector of people and their stories, and so Nick, Jonathan, and I interviewed more sources than we originally intended. We ended up quoting many in the book, but unfortunately, there was no space to directly include them all. Please know that each and every one of you contributed and you have my utmost thanks and respect, including: Roger Abramson, Woody Allen, Bea Arthur, Erica Brown, Michael Bruno, Ari Caroline, Mallika Chopra, Michael Claes, George Conrades, Todd Dagres, Steve Dietmann, Riki Drori, Natan Edelsburg, Huckleberry Elling, David Evenchick, Dr. Richard A. Friedman, E. Gordon Gee, Tamar Gordon, Jonah Greenberg, Connie Griffin, Matthew Guberman-Pfeffer, Amanda Gutterman, Diana Higbee, India Howell, Alex Konrad, Philippe Krakowsky, Alan Lightman, Lindsay Litowitz, Kirk McDonald, Noah and Ari Meyerowitz, Jack Mitchell, Joe Moscola, Dan Mullen, Pete Paxton, Vib Prasad, Maurice Reid, Ali Rezai, Mike Schmidt, Dave Schwartz, Jonathan Seelig, Jeff Smith, Mike Uretz, Tanya Valle, Stephen Valyou, Beverly Warne, Love Whelchel, and Tina Wilson.

Before and after these interviews, I had a string of pivotal conversations with old friends and new friends who helped me take the plunge. Thanks to the others who made key introductions and got me to adjust course and carry on, including: Brian Berkopec, Ethan Bronner, Buck Buchwald, Ronald Dufresne, Alex and Dan Fallon, Victor Finomore, Tyler Friesen, Jason Guberman-Pfeffer, Haim and Jamie Handwerker, Bill Heyman, Tal Keinan, Alfred Leach, Gila Lev Ran, Terry Lynam, Amy and Ronen Marcus, Felice Maranz, David Margolick, Lia Matthow, Stacy McLaughlin, Kate Mullen, Brian Mulligan, Gadi Navon, Wendy Sachs, Lara Setrakian, Danny Shea, Hamburg and Kelly Tang, Scott Tobin, Rick Wartzman, my aunt, Evelyn Weinstock, Bari Weiss, and Dana Wolfe. And most of all, thanks to my sister, Lara Greenberg Kaplan, for always believing in me and making key introductions. And to my mom, Marian Greenberg, for pep talks, unconditional love, encouragement, and for planting the notion of becoming a writer in my young brain.

Friends are needed, but I wouldn't be here without great therapists who helped shape and reshape my thinking over the years. First and foremost, my deepest gratitude to Dr. LF, my therapist, who's witnessed my life trajectory, stitched together different periods and people he never met, and whose reassuring nod, compassionate check-ins, and original observations mean the world to me.

Several people gave me a last-minute review on the manuscript, including Andrew Aoyama, David Galper, Anthony Holland, Clay Marsh, Dan Perry, and Paul Sagan. And finally, my heartfelt thanks to Tim Golden, my oldest friend, for his invaluable comments and edits.

To my colleagues at work, I am grateful for the help that each and every one of you provided while keeping the ship moving forward, including Ryan Birchmeir, Vanessa Cordova, Joe Grochmal, Larry Harris, Peter Himler, Sujin Lee, Alyssa Meyer, David Reichberg, and Dylan Spina. And thanks to my attorney, Gadi Hill.

My work as an adjunct professor at NYU and Fordham helped me better understand the mindset of first-time job seekers today. I want to thank my students for sharing their experiences.

At moments like these you reflect on the people who are no longer with us. Primitives who died in the prime of their lives: Ron Baham, Steve Frushtick, Pamela Johnston, Kirk MacLeod, Brian Maruffi, Mark Mehl, Zwika Pres, Wendy (Ziner) Ravech, Rabbi Allan Schranz, and Kyle, my longtime massage therapist who, when she was battling cancer, reminded me that her focus had returned to nature, children, and animals. All very primitive.

My dad, Tony Greenberg, embedded within me with the line "virtue is its own reward." I've tried to live up to that ever since. He's buried in Kipahulu, Maui, precisely because it is not yet fucked up and is glowing with the best natural beauty the world has to offer. You are remembered each and every day.

Stacey and my three now basically grown children are the loves of my life. Thank you to Antonia, an amazing writer in her own right, who kept track of the progress and shared great insights on my writing. She's a civilizing force, but one who has also made many successful primitive moves. Thank you to Noah, a kindred primitive spirit who always asked, "How's the book coming, Dad?" and whose relentlessness and oppositional ways will forever propel him forward. Thank you to Stella, who landed her first summer job and killed it; I hope the book serves as inspiration as you continue to blossom in high school and beyond. For them and their fellow members of Generation Z, my wish is that *Primitive* gives much food for thought as they embark on their own careers, and permission to be true to themselves and forge their own paths.

BIBLIOGRAPHY

INTRODUCTION

Harter, Jim. "Employee Engagement on the Rise in the US." *Gallup*. August 26, 2018. https://news.gallup.com/poll/241649/employee-engagement-rise.aspx.

Massachusetts Institute of Technology. "Primitive Brain Is 'Smarter' Than We Think, MIT Study Shows." Press release. February 23, 2005. http://news.mit.edu/2005/basalganglia.

Munnell, Alicia, et al. "Why Have Defined Benefit Plans Survived in the Public Sector?" Center for Retirement Research at Boston College. December 2007. http://crr.bc.edu/wp-content/uploads/2007/12/slp_2.pdf.

Wolf Shenk, Joshua. *Powers of Two: How Relationships Drive Creativity*. New York: Mariner Books, 2015.

CHAPTER ONE: RELENTLESS

"ACS Award for Team Innovation." *Chemical & Engineering News*. January 30, 2006. https://cen.acs.org/articles/84/i5/ACS-Award-Team-Innovation.html.

Anderson, Troy. *The Way of Go: 8 Ancient Strategy Secrets for Success in Business and Life*. New York: Free Press, 2004.

Cohen, Rhaina, et al. "Guys, We Have a Problem: How American Masculinity Creates Lonely Men." Podcast. *Hidden Brain*. NPR. March 19, 2018. https://www.npr.org/2018/03/19/594719471/guys-we-have-a-problem-how-american-masculinity-creates-lonely-men.

Edward Jones. "Edward Jones Ranks among FORTUNE 500 for Seventh Consecutive Year." Press release. May 21, 2019. https://www.edwardjones.com/about/media/news-releases/fortune-500-2019.html.

Franciulli, Jacquie. "Megan Mullen Helping Change the Culture at Florida." *Rival.* December 11, 2018. https://florida.rivals.com/news/megan-mullen-helping-change-the-culture-at-florida.

Lieber, Jill. "John Randle." *Sports Illustrated.* November 28, 1994. https://www.si.com/vault/1994/11/28/132707/john-randle.

Maese, Rick. "Can an American Running Legend Out-Race 60 Horses? He's Ready to Find Out." *Washington Post.* June 4, 2019. https://www.washingtonpost.com/sports/2019/06/04/can-an-american-running-legend-out-race-horses-hes-ready-find-out/.

Molin, Anna. "High-Intensity Training Can Sharply Improve Endurance." *Wall Street Journal.* November 3, 2015. https://www.wsj.com/articles/high-intensity-training-can-sharply-improve-endurance-1446566476.

Mozer, Mindy, and Ellen Rosen. "Promise Delivered: Alumnus Makes Largest Gift in RIT History." Rochester Institute of Technology. March 19, 2018. https://www.rit.edu/news/promise-delivered-alumnus-makes-largest-gift-rit-history.

Newport, Cal. *Deep Work: Rules for Focused Success in a Distracted World.* New York: Grand Central Publishing, 2016.

Pang, Alex Soojung-Kim. "Why You Should Work 4 Hours a Day, according to Science." *The Week.* May 6, 2017. https://theweek.com/articles/696644/why-should-work-4-hours-day-according-science.

Raz, Guy. "Rent the Runway: Jenn Hyman." Podcast. *How I Built This with Guy Raz.* NPR. August 7, 2017. https://www.npr.org/2017/09/21/541686055/rent-the-runway-jenn-hyman.

Smits, Garry. "Dan Mullen Learned 'Relentless Effort' During High School Days in New Hampshire." *St. Augustine Record.* August 31, 2018. https://www.staugustine.com/sports/20180831/dan-mullen-learned-relentless-effort-during-high-school-days-in-new-hampshire/1.

"Vikings' John Randle Rose to Great Heights After Humble Beginnings." *Grand Forks Herald,* August 5, 2010. https://www.grandforksherald.com/sports/2133180-vikings-john-randle-rose-great-heights-after-humble-beginnings.

CHAPTER TWO: OPPOSITIONAL

Brescoll, Victoria, and Eric Uhlmann. "Can an Angry Woman Get Ahead?: Status Conferral, Gender, and Expression of Emotion in the Workplace." *Psychological Science* 19, no. 3 (March 2008): 268–275.

Burkus, David. "How Criticism Creates Innovative Teams." *Harvard Business Review.* July 22, 2013. https://hbr.org/2013/07/how-criticism-creates-innovati.

Caesar, Ed. "The Reputation-Laundering Firm That Ruined Its Own Reputation." *New Yorker.* June 18, 2018. https://www.newyorker.com/magazine/2018/06/25/the-reputation-laundering-firm-that-ruined-its-own-reputation.

Coyle, Daniel. *The Culture Code: The Secrets of Highly Successful Groups.* New York: Bantam Books, 2018.

Deb, Sopan. "Ibtihaj Muhammad: The Olympic Fencer Is Charting Her Own Path." *New York Times.* July 24, 2018. https://www.nytimes.com/2018/07/24/books/ibtihaj-muhammad-fencing-hijab-olympics.html.

Google. "Identify Dynamics of Effective Teams." *re:Work.* https://rework.withgoogle.com/guides/understanding-team-effectiveness/steps/identify-dynamics-of-effective-teams/.

Grant, Adam. "Why I Taught Myself to Procrastinate." *New York Times.* January 16, 2016. https://www.nytimes.com/2016/01/17/opinion/sunday/why-i-taught-myself-to-procrastinate.html.

Hall, Carrie, et al. "Can Embracing Conflict Spur Positive Change?" EY Americas Family Business Services. May 10, 2019. https://www.ey.com/Publication/vwLUAssets/EY_-_Can_embracing_conflict_spur_positive_change/$FILE/ey-family-business-embracing-conflict.pdf.

Hermann, Aaron, and Hussain Rammal. "The Grounding of the 'Flying Bank.'" *Management Decision* 48, no. 7 (August 3, 2010): 1048–1062.

Jansen, Sue. "How Western PR Firms Quietly Push Putin's Agenda." *Fast Company.* July 1, 2017. https://www.fastcompany.com/40437170/russia-quiet-public-relations-war.

Jordan, Andrew. "Family Summers, Family Business." LinkedIn. August 28, 2017. https://www.linkedin.com/pulse/family-summers-business-andrew-aj-jordan.

Kashdan, Todd. "Companies Value Curiosity but Stifle It Anyway." *Harvard Business Review.* October 21, 2015. https://hbr.org/2015/10/companies-value-curiosity-but-stifle-it-anyway.

Klotz, Anthony, et al. "Good Actors but Bad Apples: Deviant Consequences of Daily Impression Management at Work." *Journal of Applied Science* 103, no. 10 (June 25, 2018): 1145–1154.

Kottasova, Ivana. "Putin Drops His American PR Company." *CNN*. March 12, 2015. https://money.cnn.com/2015/03/12/media/russia-putin-pr-ketchum/index.html.

Lehrer, Jonah. "Groupthink," *New Yorker.* January 22, 2012. https://www.newyorker.com/magazine/2012/01/30/groupthink.

Ludwig, Arnold. *The Price of Greatness: Resolving the Creativity and Madness Controversy.* New York: The Guildford Press, 1995.

Maslin, Janet. "With Just Months Left to Live, a Boss Offers a New Mission Statement: Seize the Day." *New York Times.* January 30, 2006. https://www.nytimes.com/2006/01/30/books/with-just-months-left-to-live-a-boss-offers-a-new-mission-statement.html.

Nelson, Christopher. "Latest Research Says Praising Employees Boosts Productivity After All." *Forbes.* November 1, 2015. https://www.forbes.com/sites/christophernelson/2015/11/01/latest-research-says-praising-employees-boosts-productivity-after-all/#63ad49e85f80.

Oppong, Thomas. "For a More Creative Brain, Embrace Constraints (Limitations Inspire Better Thinking)." *Medium,* January 18, 2018. https://medium.com/swlh/for-a-more-creative-brain-embrace-constraints-5a588c8a8619.

———. "Stop Thinking You Have All the Answers (The Best Ways to Harness the Power of Questions)." *Medium.* April 19, 2017. https://medium.com/personal-growth/stop-thinking-you-have-all-the-answers-never-stop-questioning-e17bfde31e08.

Ottesen, KK. "U.S. Fencer Ibtihaj Muhammad: 'Don't Be Afraid to Reject Someone's Disbelief in You.'" *Washington Post Magazine.* September 24, 2019. https://www.washingtonpost.com/lifestyle/magazine/us-fencer-ibtihaj-muhammad-dont-be-afraid-to-reject-someones-disbelief-in-you/2019/09/20/c0c798fe-c8ef-11e9-be05-f76ac4ec618c_story.html.

Rao, Hayagreeva, Robert Sutton, and Allen Webb. "Innovation Lessons from Pixar: An Interview with Oscar-Winning Director Brad Bird." *McKinsey Quarterly.* April 2008. https://www.mckinsey.com/business-functions/strategy-and-corporate-finance/our-insights/innovation-lessons-from-pixar-an-interview-with-oscar-winning-director-brad-bird.

Setrakian, Lara. "I'm One of Mark Halperin's Accusers. He's Part of a Bigger Problem We Need to Fix." *Washington Post.* October 27, 2017. https://www.washingtonpost.com/opinions/im-one-of-mark-halperins

-accusers-hes-part-of-a-bigger-problem-we-need-to-fix/2017/10/27
/a304f5e0-ba65-11e7-be94-fabb0f1e9ffb_story.html

Sonenshein, Scott. "How Constraints Force Your Brain to Be More Creative."
Fast Company. February 7, 2017. https://www.fastcompany.com/3067925
/how-constraints-force-your-brain-to-be-more-creative.

Stokes, Patricia. *Creativity from Constraints: The Psychology of Breakthroughs.* New
York: Springer Publishing, 2006.

Woloch, Nancy. "Eleanor Roosevelt's White House Press Conferences."
National Women's History Museum. September 22, 2017. https://
www.womenshistory.org/articles/eleanor-roosevelts-white-house-press
-conferences.

CHAPTER THREE: AGNOSTIC

Ashcraft, Brian. "The Nintendo They've Tried to Forget: Gambling, Gangsters,
and Love Hotels." *Kotaku.* March 22, 2011. https://kotaku.com/the-nintendo
-theyve-tried-to-forget-gambling-gangster-5784314.

Bradley Hagerty, Barbara. "Quit Your Job." *The Atlantic.* April 2016. https://
www.theatlantic.com/magazine/archive/2016/04/quit-your-job/471501/.

Brown, Erica. *Take Your Soul to Work: 365 Meditations on Every Day Leadership.* New
York: Simon and Schuster, 2015.

Eban, Katherine. "The Hidden Dangers of Outsourcing Radiology." *SELF.*
November 18, 2011. https://www.self.com/story/outsourcing-radiology
-dangers.

Griffin, Oliver. "How Artificial Intelligence Will Impact Accounting." The
Institute of Chartered Accountants in England and Wales. October 6,
2016. https://economia.icaew.com/features/october-2016/how-artificial
-intelligence-will-impact-accounting.

Jenkins, Aric. "Robots Could Steal 40% of U.S. Jobs by 2030." *Fortune.* March 24,
2017. https://fortune.com/2017/03/24/pwc-robots-jobs-study/.

Joelving, Frederik. "How You Learn More from Success Than Failure." *Scientific
American.* November 1, 2009. https://www.scientificamerican.com/article
/why-success-breeds-success/.

Keng, Cameron. "Employees Who Stay in Companies Longer Than Two Years
Get Paid 50% Less." *Forbes.* June 22, 2014. https://www.forbes.com/sites
/cameronkeng/2014/06/22/employees-that-stay-in-companies-longer
-than-2-years-get-paid-50-less/#7000452be07f.

Lobenstine, Margaret. *The Renaissance Soul: Life Design for People with Too Many Passions to Pick Just One.* New York: Harmony, 2006.

Mangan, Dan. "Lawyers Could Be the Next Profession to Be Replaced by Computers." *CNBC.* February 17, 2017. https://www.cnbc.com/2017/02/17/lawyers-could-be-replaced-by-artificial-intelligence.html.

McGoldrick, Debbie. "When You Dream, You Can Succeed—Grand Marshal of NYC's St. Patrick's Day Parade." *Irish Central.* March 13, 2017. https://www.irishcentral.com/news/irishvoice/when-you-dream-you-can-succeed-grand-marshal-of-nyc-s-st-patrick-s-day-parade.

Murray, Charles. *Human Accomplishment: The Pursuit of Excellence in the Arts and Sciences, 800 BC to 1950.* New York: Harper, 2003.

Nelkin, Stacey, and Paul Schienberg. *You Can't Afford to Break Up: How an Empty Wallet and a Dirty Mind Can Save Your Relationship.* New York: iUniverse, 2009.

Paltrow, Scot, and Jonathan Weber. "$8-Billion Loss Posted by IBM; More Layoffs Set." *Los Angeles Times.* July 28, 1993. https://www.latimes.com/archives/la-xpm-1993-07-28-mn-17823-story.html.

"Play-Doh Was Originally Supposed to Clean Your Walls." Blog. *Chicago Tribune.* December 31, 2015. https://www.chicagotribune.com/redeye/redeye-the-surprising-history-of-playdoh-20151231-story.html.

Popova, Maria. "Why Success Breeds Success: The Science of 'The Winner Effect.'" *Brain Pickings.* https://www.brainpickings.org/2012/08/09/jonh-coates-hour-between-dog-and-wolf-winner-effect/.

"Purpose in Life and Alzheimer's." Rush University Medical Center. https://www.rush.edu/health-wellness/discover-health/purpose-life-and-alzheimers.

Rana, Zat. "The Expert Generalist: Why the Future Belongs to Polymaths." *Medium.* March 1, 2018. https://medium.com/@ztrana/the-expert-generalist-why-the-future-belongs-to-polymaths-46b0e9edc7bc.

Simmons, Michael. "People Who Have 'Too Many Interests' Are More Likely to Be Successful According to Research." *Medium.* April 5, 2018. https://medium.com/accelerated-intelligence/modern-polymath-81f882ce52db.

"World Gym Honors Mike Uretz With Joe Gold Lifetime Acheivement [*sic*] Award." *Club Insider.* December 17, 2015. https://www.clubinsideronline.com/news/chains/world-gym-honors-mike-uretz-with-joe-gold-lifetime-acheivement-award/.

Zittrain, Jonathan. "The Internet Creates a New Kind of Sweatshop." *Newsweek.* December 7. 2009. https://www.newsweek.com/internet-creates-new-kind-sweatshop-75751.

CHAPTER FOUR: MESSIANIC

Brown, Eliot. "How Adam Neumann's Over-the-Top Style Built WeWork. 'This Is Not the Way Everybody Behaves.'" *Wall Street Journal.* September 18, 2019. https://www.wsj.com/articles/this-is-not-the-way-everybody -behaves-how-adam-neumanns-over-the-top-style-built-wework-115688 23827.

Carey, Benedict. "Chip, Implanted in Brain, Helps Paralyzed Man Regain Control of Hand." *New York Times.* April 13, 2016. https:// www.nytimes.com/2016/04/14/health/paralysis-limb-reanimation-brain -chip.html.

Chan, Nathan. "179: How Kiva's Jessica Jackley Turned a Simple Idea into $1B in Microloans." *Foundr.* December 21, 2017. https://foundr.com/micro -loans-jessica-jackley-kiva/.

Hoffman, Reid. "What Great Founders Do at Night." Podcast. *Masters of Scale.* October 3, 2018. https://mastersofscale.com/arianna-huffington-what-great -founders-do-at-night/.

Huffington, Arianna. "10 Years Ago I Collapsed from Burnout and Exhaustion, and It's the Best Thing That Could Have Happened to Me." *Medium.* April 6, 2017. https://medium.com/thrive-global/10-years-ago -i-collapsed-from-burnout-and-exhaustion-and-its-the-best-thing-that -could-have-b1409f16585d.

Kessler, Sarah. "Adam Neumann's $16 Billion Neo-Utopian Play to Turn WeWork into WeWorld." *Fast Company.* March 14, 2016. https://www .fastcompany.com/3057415/adam-neumanns-16-billion-neo-utopian-play -to-turn-wework-into-wewo.

Matuluko, Muyiwa. "Meet Tayo Oviosu, the Man Whose Financial Services Company Has a Wider Reach Than All Banks in Nigeria Combined." *Techpoint Africa.* April 10, 2017. https://techpoint.africa/2017/04/10/tayo -oviosu-paga-founder-ceo/.

Meyrowitz, Carol. "The CEO of TJX on How to Train First-Class Buyers." *Harvard Business Review.* May 2014. https://hbr.org/2014/05/the-ceo-of -tjx-on-how-to-train-first-class-buyers.

Oviosu, Tayo. "If You Could Wave a Magic Wand to Change 1 Thing, What Would It Be?" *Moguldom Nation.* July 23, 2018. https://moguldom.com /152061/paga-founder-could-wave-a-magic-wand-to-change-1-thing-what -would-it-be-and-why/.

Pennington, Randy. "Is Passion Really What We Need to Succeed?"

Huffington Post. June 6, 2016. https://www.huffpost.com/entry/is-passion
-really-what-we_b_10310662.

Umoh, Ruth. "Arianna Huffington Says She Became Successful After She
Quit One Common Bad Habit." *CNBC.* March 11, 2018. https://www
.cnbc.com/2018/03/11/arianna-huffington-became-successful-after-she
-started-sleeping-well.html.

Vedantam, Shankar, et al. "Finding Meaning at Work: How We Shape and Think
About Our Jobs." Podcast. *Hidden Brain.* NPR. September 12, 2019. https://
www.npr.org/2019/09/12/760255265/finding-meaning-at-work-how-we
-shape-and-think-about-our-jobs.

Zax, David. "Want to Be Happier at Work? Learn How from These 'Job
Crafters.'" *Fast Company.* June 3, 2013. https://www.fastcompany.com
/3011081/want-to-be-happier-at-work-learn-how-from-these-job-crafters.

CHAPTER FIVE: INSECURE

Abrams, Abigail. "Yes, Impostor Syndrome Is Real. Here's How to Deal With It."
Time. June 20, 2018. https://time.com/5312483/how-to-deal-with-impostor
-syndrome/.

Chamorro-Premuzic, Tomas. *Confidence: How Much You Really Need and How to Get
It.* New York: Plume, 2014.

———. "Less-Confident People Are More Successful." *Harvard Business
Review.* July 6, 2012. https://hbr.org/2012/07/less-confident-people-are
-more-su.

Grove, Andrew. *Only the Paranoid Survive: How to Identify and Exploit the
Crisis Points That Challenge Every Business.* New York: Doubleday,
1996.

Kramer, Roderick. "When Paranoia Makes Sense." *Harvard Business Review.* July
2002. https://hbr.org/2002/07/when-paranoia-makes-sense.

Lebowitz, Shana. "Richard Branson Says He Didn't Know the Difference
Between 'Net' and 'Gross' Until Age 50—And It Didn't Stop Him
Building an Empire." *Business Insider.* February 28, 2018. https://www
.businessinsider.com/richard-branson-net-vs-gross-dyslexia-2018-2.

Page, Danielle. "How Impostor Syndrome Is Holding You Back at Work."
NBC News. October 25, 2017. https://www.nbcnews.com/better/health
/how-impostor-syndrome-holding-you-back-work-ncna814231.

Raz, Guy. "Lady Gaga & Atom Factory: Troy Carter." Podcast. *How I Built*

This with Guy Raz. NPR. May 28, 2018. https://www.npr.org/2018/05/24/614081933/lady-gaga-atom-factory-troy-carter.

Tenney, Elizabeth, Nathan Meikle, and David Hunsaker. "Research: When Overconfidence Is an Asset, and When It's a Liability." *Harvard Business Review.* December 11, 2018. https://hbr.org/2018/12/research-when-overconfidence-is-an-asset-and-when-its-a-liability.

Timashev, Ratmir. "Why Paranoia Is Necessary for Success," *Fortune.* February 2, 2016. https://fortune.com/2016/02/02/paranoia-necessary-success/.

Vanderkam, Laura. "Why Insecurity May Be the Key to Success." *Fast Company.* November 25, 2013. https://www.fastcompany.com/3022152/why-insecurity-may-be-the-key-to-success.

CHAPTER SIX: NUTS

Arthur, Bea. "Failing Forward: Lessons Learned from the End of a Startup." *Forbes.* June 15, 2016. https://www.forbes.com/sites/beaarthur/2016/06/15/failing-forward-lessons-learned-from-the-end-of-a-startup/#273796357d86.

Bartholomew, Douglas. "From Wrecks to Riches: 'I Only Rent to Nice People,' Says the Founder of Rent-A-Wreck.: A Portrait of an Uncommon Entrepreneur." *Los Angeles Times.* December 14, 1986. https://www.latimes.com/archives/la-xpm-1986-12-14-tm-2804-story.html.

Davenport, Christian. *The Space Barons: Elon Musk, Jeff Bezos, and the Quest to Colonize the Cosmos.* New York: Hachette, 2018.

Engber, Daniel. "What Makes Nuts So Crazy?" *Slate.* April 10, 2006. https://slate.com/news-and-politics/2006/04/what-makes-nuts-so-crazy.html.

Fagan, Kate. "Bikram Yoga's Moral Dilemma." *espnW.* November 9, 2018. http://www.espn.com/espnw/culture/feature/article/23539292/after-serious-allegations-founder-bikram-yoga-practitioners-crossroads.

Freedlander, David. "'I Want Him on Everything': Meet the Woman Behind the Buttigieg Media Frenzy." *Politico.* April 29, 2019. https://www.politico.com/magazine/story/2019/04/29/lis-smith-buttigieg-2020-president-campaign-manager-226756.

"Going with Your Gut Feeling: Intuition Alone Can Guide Right Choice, Study Suggests." *Science Daily.* November 8, 2012. https://www.sciencedaily.com/releases/2012/11/121108131724.htm.

Jamil, Suzi. "How to Harness Humans' Inherent Tendency towards Irrationality."

Think Inc. July 6, 2018. https://thinkinc.org.au/how-to-harness-humans -inherent-tendency-towards-irrationality/.

Kane, Becky. "The Science of Analysis Paralysis: How Overthinking Kills Your Productivity & What You Can Do About It." *Doist.* https://doist.com/blog /analysis-paralysis-and-your-productivity/.

Krogue, Ken. "Behind the Cloud—Part 2—The Marketing Playbook." Inside Sales. December 9, 2009. https://blog.insidesales.com/kens-notes/behind -the-cloud-part-2/.

Montagne, Renee. "Preschoolers Outsmart College Students in Figuring Out Gadgets." Podcast. *The Shots.* NPR. June 30, 2014. https://www.npr.org/templates /transcript/transcript.php?storyId=325230618?storyId=325230618.

"New Survey Reveals Extent, Impact of Information Overload on Workers; From Boston to Beijing, Professionals Feel Overwhelmed, Demoralized." LexisNexis. October 20, 2010. https://www.lexisnexis.com/en-us/about -us/media/press-release.page?id=128751276114739.

Oremus, Will. "What Fuels the Rocket Man?" *Slate.* May 21, 2015. https://slate.com /business/2015/05/elon-musk-biography-review-how-did-a-sci-fi-nut-with -a-hero-complex-becoming-a-world-changing-industrialist.html.

Paskowitz, Dorian. *Surfing and Health.* Honolulu: Juliette Publishing, 2007.

Pray, Doug, dir. *Surfwise.* Motion picture. United States: Magnolia Pictures, 2007.

Raz, Guy. "Zappos: Tony Hsieh." Podcast. *How I Built This with Guy Raz.* NPR. January 23, 2017. https://www.npr.org/2017/01/23/510576153 /zappos-tony-hsieh.

Santos, Laurie, and Alexandra Rosati, "The Evolutionary Routes of Human Decision Making." *Annual Review of Psychology* 66 (June 2, 2015): 321–347.

Schmidt, Samantha. "Arrest Warrant Issued for Bikram Choudhury, the Hot-Yoga Guru Accused of Sexual Harassment." *Washington Post.* May 26, 2017. https://www.washingtonpost.com/news/morning-mix/wp/2017 /05/26/arrest-warrant-issued-for-bikram-choudhury-the-hot-yoga-guru -accused-of-sexual-harassment/.

Synnott, Mark. "Exclusive: Alex Honnold Completes the Most Dangerous Free-Solo Ascent Ever." *National Geographic.* October 3, 2018. https://www .nationalgeographic.com/adventure/features/athletes/alex-honnold/most -dangerous-free-solo-climb-yosemite-national-park-el-capitan/.

"The Effectiveness of Instinct in Decision Making." Tel Aviv University. November 15, 2012. https://english.tau.ac.il/news/instinct.

Wang, Victoria, and Candice Helfand-Rogers. "Bringing Car Confidence to Women." The Story Exchange. June 15, 2016. https://thestoryexchange .org/good-audra-fordin/.

"Why You Should Have a Child-Like Imagination (and the Research That Proves It)." Ideas To Go. June 2, 2017. https://www.ideastogo.com /articles-on-innovation/why-you-should-have-a-child-like-imagination -and-the-research-that-proves-it.

Zatat, Narjas. "Schools Are 'Factories for Humans' and Dumb Down Genius Children, Study Finds." *The Independent.* January 24, 2018. https://www.indy100 .com/article/genius-children-schools-factories-humans-dumb-down-clever -kids-nasa-dr-george-land-tedx-8175136.

CHAPTER SEVEN: GALLANT

"Business Roundtable Redefines the Purpose of a Corporation to Promote 'An Economy That Serves All Americans.'" Business Roundtable. August 19, 2019. https://www.businessroundtable.org/business-roundtable -redefines-the-purpose-of-a-corporation-to-promote-an-economy-that -serves-all-americans.

Grant, Adam. *Give and Take: A Revolutionary Approach to Success.* New York: Viking, 2013.

Greenfield, Kent. "The Impact of 'Going Private' on Corporate Stakeholders." *Brooklyn Journal of Corporate, Financial & Commercial Law* 3, no. 1 (December 4, 2008): 75–88.

Laughland, Oliver, and Tom Silverstone. "Liquid Genocide: Alcohol Destroyed Pine Ridge Reservation—Then They Fought Back." *The Guardian.* September 29, 2017. https://www.theguardian.com/society/2017/sep /29/pine-ridge-indian-reservation-south-dakota.

Marsh, Abigail. *The Fear Factor: How One Emotion Connects Altruists, Psychopaths, and Everyone In-Between.* New York: Basic Books, 2017.

Pearce, Ed. "Tea Bag." *Encyclopedia of Trivia.* August 13, 2018. https:// encyclopaediaoftrivia.blogspot.com/2018/08/tea-bag.html.

Porter, Gareth. "How the U.S. Quietly Lost the IED War in Afghanistan." *Inter Press Service,* October 9, 2012. http://www.ipsnews.net/2012/10/how-the -u-s-quietly-lost-the-ied-war-in-afghanistan/.

Purcell, Amanda. "Wounded Vet Gets New 'Smart' Home in Millerton." *Poughkeepsie Journal,* June 23, 2016. https://www.poughkeepsiejournal.com

/story/news/2016/06/23/wounded-vet-gets-new-smart-home-millerton /86289024/.

Strochlic, Nina. "How Fear Makes You Do Good or Evil." *National Geographic.* January 3, 2018. https://www.nationalgeographic.com/news/2018/01/fear -factor-abigail-marsh-psychopath-altruism/.

Sullivan, Meg. "Your Brain Might Be Hard-Wired for Altruism." University of California, Los Angeles. March 18, 2016. http://newsroom.ucla.edu /releases/your-brain-might-be-hard-wired-for-altruism.

"The Children's Village." *60 Minutes.* July 31, 2016. https://www.cbsnews.com /news/60-minutes-tanzania-rift-valley-childrens-village-2/.

Weisberger, Mindy. "Your Giving Brain: Are Humans 'Hardwired' for Generosity?" *Live Science.* December 19, 2016. https://www.livescience.com /57255-humans-hardwired-for-altruism.html.

"Women Airline Pilots: A Tiny Percentage, and Only Growing Slowly." CAPA Centre for Aviation. August 7, 2018. https://centreforaviation.com/analysis /reports/women-airline-pilots-a-tiny-percentage-and-only-growing-slowly -432247.

NOTES

INTRODUCTION

3 **Gallup found that…most of the respondents were still not emotionally connected to their work:** Jim Harter, "Employee Engagement on the Rise in the US," Gallup, August 26, 2018, https://news.gallup.com/poll/241649/employee-engagement-rise.aspx.

3 **"I wasn't interested in people's time sheets":** Interview with Michael Claes, June 30, 2019.

6 **"Culture is essentially giving the message that people should be safe":** Interview with Richard A. Friedman (conducted by Jonathan Schienberg), March 1, 2019.

7 **"If your job is boring and repetitive":** Annie Nova and John Schoen, "Automation Threatening 25% of Jobs in the US, Especially the 'Boring and Repetitive' Ones: Brookings Study," *CNBC*, January 25, 2019, https://www.cnbc.com/2019/01/25/these-workers-face-the-highest-risk-of-losing-their-jobs-to-automation.html.

15 **"a total civilizing factor":** Interview with Alex Konrad, May 7, 2019.

15 **"for centuries, the myth of the lone genius":** Joshua Wolf Shenk, *Powers of Two: How Relationships Drive Creativity* (New York: Mariner Books, 2015), p. xv.

CHAPTER ONE: RELENTLESS

22 **"Work, try hard, believe you can succeed, get up and try again"**: Allison Pearson, "Why David Cameron Is Right to Praise 'Tiger Mums,'" *The Telegraph*, January 12, 2016, https://www.telegraph.co.uk /education/secondaryeducation/12095876/Why-David-Cameron-is -right-to-praise-Tiger-Mums.html.

27 **"Throw things around, because people have got to know that you feel strongly about it"**: Kathleen Elkins, "PepsiCo CEO Indra Nooyi on Why Steve Jobs Advised Her to Throw Tantrums," *Yahoo! Finance*, November 10, 2016, https://finance.yahoo.com/news/pepsico-ceo-indra -nooyi-why-183526111.html?soc_src=social-sh&soc_trk=pi.

29 **"If someone asked me to describe Dan as an athlete and a person"**: Garry Smits, "Dan Mullen Learned 'Relentless Effort' During High School Days in New Hampshire," *St. Augustine Record*, August 31, 2018, https:// www.staugustine.com/sports/20180831/dan-mullen-learned-relentless -effort-during-high-school-days-in-new-hampshire/1.

30 **"treat every player on the team like they're our own kids"**: Heather Crawford, "First Family of Florida Football: It Was Meant to Be," *First Coast News*, February 5, 2018, https://www.firstcoastnews.com/article/sports /college/florida-gators/first-family-of-florida-football-it-was-meant-to -be/77-514627473.

30 **"Michael Jordan plays ball"**: "Thank You for Smoking," Quotes.net, https://www.quotes.net/mquote/129644.

36 **"When you wake up in the morning and look at emails"**: Sarah Berger, "'Shark Tank' Star Daymond John's Email Rule Is the Most Important Part of His Morning Routine," *CNBC*, January 7, 2019, https://www.cnbc.com/2019/01/07/shark-tank-star-daymond-johns -morning-routine-email-rule.html.

37 **"Every day I seated myself at my work table"**: Larry Maguire, "Why Creativity Flourishes in Solitude," *Medium*, July 17, 2019, https://medium.com /the-reflectionist/why-creativity-flourishes-in-solitude-72bac63e6684.

39 **"half our waking minds be designated and saved for quiet reflection"**:

Alan Lightman, "Why We Owe It to Ourselves to Spend Quiet Time Alone Every Day," Ideas.Ted.Com, May 15, 2018, https://ideas.ted.com /why-we-owe-it-to-ourselves-to-spend-quiet-time-alone-every-day/.

40 **"During that amazing run"**: "Austin McChord," General Catalyst, https:// www.generalcatalyst.com/team/austin-mcchord/.

CHAPTER TWO: OPPOSITIONAL

49 **"They began talking and thinking strategically"**: Daniel Coyle, *The Culture Code: The Secrets of Highly Successful Groups* (New York: Bantam Books, 2018), p. xvi.

50 **"no one on the team will embarrass or punish anyone else for admitting a mistake"**: Google, "Identify Dynamics of Effective Teams," *re:Work*, https://rework.withgoogle.com/guides/understanding-team-effectiveness /steps/identify-dynamics-of-effective-teams/.

50 **"While the instruction 'do not criticize' is often cited as the important instruction in brainstorming**: David Burkus, "How Criticism Creates Innovative Teams," *Harvard Business Review,* July 22, 2013, https://hbr.org /2013/07/how-criticism-creates-innovati.

51 **"conflict appropriately when it arises"**: Carrie Hall, et al., "Can Embracing Conflict Spur Positive Change?" EY Americas Family Business Services, May 10, 2019, https://www.ey.com/Publication /vwLUAssets/EY_-_Can_embracing_conflict_spur_positive_change /$FILE/ey-family-business-embracing-conflict.pdf.

52 **The fact that none of the board members appeared to oppose Swissair's decision**: Aaron Hermann and Hussain Rammal, "The Grounding of the 'Flying Bank,'" *Management Decision* 48, no. 7 (August 3, 2010): 1048–1062.

53 **"This is never going to work in a million years"**: Interview with Jonathan Seelig, May 8, 2019.

54 **"As we grow older, curiosity tends to be wrung out of us"**: Todd

Kashdan, "Companies Value Curiosity but Stifle It Anyway," *Harvard Business Review,* October 21, 2015, https://hbr.org/2015/10/companies -value-curiosity-but-stifle-it-anyway.

54 **"good actors but bad apples":** Anthony Klotz, et al., "Good Actors but Bad Apples: Deviant Consequences of Daily Impression Management at Work," *Journal of Applied Science* 103, no. 10 (June 25, 2018): 1145–1154.

54 **"We run this company on questions, not answers":** Jeremy Caplan, "Google's Chief Looks Ahead," *Time,* October 2, 2006, http://content .time.com/time/business/article/0,8599,1541446,00.html.

55 **"I don't know what sport that is":** Aimee Berg, "Fencer with Headscarf Is a Cut Above the Rest," *Wall Street Journal,* June 24, 2011, https://www.wsj .com/articles/SB10001424052702304569504576404011992467534.

56 **"the more constrained the solution paths, the more variable, the more creative the problem solvers":** Patricia Stokes, *Creativity from Constraints: The Psychology of Breakthroughs* (New York: Springer Publishing, 2006), p. xii.

57 **"psychological unease":** Arnold Ludwig, *The Price of Greatness: Resolving the Creativity and Madness Controversy* (New York: The Guildford Press, 1995), p. 11.

57 **"Psychologists have coined a term for my condition":** Adam Grant, "Why I Taught Myself to Procrastinate," *New York Times,* January 16, 2016, https://www.nytimes.com/2016/01/17/opinion/sunday/why -i-taught-myself-to-procrastinate.html.

61 **"well-behaved women seldom make history":** Quote Investigator, "Well-Behaved Women Seldon Make History," https://quoteinvestigator.com /2012/11/03/well-behaved-women/.

62 **"The only reason I have a bad reputation is because I'm a girl":** Jaan Uhelszki, "Joan Jett," *Classic Rock,* February 1, 2018, https://www.pressreader .com/@Michael_Nichols%60/281483571811934.

62 **"I feel compelled to come forward":** Lara Setrakian, "I'm One of Mark Halperin's Accusers. He's Part of a Bigger Problem We Need to Fix," *Washington Post,* October 27, 2017.

63 **"women who expressed anger were consistently accorded lower status":** Victoria Brescoll and Eric Uhlmann, "Can an Angry Woman Get

Ahead?: Status Conferral, Gender, and Expression of Emotion in the Workplace," *Psychological Science* 19, no. 3 (March, 2008): 268–275.

64 **"top performers need to know their efforts are recognized and valued"**: Annamarie Mann and Nate Dvorak, "Employee Recognition: Low Cost, High Impact," Gallup, June 28, 2016, https://www.gallup.com/workplace/236441/employee-recognition-low-cost-high-impact.aspx.

64 **"If you asked Danny to give you a truly honest assessment"**: Interview with Jonathan Seelig, May 8, 2019.

CHAPTER THREE: AGNOSTIC

69 **"I feel like when I take a new position"**: Interview with Love Whelchel, March 2, 2019.

72 **"In essence, I've just followed my curiosity"**: Interview with Tanya Valle, April 2, 2019.

75 **"digital sweatshops"**: Jonathan Zittrain, "The Internet Creates a New Kind of Sweatshop," *Newsweek,* December 7, 2009, https://www.newsweek.com/internet-creates-new-kind-sweatshop-75751.

75 **"They show up; they get their paycheck and do the minimum required"**: Barbara Bradley Hagerty, "Quit Your Job," *The Atlantic,* April 2016, https://www.theatlantic.com/magazine/archive/2016/04/quit-your-job/471501/.

75 **"There's a difference between twenty years of experience"**: Ibid.

75 **"had a substantially reduced risk of developing Alzheimer's disease"**: "Purpose in Life and Alzheimer's," Rush University Medical Center, https://www.rush.edu/health-wellness/discover-health/purpose-life-and-alzheimers.

76 **"Any university president worth his or her salt"**: Interview with E. Gordon Gee, April 11, 2019.

79 **"Theoretical physicists do their best work at a young age"**: Interview with Alan Lightman, March 29, 2019.

85 **"when we are rejected, the door before us becomes a wall"**: Erica Brown, *Take Your Soul to Work: 365 Meditations on Every Day Leadership* (New York: Simon and Schuster, 2015), p. 20.

87 **"Success has a much greater influence on the brain than failure"**: Frederik Joelving, "How You Learn More from Success Than Failure," *Scientific American*, November 1, 2009, https://www.scientificamerican.com/article/why-success-breeds-success/.

89–90 **"Well, then I think you should take over HR"**: Interview with Joe Moscola, April 15, 2019.

CHAPTER FOUR: MESSIANIC

101 **"up to 87.7 percent of America's workforce is not able to contribute to their full potential"**: Randy Pennington, "Is Passion Really What We Need to Succeed?" *Huffington Post*, June 6, 2016, https://www.huffpost.com/entry/is-passion-really-what-we_b_10310662.

101 **"The success at the *Huffington Post*"**: Ruth Umoh, "Arianna Huffington Says She Became Successful After She Quit One Common Bad Habit," *CNBC*, March 11, 2018, https://www.cnbc.com/2018/03/11/arianna-huffington-became-successful-after-she-started-sleeping-well.html.

104 **"Silicon Valley's Donald Trump"**: Helaine Olen, "What the Fate of Silicon Valley's Donald Trump Can Teach Us," *Washington Post*, September 25, 2019, https://www.washingtonpost.com/opinions/2019/09/25/what-fate-silicon-valleys-donald-trump-can-teach-us/.

104 **"a payout per share worth substantially less"**: Eliot Brown, "How Adam Neumann's Over-the-Top Style Built WeWork. 'This Is Not the Way Everybody Behaves,'" *Wall Street Journal*, September 18, 2019, https://www.wsj.com/articles/this-is-not-the-way-everybody-behaves-how-adam-neumanns-over-the-top-style-built-wework-11568823827.

105 **"rich relational terms"**: David Zax, "Want to Be Happier at Work? Learn How from These 'Job Crafters,'" *Fast Company*, June 3, 2013,

https://www.fastcompany.com/3011081/want-to-be-happier-at-work
-learn-how-from-these-job-crafters.

114 **"I've been wondering what role our business could play in the world
around us"**: Tayo Oviosu, "If You Could Wave a Magic Wand to
Change 1 Thing, What Would It Be?" *Moguldom Nation,* July 23, 2018,
https://moguldom.com/152061/paga-founder-could-wave-a-magic-wand
-to-change-1-thing-what-would-it-be-and-why/.

115 **"They are isolated, punished, and pushed out"**: American Civil Liberties
Union, "School-to-Prison Pipeline," https://www.aclu.org/issues/juvenile
-justice/school-prison-pipeline.

115 **"It's a violent culture"**: Interview with Maurice Reid, June 1, 2019.

CHAPTER FIVE: INSECURE

124 **"When I first started teaching"**: Laura Vanderkam, "Why Insecurity May
Be the Key to Success," *Fast Company,* November 25, 2013, https://www
.fastcompany.com/3022152/why-insecurity-may-be-the-key-to-success.

124 **"Although society places a great deal of importance on being confident"**: Tomas Chamorro-Premuzic, *Confidence: How Much You Really Need
and How to Get It* (New York: Plume, 2014), p. 73.

126 **"Fooled 'em again"**: Interview with Jonathan Schienberg, April 9, 2019.

126 **"not the world's greatest manager"**: Interview with Riki Drori, May 6, 2019.

128 **"It is therefore time to debunk the myth"**: Tomas Chamorro-Premuzic,
"Less-Confident People Are More Successful," *Harvard Business Review,* July
6, 2012, https://hbr.org/2012/07/less-confident-people-are-more-su.

128 **"The results replicated our previous studies"**: Elizabeth Tenney,
Nathan Meikle, and David Hunsaker, "Research: When Overconfidence
Is an Asset, and When It's a Liability," *Harvard Business Review,* December 11, 2018, https://hbr.org/2018/12/research-when-overconfidence
-is-an-asset-and-when-its-a-liability.

129 **"Well, I think we tried very hard not to be overconfident":** Christine Riordan, "Three Ways Overconfidence Can Make a Fool of You," *Forbes,* January 8, 2013, https://www.forbes.com/sites/forbesleadershipforum/2013/01/08/three-ways-overconfidence-can-make-a-fool-of-you/#52f1d95537fb.

129 **"I have written eleven books":** Carl Richards, "Learning to Deal with the Impostor Syndrome," *New York Times,* October 26, 2015, https://www.nytimes.com/2015/10/26/your-money/learning-to-deal-with-the-impostor-syndrome.html.

129–130 **"I am always looking over my shoulder wondering if I measure up":** Jennifer Ludden, "Sotomayor: 'Always Looking Over My Shoulder,'" *NPR,* May 26, 2009, https://www.npr.org/templates/story/story.php?storyId=104538436.

130 **"No matter what we've done, there comes a point":** Terry Gross, "Tom Hanks Says Self-Doubt Is 'A High-Wire Act That We All Walk,'" podcast, *Fresh Air,* NPR, April 26, 2016, https://www.npr.org/2016/04/26/475573489/tom-hanks-says-self-doubt-is-a-high-wire-act-that-we-all-walk.

130 **"Every time I was called on in class":** Julie Ma, "25 Famous Women on Impostor Syndrome and Self-Doubt," *The Cut,* January 12, 2017, https://www.thecut.com/2017/01/25-famous-women-on-impostor-syndrome-and-self-doubt.html.

130 **"I have to admit that today, even twelve years after graduation":** Aly Weisman, "Natalie Portman Reveals Her 'Dark Moments' in College During Powerful Harvard Commencement Speech," *Business Insider,* May 30, 2015, https://www.businessinsider.com/natalie-portman-harvard-commencement-speech-2015-5.

130 **"I am not a writer":** Maria Popova, "How Steinbeck Used the Diary as a Tool of Discipline, a Hedge against Self-Doubt, and a Pacemaker for the Heartbeat of Creative Work," *Brain Pickings,* https://www.brainpickings.org/2015/03/02/john-steinbeck-working-days/.

133 **"Is this good news or bad news?":** Shana Lebowitz, "Richard Branson Says He Didn't Know the Difference Between 'Net' and 'Gross' Until Age 50—And It Didn't Stop Him Building an Empire," *Business Insider,*

February 28, 2018, https://www.businessinsider.com/richard-branson -net-vs-gross-dyslexia-2018-2.

133 **"If you have a learning disability, you become a very good delegator"**: Ibid.

136 **"financial PTSD"**: Guy Raz, "Lady Gaga & Atom Factory: Troy Carter," podcast, *How I Built This with Guy Raz*, NPR, May 28, 2018, https://www .npr.org/2018/05/24/614081933/lady-gaga-atom-factory-troy-carter.

137 **"The paranoid person does not project onto the sky, so to speak"**: Roderick Kramer, "When Paranoia Makes Sense," *Harvard Business Review*, July 2002, https://hbr.org/2002/07/when-paranoia-makes-sense.

137 **"The best way to maintain a company's success is to always be paranoid"**: Ratmir Timashev, "Why Paranoia Is Necessary for Success," *Fortune*, February 2, 2016, https://fortune.com/2016/02/02/paranoia -necessary-success/.

138 **"Prudent paranoia"**: Roderick Kramer, "When Paranoia Makes Sense," *Harvard Business Review*, July 2002, https://hbr.org/2002/07/when-paranoia -makes-sense.

CHAPTER SIX: NUTS

142 **"Guys, there it is"**: Doug Pray, dir., *Surfwise*, motion picture, United States: Magnolia Pictures, 2007.

143 **"was worried about my way of life as a surfing doctor"**: Dorian Paskowitz, *Surfing and Health* (Honolulu: Juliette Publishing, 2007), p. 180.

144 **"We were simply *messhugge* [*sic*]"**: Ibid., p. 181.

146 **"I'm actually not passionate about shoes at all"**: Guy Raz, "Zappos: Tony Hsieh," podcast, *How I Built This with Guy Raz*, NPR, January 23, 2017, https://www.npr.org/2017/01/23/510576153/zappos-tony-hsieh.

146 **"Choudhury had allegedly violated women under his tutelage"**: Kate Fagan, "Bikram Yoga's Moral Dilemma," *espnW*, November 9, 2018,

http://www.espn.com/espnw/culture/feature/article/23539292/after
-serious-allegations-founder-bikram-yoga-practitioners-crossroads.

147 **"The best part about going through hell is that you come out on fire!"**: Bea Arthur, "Failing Forward: Lessons Learned from the End of a Startup," *Forbes*, June 15, 2016, https://www.forbes.com/sites/beaarthur /2016/06/15/failing-forward-lessons-learned-from-the-end-of-a-startup /#273796357d86.

148 **"I had exactly $2.45, and I'm ready to go see this play"**: Interview with Bea Arthur, July 16, 2019.

148 **"Now I always trust my gut"**: "Finding Balance with What You Do & Who You Are | Bea Arthur," Triple F.A.T. Goose, https://triplefatgoose .com/blogs/down-time/bea-arthur-finding-balance-with-what-you-do -and-who-you-are.

150 **"Rationality has to be defined according to how well you accomplish some goals"**: Suzi Jamil, "How to Harness Humans' Inherent Tendency Towards Irrationality," Think Inc., July 6, 2018, https://thinkinc.org.au /how-to-harness-humans-inherent-tendency-towards-irrationality/.

152 **"There was some skepticism about my ability to handle the challenges"**: Victoria Wang and Candice Helfand-Rogers, "Bringing Car Confidence to Women," The Story Exchange, June 15, 2016, https:// thestoryexchange.org/good-audra-fordin/.

153 **"Of all the definitions of man," the French journalist Anatole France once wrote:** Laurie Santos and Alexandra Rosati, "The Evolutionary Routes of Human Decision Making," *Annual Review of Psychology* 66 (June 2, 2015): 321–347.

153 **"I have never put much weight on focus groups"**: Interview with Michael Bruno, May 8, 2019.

154 **"Speed is the ultimate competitive advantage"**: "About Roger Abramson," Abramson Accelerator, https://www.abramsonaccel.com/our-roots.

154 **"I pretty much always go with my gut no matter what"**: Interview with Roger Abramson, June 5, 2019.

157 **"When you look at what's happening inside the brain"**: Narjas Zatat, "Schools Are 'Factories for Humans' and Dumb Down Genius Children,

Study Finds," *The Independent,* January 24, 2018, https://www
.indy100.com/article/genius-children-schools-factories-humans-dumb
-down-clever-kids-nasa-dr-george-land-tedx-8175136.

157 **"What we discovered, to our surprise"**: Renee Montagne, "Preschoolers
Outsmart College Students in Figuring Out Gadgets," podcast, *The
Shots*, NPR, June 30, 2014, https://www.npr.org/templates/transcript
/transcript.php?storyId=325230618?storyId=325230618.

159 **"I was told by everyone that you do not sue NASA"**: Christian Davenport, *The Space Barons: Elon Musk, Jeff Bezos, and the Quest to Colonize the
Cosmos* (New York: Hachette, 2018), p. 48.

160 **"a very unusual cat"**: Interview with Philippe Krakowsky, July 2, 2019.

161 **"Listen—I'm going to ask the fucking questions here"**: Interview with
Todd Dagres, June 1, 2019.

162 **"She puts the word *fuck* through every part of speech the word
can be bent into"**: David Freedlander, "'I Want Him on Everything':
Meet the Woman Behind the Buttigieg Media Frenzy," *Politico,* April
29, 2019, https://www.politico.com/magazine/story/2019/04/29/lis
-smith-buttigieg-2020-president-campaign-manager-226756.

164 **"I had never done anything like it before"**: Interview with Vibhav Prasad,
June 11, 2019.

CHAPTER SEVEN: GALLANT

166 **"I would say around 120 kids would claim me as mom"**: Interview with
India Howell, July 19, 2019.

166 **"My kids aren't orphans"**: "The Children's Village," *60 Minutes,* July 31,
2016, https://www.cbsnews.com/news/60-minutes-tanzania-rift-valley
-childrens-village-2/.

170 **"Knocking out these areas appears to free your ability to feel for
others"**: Mindy Weisberger, "Your Giving Brain: Are Humans

'Hardwired' for Generosity?" *Live Science*, December 19, 2016, https://www.livescience.com/57255-humans-hardwired-for-altruism.html.

170 **"Life in the jungle may be bloody, but it is not devoid of love and loyalty":** Judith Rich Harris, *The Nurture Assumption: Why Children Turn Out the Way They Do* (New York: Simon and Schuster, 1999), p. 149.

171 **There is a Hebrew word *achrayut*:** "Bereishit (5774—Taking Responsibility," The Office of Rabbi Jonathan Sacks, September 28, 2013, http://rabbisacks.org/bereishit-5774-taking-responsibility/.

172 **"Then I suddenly remembered," Kirk recounted to me:** Interview with Kirk McDonald, July 11, 2019.

174 **In another study of six hundred medical students in Belgium:** Adam Grant, *Give and Take: A Revolutionary Approach to Success* (New York: Viking, 2013), p. 6.

175 **"Hollywood's Mr. Nice Guy":** Ned Zeman, "Ron Meyer, Hollywood's Mr. Nice Guy," *Wall Street Journal Magazine*, September 28, 2016, https://www.wsj.com/articles/ron-meyer-hollywoods-mr-nice-guy-1475076890.

177 **"Our results, however, suggest that they may be more successful":** Katherine Nelson et al., "Do Unto Others or Treat Yourself? The Effects of Prosocial and Self-Focused Behavior on Psychological Flourishing," *Emotion* 16, no. 6 (April 21, 2016): 850–861.

178 **"That job wasn't for everyone":** Interview with Stephen Valyou, August 11, 2019.

180 **"People who are highly altruistic are really good at recognizing other people's fear":** Nina Strochlic, "How Fear Makes You Do Good or Evil," *National Geographic*, January 3, 2018, https://www.nationalgeographic.com/news/2018/01/fear-factor-abigail-marsh-psychopath-altruism/.

182 **"We took over because of the mission":** Interview with Ari and Noah Meyerowitz, June 14, 2019.

184 **"Part of what happens to nurses is they give so much of themselves":** Interview with Beverly Warne, August 6, 2019.

186 **"They would have pushed me and pushed me until I gave up":** Interview with Diana Higbee, July 13, 2019.

187 **"My soul was just empty"**: Interview with Jane, April 1, 2019.

190 **"I have a responsibility to the worker, both blue-collar and white-collar"**: Kent Greenfield, "The Impact of 'Going Private' on Corporate Stakeholders," *Brooklyn Journal of Corporate, Financial & Commercial Law* 3, no. 1 (December 4, 2008): 75–88.

191 **"While each of our individual companies serves its own corporate purpose"**: "Business Roundtable Redefines the Purpose of a Corporation to Promote 'An Economy That Serves All Americans,'" Business Roundtable, August 19, 2019, https://www.businessroundtable.org/business-roundtable-redefines-the-purpose-of-a-corporation-to-promote-an-economy-that-serves-all-americans.

CONCLUSION

193 **"I wish I could encourage you to major in English instead of chemistry"**: Email interview with Matthew Guberman, July 7, 2017.

INDEX